OUT OF CONTROL:
The Last Days of The Clash

WRITTEN BY VINCE WHITE

a **T✺RGET** *MOVING* publication

First published in Great Britain in 2007 by Moving Target
84-86 Blenheim Crescent, London W11 1NZ

Copyright © Vince White 2007

The right of Vince White to be identified as the author of this work has been asserted by him in accordance with the Copyright, Designs and Patents Act 1988.

All rights reserved. No part of this publication may be reproduced in any material form (including photocopying or storing it in any medium by electronic means and whether or not transiently or incidentally to some other use of publication) without the written permission of the copyright owner. Applications for the copyright owner's written permission to reproduce any part of this publication should be addressed to the publisher.
Any person who does any unauthorised act in relation to this publication may be liable to criminal prosecution and civil claims for damages.

Moving Target asserts that this song, 'OUT OF CONTROL' has been unedited, unproduced and untampered with in any way by any Authority and left in its raw state. Any spelling mistakes, typos or grammatical 'errors' remain at the insistence of the author.

ISBN 978-0-9555038-0-1

Printed and bound in Great Britain by Biddles Ltd, King's Lynn, Norfolk

Lao Tsu: 'Tao-Tae Ching':
"The people with no one to command them would of themselves become harmonious."

OUT OF CONTROL

INTRO		3
VERSE	IN SEARCH OF SPACE	7
2nd VERSE	A CAREER OPPORTUNITY	17
CHORUS	WHAT'S MY NAME?	31
VERSE	CALIFORNIA DREAMIN'	58
CHORUS	SAFE EUROPEAN TOILET	86
MID 8	BORED WITH THE U.S.A.	103
SOLO	WHO PUT THAT HEAD?	166
VERSE	THE CLAMPDOWN	204
CHORUS	THIS IS ENGLAND	224
2nd CHORUS	COMPLETE CONTROL	239
OUTRO	TRAINS IN VAIN	269
CODA		287

OUT OF CONTROL:
The Last Days of The Clash

INTRO:

I didn't really want to write this book. Playing guitar for the Clash was the best and the worst of times for me. And there were a lot more worst times than best ones. Frankly, I don't give a shit. It's history and I learnt a lot from the experience but I didn't think I would be able to fill up more than a couple of pages with words if I only thought of happy times. So the prospect was a bit daunting.

Anyway, cut to the chase, fact is, I have a large outstanding bar tab courtesy of Lloyds TSB *Mastercard* and it needs paying off. I've always disliked working for anyone and couldn't think of a better way to earn a few quid than sitting on my arse and telling a story. People are always asking me 'what was it like?' or 'what happened?' and so here's my version of events. I hope you find something of interest and value here. What's said here represents me and no one else who was involved or record companies or anything or anybody else.

THE CLASH. I can't believe the power that name still has over people the world over. It's almost as if the *name* itself means more than the actual people involved or the music. Like a cult or an institution of sorts. I wonder if the same group of people with the same songs and artwork etc. would have been so successful if the group had been called 'The Smash' or *'The Flash!!'* But then The Clash cast a spell over *me* in 1978 and 1979 and so I understand what it did to me. But back then I was spotty. I had an excuse. What worries me now is these fucking fifty year olds still banging on about it. I just don't get it anymore because what I *imagined* when I was leaping around near the stage as a teenager was that the Clash were *humanitarians*, who believed in equality and justice and freedom and rights, the voices of people like me, people who were pissed off with the world, *individuals*, angry and indignant and tired of being pushed around and told what to do and think by the state. What I *found* when I actually joined the band was a SMUG, joyless and oppressive totalitarian dictatorship that would've shocked Stalin.

Of course, choosing *me* as one of two new guitarists to replace Mick Jones could easily be put down to my amazing good looks, incredible personality, charisma and style. But then again, it could also be said that pulling in a complete unknown was a cynical and contemptuous way of reinforcing the illusion of socialist equality and credibility. An important element in winning over the public's 'vote'. That the Clash was a 'street' band. That the band was 'of the people and for the people' and *'We* are the Clash' and all that bollocks and that the 'people' were it and owned it. The reality was that the dictators behind the scene owned everything and all the power and all the money like they do in real life politics. I can personally testify that they weren't in a hurry to redistribute any of it.

But don't worry. I'm not gonna complain about my useless employment! After all, I could've jacked it in at any time. This is a story of how I tried and failed to keep my mouth shut, tried and failed to pretend and get what I could out of the experience while all the time thinking of the money I never got!

VERSE:

IN SEARCH OF SPACE

I grew up in the Hampshire countryside. I hated my parents. I learnt by the age of 5 that there was something very wrong with the world. These oppressors, my parents, were a male and a female. The male was big and powerful and always seemed to be angry with me. He kept beating me every day for reasons I could never fathom. When I was bad I was beaten. When I was good I was beaten. There was no sense to it. The female was cold and aloof and never made any physical contact. Like Dorothy, I started off down the road of life sandwiched between the cowardly lion and a tin person. I thought my parents must be imposters. I often wondered who my real parents might be. Other kids had real parents. I would go for tea round other kid's houses and I would forget about things. But the time would always come when I had to leave the warmth and friendship of the occasion and return to my house. My house had a grey roof on it. The thought of returning to that grey roof would fill me with a dark anxiety. If I arrived too late I knew I would get beaten. If I arrived on time I would get beaten. When I got home I would get sent to my room and then beaten. I would lie there in bed often wishing someone official would knock on the door and take me away into care. I had a very low self esteem.

I started playing guitar when I was 15. At that time I was listening to guitarists like Brian May and Jimmy Page and the guy from Deep Purple but what they were doing seemed so difficult and a million miles away. I felt I could never get to where they were. It made me feel even more inadequate. Then things changed. Punk happened. It was like someone had thrown me a lifeline. I bought the Lurkers. The Vibrators. The Stranglers. The Damned. The Sex Pistols. Someone leant me a copy of 'White Riot' by the Clash. These seven inch pieces of plastic seemed to sympathise with my situation. They were angry and indignant like me. It was encouraging. They became my friends. The guitar on those records was simple and I found I could play it easily. It gave me a lot of confidence.

My beatings had changed by then. Now I was a bit older, instead of a belt whipping I was getting thrown against walls, receiving grown up punches and sudden, unexpected whacks around the head. I tried to fight back but I was skinny and not very strong. It only made things worse so I gave up and just took it.

I was very angry about it all and all that anger went into the sound of a distorted bar chord. I realised you could just play the same chord and move it up and down the fretboard without thinking about it too much. You could just enjoy the feeling and the sound of it without trying too hard. Punk became big news then and the Sex Pistols were really sticking it to them. I suddenly stopped worrying about my oppressors. I'd found something that filled me with power. Something big. My beatings didn't hurt anymore. When my male oppressor had finished I simply asked, *why have you stopped?* Couldn't I have some *more?* He walked out with a confused look and the beatings stopped.

Two years before I joined the Clash I'd been at University College, London studying for an Astronomy degree. I had no idea how I'd got there studying such a subject. Like everything else in my life, the decision to go was simply the result of some powerful, vague impulse that just came to me in a moment in time. All I knew was I was looking for something. I had no idea what it was I was looking for. My thought was just to get away from home. I knew there would be a big future for me once I'd done that.

I was late with my University application and had to decide quickly. One afternoon I was practising guitar round my mate's house knowing I had to get down to it. We were jamming along to Hawkwind's 'Master Of The Universe' which was a big favourite of mine. I looked at all the possibilities in the handbook. I looked at the sun burning outside through the window. I rapidly filled out the form putting down Astronomy for five places that did it. I was suddenly convinced that Astronomy students *had* to be a fine, interesting, crazy fun bunch. The first three were in London. London was where it was all happening. I'd get in a band there too. It would be a laugh. It would be great. It was done. I put the form in the envelope, ready for posting. Went back to practising bar chords with my mate.

One thing just led to another thing. My idea was that after I left university I might become an Astronaut. After all, I reasoned, there had to be a demand for astronomers in Outer Space, didn't there? Things would always start out like that. With a direction of sorts. But usually it was just the result of thinking about the grandest idea imaginable with the belief that, somehow, things would just work out by themselves.

I was a bit surprised when on arriving in London in late '78 that things fell apart before my eyes. Soon after arriving, someone in the halls of residence had offered me a red star. A red star was a tab of L.S.D. They were still the powerful doses then like people took in the 60's. It seemed like a good idea at the time. It was too much. I went mad. After I came down I wasn't the same person anymore. I began thinking too much and started a lot of unhealthy, obsessive questioning into the nature of things. Overnight the whole house came tumbling down. Life turned from a positive image into a negative one. It still had all the same *outlines* so you could recognize where you had to move around and that, but with the *content* all reversed. I began obsessively reading shit trying to figure out what was going on. I read a book called 'The Selfish Gene' about evolution. It blew my mind. I could just see it and it made complete sense. Complex molecules battling it out over aeons and getting bigger and bigger and reproducing and replicating and getting more complex and going on and on reproducing and devouring each other over incredible time and producing what? Life. Animals. Me. An 'evolved' ape. One of six billion other apes all crawling around on a piece of rock that was spinning around a large ball of burning hydrogen amongst countless billions of other burning balls in infinite time and space spinning out going around nowhere without rhyme or reason.

It was a bit of a shock. As a kid growing up through the 60's you'd been led to expect a great future when you finally grew up full of technological wonder and miracles. What I discovered was that life was actually full of nothing. Instead of hover cars, sipping martini on yachts, incredible pneumatic James Bond women, trips to the moon and mars I was presented with the dole queue. With emptiness. Isolation. Soulless, suspicious eyes on every street corner. Poverty. Internal and exterior horror. Pointlessness. A universal senseless sadness and deadness at the root of all things. I felt utterly cheated. I realised I'd been conned. It was all a big mistake. I was furious. I wanted my money back.

I moved on into the 1980's struggling to complete the rest of my University degree with an overpowering sense of futility about everything and not knowing what to do about it. After I graduated I carried on wandering through this new inverted image of the world dazed and lost, wondering what the hell had happened. It was like I'd been gazing excitedly at all my Christmas presents under the tree of life only to open them and find what? A bottle of deodorant. An empty leather wallet. A book about India that didn't have any pictures in it. And the biggest most exciting looking one? A foot pump that could blow up lidos and beach balls. People told me I was lucky. I'd gone to university. I had an education.

Soon after graduating, I sat down with myself and made a serious decision. Then and there I understood that there were only three things that could stop all the horror. The first was alcohol. The second was girls. And the third was the sound of distorted electric guitar. I resolved to pursue all three with vigour. It was the only logical solution. Punk rock music was a bit old hat by 1981 but I simply went back to it. I played 'Never Mind The Bollocks' and the first Clash album everyday and almost non-stop. It suddenly made more sense than ever. It provided a kind of relief.

None of my friends seemed to understand what was wrong with me. I couldn't talk to anyone about my problem. Everyone I met seemed to accept all the appearances of reality as truth. Like a giant conspiracy of assumptions that said a bus was a bus. But a bus wasn't a bus. It was an obscene red metal object that moved down the street carrying blank faces that had come from nowhere and was going absolutely nowhere. I would try and explain what I was feeling to my mates but a proper exchange of ideas never really happened. I got back from them what I always did. Either complete avoidance or non comprehension.

Most of my friends began moving on from the university I was at and the drinking and parties and girls and gigs and such to find new lives with marriage and good jobs with big companies. I just simply held on. There was nowhere for me to go. I dutifully went to a couple of interviews with 'Kodak' and 'British Petroleum' who came round interviewing graduates on the university 'milk round.' The idea was that I might perform scientific research with them. I had the relevant qualifications for it and it was sort of the expected thing to do. At each interview I sat down and me and the interviewer eyed each other. Within a split second it was obvious to both of us that it wouldn't work. But he would carry on asking questions. I carried on answering them. I went on in my best phoney way knowing I wasn't convincing anybody. I wasn't a much of a con man. I filled out application forms. The last part was always the hardest. What are your interests? I couldn't put down drinking, fucking and playing the guitar so I made things up. Complete nonsense. I was ambitious. I was the member of various societies and played sports and loved being part of a team. I liked working with others. The interviewer looked up from my form and smiled. He wasn't stupid. He knew right off I hated people. And he was right of course.

I was relieved when the interviews were over. I could tell the interviewers were relieved too. Each time, I went immediately to the pub afterwards and got really drunk.

It was all a bit embarrassing to still be hanging around the university bar after graduating, signing on the dole and carrying on with all the parties and that as new people moved in and the old ones moved on to earn money and have proper lives. I was supposed to have left. I decided there was only one thing I could do. And that was to become a rock star. I would show them.

I set about finding a way to make it happen. I got something together with friends. We bashed around for months getting nowhere. It was useless. I felt I had to take drastic action. On the spur of the moment, I quit, packed up my things and moved up to Liverpool. I got something together up there with some ex members of the band 'Dead or Alive'. Before they became the pop version. Then they were alternative. Like Echo and the Bunnymen and all that. The London punk scene was long over. It was all happening up North then. I moved into a flat in Birkenhead and commuted to rehearsal on the Mersey ferry. But nothing happened. Day after day my existential misery only escalated. People up there were even more desperate than me. I kept getting into fights. I came home each night from the pub covered in blood. Just getting a portion of curry and chips after the pub shut became a problem. It was my accent. They thought I was a privileged southern *bastard.* Therefore I *was.* Their minds were made up.

'You wanna make something of it?'
'You CUNT!'
BANG!

It was like that nearly every night.

My flat got broken into three times. Everything I owned was taken. All my records. Record player. Clothes. I'd had enough. I miserably gave up and returned to London with my tail between my legs. Fucking Scousers and their stupid fucking Beatles. They could keep it.

Back in London I got a job in a warehouse near King's Cross and found a bedsit in Finsbury Park. It was then I met the Whale. It was my nickname for her. Her real name was Jane. Of course she wasn't a whale. She was georgeous. A real honey. She had class. A great 19 year old body, black spiky hair, white pearly skin and film star lips. I was immensely proud. She was a real head spinner. Every night I would come home from the warehouse and start drinking beers while she would cook up some terrible meal of rice and peppers and stuff. Girly food. I would pretend it was like the best thing I'd ever tasted.

The street outside was full of prostitutes and kerb crawlers. Mostly I would have to go to the off licence myself because of the constant hassle the Whale would get. Being there with her was a safe haven of sorts. It quenched the non specific constant grumbling anxiety I felt towards the world.

I put another band together. This was going to be *it*. We began rehearsals. Got a couple of gigs. We were on our way. We were going to make it.

But then for some reason I started having dreams about deserts. In these dreams I was Lawrence of Arabia roaming around this great expanse of sand every night dressed in long white robes. Lots of long horizons with a purple moon in the darkness. I began having them at work in the day too. Hazy sun filled misty images of pyramids and hot othernesses. I got books from the library and persuaded the Whale.

'Look, babe! We're going to Egypt!'

'What?'

'I've *decided*. Don't worry. You'll love it! I'm off to work. I want you to book two flights to Egypt. We're going on holiday! Whooh!'

The Whale got the tickets and we were off. It was fantastic. It was rock'n'roll. It was poor there. A pound went a million miles and no one seemed to be bothered about trying to *be* anything. It was hot. Exotic. You didn't have to do anything except move around and hang around in the sun and look at pyramids and things or sit on a beach and drink beer. I loved it.

But by the time I got back the band had had enough. It was over already before it started. Our drummer had found another situation. The others had lost interest.

'Look guys. Don't give up on this. Don't you *realise!* This is going to be MASSIVE!' I yelled.

But they weren't convinced.

I went back to work. I was pissed off. Wankers! What's the matter with them? Don't they get it? I bought a copy of the

Melody Maker on the way in. I looked through the wanted column. In it was a three column advert in black.

'WILD GUITARIST WANTED'

It said something else about being over a certain height. I didn't like the wording. Who the hell would say they *wanted* you to be 'Wild'? Like you could just turn it on like a switch. It sounded stupid. You either were a wild person or you weren't. It put me off a bit because I felt some things were better left unsaid. I pulled 10p out my pocket, stuck it in the phone box and rang the number.

It immediately answered.

'Yeah, OK, I saw your ad. I play the guitar. And I'm fucking good.'

'Oh, *great*.' A female voice began, enthusiastically.

Then she began asking me strange questions which had nothing at all to do with music.

'Do you have a passport?'
'Yeah.'
'Do you have a criminal record?'
'*What?*'
'Have you been convicted of anything?'
'Jumping the tube'.
'Do you have any criminal offences that would prevent you from travelling to the United States?'
'No. Not that I know of.'
'How tall are you?'
'Oh. Around six foot.'
'Great. What kind of books do you read?'
'What kind of *books*? Are you having a laugh?'
'What are you reading at the moment?'
'I'm reading something by J.G. Ballard. Do you know him?'

'Yes. And what kind of music?'
'Rock. Punk rock. Anything with balls.'
'Brilliant!'

She gave me the date of the audition. It was at the Electric Ballroom in Camden. Turn up anytime in the afternoon.
 I put the phone down. Fuck. That was weird. I made a note of the date in my diary.

2ND VERSE:

A CAREER OPPORTUNITY

I'd only been to the Electric Ballroom at night to see bands. In fact, I can't remember going out anywhere before then for any other reason. No 'club' nights or dancing or anything like that. That was for *girls*. I only ever went out to see *bands*. The Ramones there in late '78 stands out in my mind. Leaping about down the front like an idiot with a few hundred other idiots drenched in hot sweat and violently caught up in the whole energy abandon thing. It was fucking great. But what was *this*?

It was dark and musty in there. The smell of stale smoke and booze hung in the air. The atmosphere felt very polite and serene and it was just like we'd walked into church or something. I arrived with my sister, Sammy and we found an empty table as far back as possible.

On the stage was a 100 watt Marshall stack. Next to it, sitting on a table was a TEAC reel to reel tape machine playing two tracks of backing music. One track was a blues thing recorded with a drum machine and the other was a kind of modern hip-hop drum loop. At that time a lot of bands were using taped backing tracks and drum machines. O.M.D. Depeche Mode. There are a few others I can't bring myself to mention.

There must have been a hundred guitarists in there. A long queue had formed by the left side of the room and one by one people filed up on the stage to play along. In front was a long table where our judges sat. There were three of them. A couple of guys and a nice looking blonde. I didn't have a clue who they were. I didn't recognize anyone. It seemed like something big. But then again you wondered if it just more con. Thinking about it now, it was just like an 80's version of the modern 'Pop Idol' show. I had no idea, of course, I was auditioning for the biggest boy band going. There was a rumour going around that it was the Clash but nothing was certain and there were other rumours going around regarding Ten Pole Tudor. Then again, it could have been 'Marian and her Rocking Boatmen' for all I knew.

I'd never been to an audition before and even though it's acceptable procedure in 'the business' something about it pissed me off. The idea I was going to be *evaluated* annoyed me the most. It was painful to watch people get up there and perform like monkeys. It seemed humiliating.

And for WHAT? *WHO THE HELL DO THESE PEOPLE THINK THEY ARE?*

I began to feel intimidated by the standard of play. One heavy metal dude with weeping willow hair leapt up there with his white Flying V guitar and began totally freaking and rocking out! I mean, his fingers were like a pneumatic blur of precision and it was like …….he…………….*KNEW* WHAT HE WAS DOING!

I'd no idea what I was doing. I got my guitar out and figured out what key the blues track was in. My sister was looking after my shopping bag. In that bag were four cans of Tennant's Super strength lager. It was a staple part of my daily diet. In a weird mixture of excitement and depression I began digging into them.

Things weren't looking good. I'd taken another day off work for the audition and now my arse at the warehouse was really on the line. Only the day before Mr. Winstanley had summoned me to his office.

'I'm issuing you a formal warning,' he'd announced matter of factly, handing over a type written sheet. 'Not only have you been off 3 days sick last month but your *Time* keeping…….'

He watched me gravely, but also in a very *concerned* way as though he really *cared.* He was the middle aged, balding, *reasonable* guy who was only doing his job after all.

'……you were more than 10 minutes late for work everyday last week.'

I had nothing to say. He was expecting some sort of explanation but I really had none. Except that I hated getting out of bed in the morning and travelling down the tube with a lot of sad looking people who, like me, were about to spend long hours watching the clock and listening to Radio 1's Steve Wright in the afternoon. I would try and time every morning departure with military split second precision.

I eventually answered like I always did with authority figures. The police, doctors, teachers, my father……..or any other kind of dumb socialist fuck in a suit or uniform who felt they had power over me. I played soppy pretend doggie gone belly up.

'I'm sorry sir. It won't happen again.'

'Well, if your time keeping doesn't come up to scratch Gregory, I'm afraid, as you well know, I'll have no choice but to issue you a second notice.'
'Yessir. I understand. It won't happen again.'

That was it. A second written notice meant I was fired. And here I was taking more time off. I didn't want to get fired. Most the guys I worked with were a good laugh and made the whole thing bearable. I'd seen far worse jobs. Chicken factory packer. Office temp. Door to door encyclopaedia's. And this one seemed to be holding me together. Just.

I waited right until the end. Best check out all the competition first, I thought. A couple of hours had passed by then and less than a dozen or so of us were left.

'I'm a fucking professional!' I laughed to myself as I emptied my last canister of Tennent's Super rocket fuel. I picked up my guitar and joined the back of the queue. Sammy wished me luck.

'Ah! Don't worry. It's a piece of piss!'

I suddenly became very nervous. As I edged forward only one thing seemed to come through in my alcoholic haze.

STAND OUT. DO SOMETHING DIFFERENT. GET FUCKING NOTICED.

The panel looked utterly bored and it suddenly it seemed like a good idea to have some fun with them.

'Hey, *YOU LOT!!* What the fuck's going *ON* here?'

Silence.

'Well, I can tell *YOU*, that this gig had better be for nothing less than the *ROLLING FUCKING STONES*......................*or*............... *well.........all I can say*

A CAREER OPPORTUNITY

is…… you better not be WASTING MY BLOODY TIME!!!THAT'S ALL!!!'

Someone on the panel smiled and mumbled something I couldn't hear.
I tried chatting with the guy next to me.

'What a load of CRAP, eh?' I said, loudly, making sure the panel could hear. 'I could be at home right now getting a good BLOW JOB!!!! Coming down here…….EH?…it's fuckin' BOLLOCKS!!!...…….THAT'S WHAT IT IS……….EH?!! what do you think, mate? EH?'
He half laughed, politely, but said nothing.

It was nearly my turn. I tried hard to focus. I was pretty drunk. I knew I had to keep it together because on some level, intuitive I suppose, I knew that despite all appearances that this was *IT*.
Suddenly it was my turn. I put on my best cocky swagger, climbed up, plugged in my guitar and turned all the amplifier knobs up to number 11 and crashed out the biggest E- chord I think I'd ever heard and just stood there. The noise was intoxicating. It felt great just *being* there, feeling this awesome sense of power reverberating through me.
The tape started playing and I dived headlong into the moment, blasting out blues riffs in mad succession dimly aware that there was a twelve bar progression going on as well. None of it made any sense. I began vomiting guitar. Haphazard. Demented. The hip hop track came. NO IDEA. Just more noise and guitar stabs looking for a home.
It was all over in a flash. I was angry. I hadn't been able to find anything to work on that stupid funky track. Fucking modern stupid funky tracks. I snapped out the guitar lead and stormed off the stage and quickly got back to our table. I'd packed my

guitar and was about to walk out when someone ran up. It was one of the panel. The pretty looking girl.
'Can I just confirm your number with you Greg?'
I looked her up and down as she read out my digits.
'Yeah. That's it.'
'Good. We'll be in touch.'
'Ok, whatever.'

Sammy and I stepped out into street. Into another grey, dreary Camden afternoon. We walked in silence to the 29 bus stop. God, I was depressed. I thought nothing more about it.

The warehouse was getting to be a real drag. It was a big new food and drink wholesalers near King's Cross. 'Baby Jane' and 'Karma Chameleon' were blasting out relentlessly every few minutes through every corner of the building. It drove me nuts. But it was mindless and that suited me down to the ground. I wanted to numb my brain. I thought too much. I desperately wanted to switch off. Minutes would slowly evolve into hours into days and then weeks would suddenly have gone by.
I worked in the 'goods-in' section. My job was to unpack the incoming boxes and label all the stuff inside with sticky blue price tags. Two years ago at University I was working out Einstein's theory's of relativity. Was this the best I could do? Sometimes the labels would change colour and we'd get white ones. Most of the time they just stayed blue.

There were five of us in my 'gang'. Ken, I liked the most. He was a blonde haired skinny Rockabilly and a real nervous live wire who had no trouble expressing himself. I couldn't express myself at all. I seemed to be frozen. I had no idea how people did it. *Communicate* that is. I often watched in sheer admiration at those who could seem to do it so effortlessly.

Ken and Waz drifted around the main warehouse loading shelves. Bob was the butcher and Harry was in some kind of minor executive position. He was supposed to be our supervisor or something. Like us, though, he really didn't give a shit as long as we didn't get him into any trouble. We'd do anything to get a laugh and relieve the boredom. In my case that meant stealing. Usually booze. I'd pull out the palettes of boxes into the main warehouse where someone else would stack them on the shelves. Later I'd collect the palettes with the empty boxes, find the drinks aisle and swiftly drop a couple of bottles of Moet Chandon into one of them. I'd cart the empty boxes to the outside skip and be busy crushing them. When I was sure no one was looking I'd hide the bottles next to the fence.
After work we'd be getting in Waz's car.

'Oh, hang on I forgot something.'

I'd run over to the fence pull the bottles through and hide them under my coat. Driving back through King's Cross, we'd fire the corks out at passers by and get hammered. It felt good to do that. It wasn't a revolution but it helped. Every little victory counted. It seemed very important.

One day my supervisor called me.

'Greg, there's a phone call for you.'

I ran to the goods-in office and picked up the phone.

'Hello.'

A serious but excited male voice came on the line.

'Hi, is that Greg?'

'Yeah? Who's that?'

'Greg, you came to an audition a couple of weeks ago?'

'Oh, yeah, the Electric Ballroom thing?'

'Yes. Do you have any idea who it was for?'

'Uhm, no, not really.'

'Well, I can tell you now that it was for the *CLASH!* I'm also happy to tell you that out of all the hopefuls *you've* been selected. Congratulations!'
I didn't know what to say.
'OK. So what happens now?' I said, coolly serious.
'We'll be in touch soon to let you know when rehearsals begin. But for now, I just want to say, 'well done'.'
'Alright. Thanks'
'Speak soon. Well done.'
I put the phone down.

My mind immediately began to race. The Clash were the biggest rock band going. Their early songs had changed my life. The band that had jumped in right behind the Sex Pistols and told it how it was. They were HUGE! FUCKING HELL!
I walked slowly out into the main building. There was no one around. I looked at my watch. Of course! It was afternoon tea break. I bounded up the stairs to the cafeteria. All the guys were in there sitting at a table cracking jokes and chatting away. I slowly sat down. I waited a few seconds.
'Fucking hell!' I exclaimed suddenly. 'You'll never guess what!'
The table went quiet. I pulled out a red Marlboro and lit up.
'You know that fucking audition I went to? They've only just been on the fucking phone. You'll never guess who it was for!'
Ben looked at me and quickly looked away.
'Who?'
'It was only for the fucking *CLASH!* Not only that but they're giving *ME* the fucking job! Can you believe it?'
I took an excited drag of my cigarette.
'That's amazing,' said Ben.
He began to titter. He was very tense. His face went red. Someone else began to laugh. Suddenly the whole table erupted into uncontrolled manic laughter.

'What?' I said, *'WHAT?'*

Ben put his arm around me laughing. Head low, looking up at me ashamedly, still laughing as he tried to speak.

'It was….. Bob. He…… made……..
the…………CALL………..I'm so sorry………….'

Howls of laughter.

Slowly it began to dawn on me. THE FUCKERS.

'You bastards!'

I stopped, trying to take it all in, not knowing what to think. I looked over at Bob.

'YOU FUCKING FUCKER FUCKFACE SHITBAG!' I shouted, beginning to laugh too. It *was* funny, really, when you thought about it.

Ben kept on consoling me. 'I'm sorry. It wasn't my idea.'

'You bunch of bastards. Don't worry. I'll get you back for this.'

I got up and went back to work. I acted indifferent but I was miserable all afternoon. I didn't hate them. I was sure I'd have done the same myself.

One morning, about a week later, another call came.

'Greg. We'd like you to come to a second audition. It will be one evening next week. Have you got a pen?'

I scrambled around for one.

'Yeah?'

'Someone will meet you in the Lock Tavern in Chalk Farm Road. On Tuesday. 7pm.'

'OK. I got it.'

'You'll be taken to the band's studio and we'd like you to play along with some more tracks. It won't take long. An hour or so.'

'Alright. Who am I auditioning for?'

'I still can't say at this stage but don't worry, it will be worth your while.'

'OK, I'll be there.'

The call had come on a Friday. Friday meant lunch in the pub. I decided to keep quiet about the second audition. The five of us piled into Henry's car and we drove to a pub in York Way. It was Henry's idea. He assured us that it was excellent. They had strippers there. On the way someone rolled a joint. Waz passed it to me.

'Here, Greg, get your laughing gear around that.'
'No. I don't.'
'What?'
'Nah. Thanks.'
'Fucking hell. You're such a *weird* fucker. You *look* like a complete freak. The sort ……you know…. that takes drugs. I don't understand you.'

I said nothing.

Everyone sucked away at the joint getting high and giggling. At least they didn't start the dope talk. All that stuff about seeds and bongs and all that bollocks. I hated dope smokers and their dope talk. It didn't interest me. But there I was feeling the outsider again. I desperately wanted a drink.

It was about 1.30pm when we got to the pub. There in front of us was this young girl, around 22 with a hot figure, white as porcelain, pulling off her clothes, gyrating to Rod Stewart's 'Da Ya Think I'm Sexy.' Bubbles gyrated up through my lager. Outside, trees were gyrating in the wind. Above our heads, millions of galaxies were gyrating in eternity. What the fuck was it all about?

The end of the song came and she finally removed her g string. Shit. There were only us five, her and the bartender there. You had to laugh.

The second audition was a doddle. I was taken into the band's studio in what is now the Camden's Stable's market. I was given headphones and asked to play along with some more music. It was better this time. Real drums. It was in the kind of rocky, punky style I liked. I chopped out some tough chords and simple bluesy solo stuff while standing in front of the studio window. The window was blackened out but you could tell there were people in there. I could see some shadows moving. When it was over someone came out and thanked me for coming. I packed my guitar and left. I was pleased with what I'd done. I liked the music. Things were looking up.

Weeks passed and I didn't hear anything back so I decided to call the number and find out what was going on. I was told it was down to me and another guitarist. I had to wait. Another couple of weeks passed before I rang again. This time I was told someone would be in touch shortly. No one got in touch shortly. I let it go. I reckoned they were fucking me around.
  One day I did get a call. Be at the Lock Tavern. 7.30. This time you'll meet the band.

I arrived early. I went to the bar and got another pint of Stella. It was my second. I'd already finished off three cans of Tennant's Super on the bus down. Why change a winning formula?
  Went on drinking. After a while, I looked at my watch. It was 8.10. Fuck, have I been had *again?* I sat quietly drinking expecting one of my mates to suddenly come walking in. Around 8.20 a guy with spiky black hair came in and quickly sat next to me. He was excited.
  'Greg?'
  'Yeah.'
  'Right. Are you ready to meet the band?'
  'Yeah. Sure.'
  Do you know who this band is you're auditioning for?'
  'I've no idea.'

'I can tell you now it's for the……. CLASH.'
'OK.'
'Come on. Let's go over.'

I finished my beer, picked up my guitar and we crossed the road. I entered the rehearsal space. In there I see the famous Joe Strummer standing in front of the studio window holding his world famous Fender Telecaster. He's much shorter than I would have thought. I'm introduced to everyone. Paul Simonon the original bass player is there, smiling. Pete, the new guy behind the drums. And who's that? Nick. He's got a guitar as well. Uh-oh. Another guitarist. Ok. We all shake hands.

The booze is really beginning to kick in now. Joe comes over and shows me some chords. It's 'London Calling'. E minor. F. Joe doesn't like my black Stratocaster and neither does anyone else. Everyone agrees I should change it. I'm ok with that and suddenly I'm holding a white Telecaster and we begin playing. I realise later that swopping my guitar was probably my first big mistake but anyway, I completely forget everything. I'm transported. It sounds so fucking great and LOUD. Next song is 'Brand New Cadillac'. I insist on playing the solo as I know it from playing along to the record at home. And so it goes. I can't keep up with much and in fact I'm all over the shop. I just get involved. No one expects me to know all these songs of course. I get the feeling that something is missing though. I don't know what it is but just let go and try to fill that gap. It's easy to let go. I'm pissed.

We go on playing for a couple of hours or so. I know I'm right for this. In my mind there's absolutely no question about it. Afterwards we all go to the pub for drinks and I make sure I'm sitting next to Joe. Everyone else is giving me a wide berth and chatting a bit too self consciously for my liking.

I want to break this up tightness so I lean over towards Joe.

A CAREER OPPORTUNITY

'So, when are we gonna start playing, man? I can't fucking wait!'

He pulls back immediately, collecting himself. Eyes me irritably.

'You're assuming too much. You're still under observation,' he remarks, coldly.

'Oh. Ok.'

I shut up and lean back. Everyone carries on talking, ignoring me. It doesn't faze me in the least.

I'm asked back for a more rehearsals and it's not long before I discover that Joe and Paul Simonon, the only original members of the Clash are even bigger drinkers than me. Especially Joe. We began ending up in this Mexican restaurant after rehearsals. Joe seemed to take a lot of pleasure in showing this new kid the ropes.

He turns to me at the bar.

'You like Mescal?'

'Yeah, whatever!'

I'd never had Mescal. Not that I could remember anyway. I had no idea what it was. It made no difference to me. I probably had at sometime or other. I'd bang anything away as long as it had alcohol in it. I only cared about the effect. He summons over the barmaid and ceremoniously orders shots for everyone. Begins explaining in detail about the worm and that. How to use the salt first. Put it on the soft spot on the back of the hand between thumb and forefinger. Lick it. Knock back the drink. Then suck the lemon. It was fascinating. It was a cool, rock star's drink. We all began knocking them back. With beer. Dos Equis. Exotic for me. No sooner had we done these then another lot were ordered. Then margueritas. More Dos Equis. It was getting too much.

Joe leaned over me. His big earthy face and doleful eyes sucking me in.

'Man is *destroying* himself,' he began, in deep meaningful tones. 'The whole world is in recession. You know, there's no spirit around anymore. You know, the…….'

'Hey man! Come on. Only a few years ago they put a man on the fucking MOON! I reckon that's some kind of progress. Even a statement of man's spirit.'

'Yeah. They had a HIT with that one alright. A number one. But what did they follow it up with? Eh? *Nothing. NOTHING!!* They slid down the charts after that.'

I stared at him in disbelief. Was he joking? Comparing the wonders of space exploration with the fucking hit parade?

'Are you kidding?'

'No. They had a hit. They couldn't follow it up. They couldn't repeat it.'

We slammed another tequila.

'Tell me,' he said. 'What do you think? Do you think alcohol brings out the real man or does it create a new one. A false one?'

'The real man.'

Joe nodded in agreement.

'There's so much shit in our brains, Joe. Drink gives you a chance.'

We clinked bottles.

Joe wandered off getting drunker. At some point we all grouped around the same table. The five of us. Joe had an announcement to make:

'I just wanna say that from now on this is *it*. No more changes. We are the band. This is *it*.'

I was in. There was no clinking of glasses. No big celebration. Just another round of shots.

It was the 20th December 1983.

CHORUS:

WHAT'S MY NAME?

That night I'd arranged to meet the Whale some friends in the pub after. I walked in head down and slumped down on the seat, miserably.

'Well, how did it go?' she asked, nervously.

'Bad. Nah. I didn't get it. The fuckers.'

'Oooooh. I'm so sorry. Aaah, never mind. Let me get you a drink.'

She got up to go to the bar.

'Of COURSE I GOT IT,' I yelled, 'You dummy! What do you think? I'm a fucking genius! Don't you think these guys can recognize *quality* when they see it!'

I grabbed her waist and pulled her back down. Planted a big kiss on those pink lips and leaned back.

'Oooooh! I'm sooo happy for you! Let me get you that drink,' she said, excitedly.

I sat back and watched her strut to the bar and wait to get served. I pretended to be occupied, knowing she was smiling back at me trying to get my attention. Then I'd notice and pull a face at her. Look away. Back again. One of those silly games. I began taking everything in. Flowery red patterns on the worn carpet with cigarette holes. Paisley wallpaper five years past its sell-by date. A tired juke box in the corner that had only dozen cheesy 45's on it. It was a *real* pub. Like they all were in those days. My friends were chatting away but I didn't want to talk to anyone. I wanted to savour the moment. The Whale came back with the beer. She had a pint too. I looked at her and grinned. I realized I had it. In that moment. Everything I could want. I had it all. A pint of cold lager. The hot girl. The world famous class rock band. My world class misery miraculously disappeared. Things just couldn't be better.

The next day I went into the warehouse to quit my job. I'd given my bank details to the Clash office and was told my account would be credited weekly with a £100. It was just to start. It was £20 a week more than I was getting at the job and I was happy. The news of my joining had spread fast around the warehouse. Mr Winstanley looked drawn and tired as he wished me good luck for the future. I suddenly felt sorry for him. The big man wasn't looking so big anymore. He was losing his. Warehouse sales had fallen and head management were about to bring in a new guy to replace him and shake things up a bit.

My work mates presented me with a 'Southern Death Cult' album. They'd signed it and scrawled over it telling me not to forget my comrades in my hour of glory. And not to forget that I'd once told them that the Clash's song 'Bankrobber' was the worst song ever written. That I was a hypocrite yanky fucking hippy. Long live Rock'a'Billy and King Kurt. Best of luck you Wally. I was touched and felt sad. Sad for them. Sad for everything in a strange way.

The new Clash began rehearsing day and night up until Christmas. During that time I met Bernie Rhodes, the band's manager. He seemed really pleased with me. Much later, Joe told me Bernie had come running up to him exclaiming he'd found a real street kid. A street punk. That was funny. I'd grown up in the countryside. I was a solitary type with few friends and had never been part of any local gang. My streets had been dirt tracks through the New Forest where as a kid I'd wander alone for hours catching tadpoles and sticklebacks and caterpillars and stuff. I'd never ever seen so much as a council estate. I'd got into a couple of fights at school but mainly just to prove to myself that I could do it and wasn't a nerd. But all that cocky bravado gang fighting mentality disturbed me and there was a lot of it around where I grew up. It got you respect. But I didn't need their respect and so I avoided it. Apart from learning to play the guitar I spent my teenage years with my head in books. I painted, played local cricket and went sailing and beach fishing.

At that time Bernie seemed cool. I put complete trust in him and Joe. I guess it was the 'halo effect'. I read in some book on psychology about the 'halo effect' that successful, famous and even beautiful people can have. Part of it is that ordinary folk see successful people to be more honest and trustworthy than regular people. My first impression was his shoes. I took a profound dislike to them. They were supposed to be brothel creepers but somehow they weren't. Instead of the thick creeper sole they were about a third as thick as the real ones. For the next two years these grey, boring shoes kept turning up in front of me. I never saw him wear anything else. I didn't get it. They weren't quite brothel creepers and they weren't quite normal shoes either. Somewhere in between.

'Did you see the fight?' he asked, one evening on the way over from the pub to the rehearsal. Apparently there had been some big heavyweight world championship match on earlier in the day. I wasn't even aware of it.
'No.'
'Do you like boxing?'
'No. I think it's brutal and stupid. It's ugly. It beats me why anybody would pay to watch two human beings kick shit out of each other.'
Bernie laughed. I couldn't understand why he was laughing. Maybe he liked the idea that I was contrary. But I wasn't being contrary. I was just being honest. It seemed like I could do no wrong. Just say what you think. At last! I was being accepted for being myself! And by these great people I admired. It was too good to be true.

A tour of California had been lined up for the New Year and there were a lot of songs to learn. Nick had been rehearsing with the band for some weeks already and had most of it down. I was finding it difficult remembering all the chords and arrangements in such short time. One night, just before we broke for Christmas Joe stayed late with me to go over the parts I was having trouble with, one on one. He was very patient and warm. I liked him a lot. He was very charismatic. I hoped I would learn something. We ended up in the café over the road after and ordered dinner.

'This isn't really a bad job, you know. There's a lot worse jobs you could be doing,' he said, nonchalantly.
'Fucking right!'
'I used to dig graves before. Now that was an eye opener.'
'Ugh! What was that like?'
'Hard work. I didn't last too long though.'

Joe went on to talk about his famous Telecaster he bought in 1974 with the little money he had. Bands he'd been in. The '101 ers'. How he'd met Bernie and Mick Jones and Paul Simonon after a '101 er's' gig. How he'd been asked that night to join them. He wasn't sure if he should. The '101 er's' were doing OK. Bernie had issued him an ultimatum. He was given 24 hours to decide. He went on about how he'd come to that crucial decision and had intuitively taken a chance. It was an important moment for him and he was obviously proud of it. Joe loved reminiscing about the past. I loved listening. Suddenly without pausing.

'Look, I've something I have to tell you.'
'What?'
'Nick and Pete don't want you in the band. They're pushing to get you out. They've been on at me to get rid of you. They don't think you're good enough.'

His words hit me like stones. A long pause followed while he let them sink in. I'd only just joined. Was I being dismissed already? I said nothing and waited for him to continue.

'But, see, *I* think you got what it takes,' he said, leaning forward. 'I'm gunning for you. So is Bernie. Nick and Pete have set up a cosy little corner for themselves. Bernie and I want you in there to break it up.'

He moved his hands about as if destroying something.
'You understand?'
'Yeah, kind of.'
I didn't really understand at all. It was all very conspiratorial.
'Cosy corner?'
'Yeah. We think they'll get all safe and predictable. It's your job to keep them on their toes.'

I knew I'd been issued a mission statement from the great rock'n'roll general. I had no idea what I was supposed to do though. I was just full of gratitude that I was still in with a chance to do my thing with one of the greatest bands of all time. Joe was behind me. None of this stuff made any sense though. It left me with an uncomfortable feeling. Why couldn't we just get on with it?

We finished our dinner and Joe paid.
'What are you doing for Christmas?'
'Well, I got 47 songs to learn for one thing.'
'Look, don't worry about it. If you're not doing anything else then come over. Bring your girlfriend.'
He wrote his number down.

I went home realising there was a problem of sorts but was felt sure everything would be OK. After all, the main people were on my side weren't they? But a seed of suspicion had been sowed that set me apart from the other new guys, Nick and Pete. I didn't trust them.

I spent most of Christmas day learning Clash songs. Opened presents, had turkey dinner with the Whale, then back to the guitar. I had no intention of going over to Joe's but later in the day it got boring like it always does. Chords were coming out of my ears. Nothing more would stick. I called his number. A female voice answered and brought him to the phone. He seemed a bit cool and reserved and a little surprised to hear from me. It was awkward. Had we only been invited out of politeness? But his tone suddenly changed.
'Yeah come on over. Don't bring anything. We've some food left and we've plenty to drink.'
We got a cab to his address in Notting Hill. Walked in. It was dark, very quiet and peaceful in there. Simply decorated with wooden floors. Some plants. Very middle class. Family were there and it was kind of formal. We were introduced to Gabby, his girlfriend and in a cot next to the dining table was their new

baby girl, Jazz. What a fucking stupid name to give to a human being, I thought. But I had no interest in babies and left that bit to the Whale.

Straight away I could tell the Whale was more than a bit nervous. She'd begun hitting the red wine really hard. She was outstripping me by at least three glasses to my one. But it got her talking. Unlike me, she was a great social talker. It got everyone laughing and relaxed.

After about an hour she announced she needed the toilet. It was at the top of the stairs, facing.

She got up unsteadily. She didn't make it to the toilet. She got to the foot of the stairs and stumbled. We could hear a loud banging around out there and then some coughing. We all ran out to see what had happened. There she was lying across the bottom of the stairs heaving violently. Puke was everywhere. All over the nice, new, expensive thick carpet. Just when you thought it would stop another lot would violently come up. Tons of it. Nothing in the world could stop it.

Gabby took care of her. Got her to lie down, put a blanket over her and began cleaning up the mess while I got talking to Joe.

I picked up a Christmas card. It was to John.

'Who's John?' I asked, laughing.

'Hah! Me! John Mellor. My *real* name. You wouldn't want to know John Mellor!'

'Yeah, I would. Why not?'

'No. You wouldn't want to know *him!*' he laughed, 'Joe Strummer is *far* more interesting.'

He seemed to make a big deal out of it. Later he kept bringing up this one thing. In front of Bernie. That I'd wanted to know who John Mellor was. Like it was significant or something. I wondered then if there really was another person hidden behind a mask that was Joe Strummer. I didn't believe it possible. You are what you are, aren't you? It was only a name change. You were still the same person whatever, weren't you? I could tell it made him uncomfortable. He changed the subject.

'What size feet are you?'

'Oh. 8 or 9.'

Joe leapt up the stairs and produced a pair of boots. Motorcycle boots.

'I had these for years. I think they might fit you. Try them on.'

I pulled the boots on. They fit perfectly.

'You can have them. I got them from Sid.'

'Sid?'

'Sid Vicious.'

Joe leaned back.

'They're really great. Yeah, they really suit you.'

'Thanks.'

Around 1a.m. Joe called us a cab and we went home. We'd had a nice time. I'd got a new pair of boots. A Christmas present. A piece of punk rock history. We'd brought no presents for anyone. We'd arrived without so much as a bloody card. The Whale was feeling better. I teased her for being such a dumb-arse, puking everywhere. What a useless bloody liability she was. Still, you had to laugh.

But after Christmas the idea came for *me* to change *my* name. It began slowly as a suggestion from Joe. He said I ought to think of a new name for myself. What was wrong with my own name? 'Greg' was too American. It was no good for an English band. Soon we'd be touring in the U.S. I didn't want to change my name but everyone began piling on the pressure. I ignored it hoping they'd forget about it. But they didn't.

'Can you tell me *one* famous musician called *Gregory*?' Paul demanded in the pub.

A name popped into my head.

'Yeah, Gregory Isaacs!'

'Oh, yeah, well, I suppose but……..'
That got him. The *cool ruler*. Paul was well into reggae. But it didn't stop the pressure from keeping on dropping.

'VINCE! Vincent!' exclaimed Joe, suddenly, one lunchtime back in the pub. 'That's IT!'
Nick, Pete and Paul all agreed it was a great name. Then everyone agreed that I should be called it.

'It's ROCK'N'ROLL!'

I looked around at their happy faces. They were really enjoying all this. Joe began going on about fifties rock'n'roll. About Gene *Vincent*, the great 50's rock'n'roller and what a wild character he'd been. And *Vince* Taylor. The singer who went mad who wrote 'Brand New Cadillac'. And some other '50's icons. Joe was convinced.

'You have to see this as a great *opportunity*. You now have a fantastic chance to *REINVENT* yourself! Leave the past behind! Become a new man! Something greater!'
'Oh, I dunno. I'll have to think about it.'

I went home and miserably told the Whale about it. I didn't like the name. I saw no need to *reinvent* myself. I didn't want to be a new man. I didn't like the feel of it. I liked 50's rock'n'roll and the fun attitude of all that but only in an amused sort of way. It didn't touch me that deeply. It was too cheesy and lightweight. It wasn't really my thing. I thought all the music that had happened since then, through the 60's and 70's had been a vast improvement. My roots were in rock. It was more powerful and sexy. Heavy bluesy guitars and songs. Led Zeppelin, the Doors, AC/DC. The Sex Pistols. Punk. The Clash had been about something far more significant in my mind than Be-bop-a-bloody-fucking-lula. Or Hound Dog. I thought about thinking up a different name but I had no time to think. Every spare moment was taken up learning song arrangements and trying to remember them all. Many of the songs were being arranged differently from the recordings to perform live. And despite my brain training at college none of it was sticking in my head quickly enough.

At rehearsals the band began calling me 'Vince'. It wasn't so much the name that bothered me then as the fact that it was happening against my will. Like a conspiracy of sorts. It seemed I had no choice. But so much was happening I soon got used to it and the name began to stick. 'Oh well', I thought, 'what's in a name?' I let it go. There seemed to be far more important things to think about.

Before I joined I'd pretty much lost interest in the Clash as a band of any real importance. What had been an incredible first album and a great early string of incendiary singles had dwindled to a kind of mainstream easy listening. It had started with the 'London Calling' album. I thought the only really good thing about it was the title track and the picture on the cover. In late '79 it was the record of the moment though and I'd got into it through repeated playings. I thought it was OK. It had character. Joe's stamp was all over it. But still, it was a bit of a disappointment. But then again I also knew that you could come to like anything if you heard it enough times. After London Calling came out I went to see the Clash play at the Lyceum with a certain trepidation. I felt they were losing it. I was happily surprised to find out how great they still were live. So when their fourth album, 'Sandanista' was released I was still excited. Excited to find out what lay inside those black shiny grooves inside the mysterious red and black sleeve. I bought the triple album from Virgin records, Oxford Street on the day it was released. Rushed home. Put it on my turntable. Lowered the needle down to the first track. Soon I was moving the needle from track to track, desperately looking for something that might push my buttons. Anything. I went through all six sides but all I could find were little piles of bland, self indulgent nonsense. Children's voices and noises and meaningless bits of this and that. Hardly any good songs. Even the better songs were cover versions. Each one airbrushed, swamped in chorused guitar and mellowed. The best thing about it was the drumming. The drum sound. It held it together. God knows what it would've sounded like without it.

I was bitterly disappointed. I thought the Clash were taking the piss. I hadn't waited this time to try and get *into* it. I carefully placed the record back into the plastic bag with the receipt, ran back to the Virgin megastore and demanded my money back. I was cool about it. I didn't agree with all the moaners and whiners at the time complaining about the Clash selling out. If everybody had done what I'd done they wouldn't have been able sell anything.

My interest resurfaced with the last two singles from the 'Combat Rock' album. Even though one was about the problems of a love break up. I thought the lyrics to that were embarrassing. But they were great songs to dance to at parties and had that indefinable, special Clash magic. A return to form. But I clearly saw that all the people I knew who owned copies of 'Combat Rock' were boring. Safe and dull types who wore normal clothes and were finishing their economics or language degrees. Soft punks who wanted to be a bit hip and put a little rebellion in their lives. But not too much. You'd go to these awful college parties and there would always be a copy there. Together with a copy of 'Parellel Lines' by Blondie. So I didn't have to buy one myself to discover that apart from the singles there wasn't much else of interest on it. Punk had evolved. Of course there were those who'd stood still and kept on railing against social injustice and the like in the same style. But for me the whole thing had become like a joke that gets repeated too often. Some had gone the pop route. Some had kept the raw energy and guitars but adding more atmosphere and mood. I'd evolved with that. As well as the early punk records, by then I was also listening to bands like Joy Division and Killing Joke. 'Transmission' was a big favourite. The newer bands hinted at things in a poetic way. I liked them because they gave space to your imagination and weren't trying to tell you what to think. I really didn't need someone telling me not to heed a call to join the bloody army or what my rights were. It felt patronising. It was a million miles away from the raw, urgent power of 'Complete Control'.

Bernie kept a low profile in the beginning. Just turning up at rehearsals now and again to see how things were going. He didn't say too much. And when he did it seemed encouraging. I hoped to be friends with him. I thought I might learn something. After all, he'd managed the Sex Pistols and got the Clash off the ground. He seemed sharp and clever. I was flattered that he'd seen something in me for the job as guitarist as well as Joe and Paul.

Joe was in the driving seat then, on full steam. His energy was infectious.

I'd made it passionately clear to him how I felt about the band's music. Moments of sheer brilliance interspersed with bland, abject mediocrity. He heartily agreed. We had long heated drunken discussions about music. Joe slayed the 'Sandanista' album as a time of excessive cocaine and other drug taking and ego tripping. We seemed to connect on every level. There seemed to be no bullshit and we couldn't wait to get started on things. The reason Mick Jones had been fired was because he was lazy and didn't want to work. Paul backed Joe up, agreeing with him. It all seemed great. There was no reason not to believe either of them.

Joe began talking about a return to basics. He described his vision of a new blistering Clash burning with the fire and spirit they'd had at the beginning. A new Clash rising up from the ashes with a bunch of short, sharp songs that would redefine what the band was really about and re-establish its credibility. It sounded great, listening to him speak. It was really exciting. I was convinced. Then Joe 'suggested' I get my hair cut. Mine was longish, back-combed and spiked in the style of the time. He drew a picture of me as I was with the spikes coming down over my forehead. Underneath, he wrote: 'HIDING'. Then he drew another with short spikes all around the top of the head. Under that he wrote: 'OPEN'. He really didn't have to bother with all that. I had no qualms about getting my hair cut. It had always been short before. A hair cutter was summoned to the Clash offices in Camden and I was done. I went home and dyed it black. Now I looked exactly as I had three years previously.

What were impromptu visits by Bernie to rehearsals to see how things were going had subtly begun to turn into 'meetings'. It soon became apparent who was really in charge. Up till then I thought Joe was. But slowly dawned on me that it was Bernie who was the real leader. At these meetings only Bernie, Joe, Paul, Nick, Pete and I would be present. It seemed like the normal thing for a band and its manager to do to discuss policy and this and that. They were anything but normal.

We'd all be sitting around with our cigarettes and Bernie (the only non-smoker) would stand centre stage wearing those grey half-shoes of his. He was a short but a bit of an imposing figure. A bit intimidating. I felt there was something deeply violent, bitter and angry suppressed in him. I understood that to some extent but I had no idea where it came from in him or where it was going. He was closed and rarely showed much warmth or emotion. His ideas were abstract and encased in a hard, cold logic that was difficult to empathise with. He began running the whole show like it was a ship. I was a punk but I didn't think that discipline was necessarily a bad thing. Especially when you wanted to achieve something. I knew I needed some discipline. I knew I was a bit too impulsive and over-reactive. But as time went on this ship came more and more to resemble the H.M.S.Bounty. Everyday one or other of us began getting psychologically whipped, keel-hauled or made to walk the plank. Put on rations or fed maggot food. Usually me.

Our captain would usually begin with a monologue where every point he wanted to put across was made in a kind of obscure cryptic language. You felt that only the truly initiated could ever understand it. Odd, incomprehensible metaphors were used to explain simple things which then made little or no sense. I'm not sure anyone else understood either. Nobody would say much back and create a discussion. Sometimes Joe would nod his head and interject something in agreement like he understood. Like he was one of the initiated ones. Mostly it was one-way traffic. Paul didn't say much. I don't think anybody spoke up much out of FEAR. By the time I'd figured out one topic or got the gist of one idea he'd already moved on to something else. I would ask him to explain something again, excited, enthusiastic and anxious to understand, only to become even more confused by further explanation. It was bizarre. I decided it was all designed to keep us on our toes, mentally. Perhaps to facilitate creative thought. But one thing quickly became clear. I always came away from these 'meetings' feeling a bit demoralised. Like I could never understand this special 'something' about the world that only he was privy to. Something vague that was well above my limited understanding.

My relationship with Nick and Pete hadn't got off to a good start either. A bit forced. I made no mention of what Joe had told me about them wanting me out but it was obvious they weren't happy about me being there. Having no choice in the matter they'd adopted an attitude of polite tolerance. I was spoken to only when necessary. Nick was technically the better guitarist but that didn't bother me. I believed in myself. I had something of my own that was unique.

People said later that I was being 'moulded' and 'punked' to fit in with what the band wanted to portray. Changing name and getting a haircut was just superficial stuff to me and seemed appropriate after all. I'd changed image many times before. From Hippy to Punk to Mod to Skinhead to Goth to Rocker to whatever. It was all part of the fun of experimenting with things. In a way it was all the same. More seriously, though, it wasn't long before speaking my mind began giving me grief. Being 'OPEN' as Joe had drawn it, left things wide open for aspects of my character and personality to come under scrutiny and for 'moulding'. I thought revealing myself and my thoughts would create understanding and rapport. I was wrong.

I began sharing things with Bernie about myself I thought he'd relate to. Things that were important to me and I thought were relevant to punk rock and being in a band. There was something I liked about him for some reason. Not many people seemed to like him. He was unique. Maybe that's why I liked him. Or wanted to. He was also very irreverent about certain things. I liked that. I'd never met anyone like him before.

One day I found myself alone with him and the Clash's PR man, Kosmo, in the Clash office in Camden.

'You know, growing up I always felt like an outsider, Bernie. I always felt like I didn't fit in. I really hate the whole fucking tribal mentality thing that most people go for. Their stupid need for hierarchies.'

He stood quietly listening. I thought he'd understand this, so I went on.

'I never understood why people have the need to control and have power over each other, you know? Like bloody monkeys! Human monkeys! Put 10 in a room what do you get? Within no time you get one jumping on the back of another and trying to be top dog. Everyone finding their place. Imitating each other. Digusting!'

'Disgusting' was Bernie's favourite word. I liked it too.

I went on.

'I think the best groups are where everyone is unique and themselves, you know? With their own look and style. Not having to be like each other. Respecting differences. Each person doing their thing and contributing to the whole. A sort of synergy.'

Bernie smiled, then looked over at Kosmo.

'How is Vince with his money? What do you think? Is Vince a *saver* or a *spender?*'

'A SPENDER! *Definitely.* Give Vince a thousand dollars and he'll blow it in fucking minutes!'

'I thought so.'

I smiled. It was kind of funny. It was flattering to have people talk about you. I loved being the centre of attention. But I didn't like them talking about me objectively, as if I wasn't really there. I wasn't really too bad at looking after my money. I'd got it together to go to Egypt after all. It seemed Bernie hadn't been listening to a word I'd been saying. But he had. At the next meeting I was determined to speak up and break the empty silences. It was always Bernie's show. I wanted to get more involved. I was very excited about the future and wanted to get things moving. Perhaps then, everyone else would open up more and get talking too. I'd hardly said a word when Bernie cut me dead.

'NO!!!!!....I don't want to LISTEN to *YOU*.
..........................You're..................... SELFISH.
I know where *you're* coming from,' he spat back. He began looking around the room. Somewhere else.

'*What? What do you mean? Why?*' I asked, confused.

He spoke into space, ignoring me.

'What we have here,' he began, 'is a *LONE OPERATOR.*'

'*What?*'

'I've been watching you. I know what you're about,' he said, suddenly looking at me straight in the face. 'You're *SELFISH*. You operate purely in your own interests. You're of no use to us if you don't know how to be part of a team. To be a TEAM PLAYER.'

He looked around the room.

'Does anybody here know what I'm talking about?'

I was horrified. Horrified by what was happening. Where was this going? A sinister black hole, an obscene singularity began forming and growing in the pit of my stomach. It started sucking away at my life energy.

Joe, sitting to Bernie's right, slowly started to speak.

'Look, Vince,' he began warmly, but firmly, looking down at the carpet. 'What Bernie's saying is that you gotta drop your *EGO*............... 'See, the trouble is......... you *think* you're better than you *are*..........now, that's not necessarily a *bad* thing but.........'

It was Nick's turn to speak. He humbly and compassionately put in his bit.

'The problem I'm having with you Vince, is that you keep yourself separate. It's hard to talk to you. I really want to get some proper rapport going between us. It's important so we can really make this thing work. We need that to have a chance of getting the guitars to work together. Organically.'

I hated the word 'organic'. Fucking hippy word. Bullshit. Oh, Christ! Who's next? Oh, it's Paul's turn.

'Vince. I *like* you, right? I think you're a cool guy. And I think we can get along. What I think is……. you need to let *go* of some things. It's like Joe, right? When we first met him he was like a bloody *hippy!* But he let all that go. He moved on. He had to change.'

I appreciated his warmth. He was sympathetic. But it seemed like he was talking about something entirely different. What the fuck was going on? Pete stayed silent, gently fingering his drum sticks.

I sat still, fully immobilised, creeped out, not able to say a word.

Bernie disappeared and we adjourned to the pub. Then everyone started being nice to me. But it only served to creep me out further. It reminded me of something, a book I'd read about a guy who'd got indoctrinated into the 'Moonies' religious cult. They'd beat him down one minute and then act nice the next. In the end he got so brainwashed by it all that he had no mind left of his own.

After a couple of drinks I relaxed. Paul was especially friendly. Joe went off talking loudly to someone at the bar. Nick began talking to me about how the guitars were going to work. Then he talked to Pete. Paul talked to me about rhythm. How the bass and rhythm guitar could synchronise. Things began to lose their common sense. I became this non specific awareness right there in the pub. Detached. Just watching all the movements. Hearing sounds, nodding and watching. Joe laughing loudly. Putting his cigarette out. Hearing myself speak and saying things that just fitted in to what seemed appropriate. I noticed a fleck of tobacco on the table. I became mesmerized by it. In that speck were billions of atoms vibrating. It was all made of vibrating atoms. The table. The beer. All the people. I looked at Paul as he was talking. He was vibrating atoms. His eye was made of vibrating atoms. And if you split those atoms into smaller and smaller parts you'd end up with just vibrating energy. Waves of energy. And that was it. All of it. Me and everything and everybody and the whole UNIVERSE an infinitely complex system of vibrating and swirling waves. What a fucking show!

I left early and caught the bus back to Finsbury Park. Thinking. My mind churning over. Was I selfish? A lone operator? I didn't think so. Or *was* I? I didn't know about ego. It seemed like a bad thing. I thought ego meant you had a big head. Boastful. I wasn't boastful! All I knew was I was under pressure to comply with something I had no understanding of. To toe some undefined line. I didn't think there was much I could do about it so I decided to look at it as a test. A test of my composure. Being cool and non-reactive. But it wasn't nice being cast as a suspicious character to watch out for. Perhaps my ideas were dangerous. All it seemed I'd achieved with all my idealistic talk about abolishing hierarchies was to get one firmly established. With me at the bottom of it.

It was a relief to get home and down the pub and relax with the Whale and be with my mates. Just to be normal again. To be with normal people and forget about all this head stuff. They were excited to know how things were going. I tried not to disappoint them.

Then things began moving quickly. New beginnings always bring with them a pile of positive energy. There was way too much going on now to have time to worry about anything. Everyday there was something to do. A photo session had been organised and Kosmo got us up early one Sunday to go down to the Shepherds Bush market. We met up around Joe's to get ready. A pile of clothes were produced and dumped on the floor. I looked at it. It was great stuff. I was in my element and greedily began digging in. I loved clothes and dressing up. Some of it was stuff from the early days of the band. Jackets and shirts that had been specially designed. I chose a black military shirt with red stripes down the side and red under the collar and a double stripe and a red patch on the front. Fucking cool! Joe produced a pair of leather trousers with zips on the pockets and buckles in odd places. He presented them to me, Kosmo watched over us. I grabbed them. Joe said I could keep them. Wicked! I'd never seen such brilliant clothes. I felt like a kid let loose in a sweet shop. Kosmo made sure we didn't all wear the same colour. There had to be some balance in the shades for a black and white picture. Clothes were really mine and Paul's thing. I was passionate about them. Joe and the others didn't seem all that bothered. We were driven down to Shepherds Bush for the session. Wandered around the freezing, deserted streets wearing our leather jackets while the photographer snapped us. Stand here. Stand there. Bit forward. To the left. Hand down a bit. Joe, you go over there. Pete to the front. It seemed to go on for hours. Millions of pictures were taken. Just to get one. It got a bit tedious but grouped together like that made it seem like we were now really a band. The images were developed and they looked good. They seemed to confirm it.

More rehearsing. We're working out some new songs for the tour. One is called 'Are You Ready For War'. Another is called 'We Are The Clash'. And 'The Three Card Trick'. Another meeting in the rehearsal room. I'd decided to keep my head down and my mouth shut after the last one. I knew I had my right of free speech but I'd have to be really pretty dumb enough to try it out again.
Some reporter guy was arriving with a photographer. For a U.S. rag. The photographer took pictures of us in the rehearsal space. They were going to do an article on the new band and they wanted to interview us. We were briefed on what to say. Or rather, what not to say.

'Well, be yourself. But don't say 'It's like a dream come true!' warned Kosmo, quietly, running around like a nervous housewife.

'Oh, fucking hell! Don't be stupid! Don't *worry!*'

One by one we had interviews. It was a bit like being at school, all this stuff going on. Go here, go there. It wasn't much of an interview. Just boring stuff about how I'd auditioned. What bands had I been in? Was I a fan of the Clash before? Yeah of course! It was all a bit shallow and pointless, really. But it made you feel important. People were interested in what you had to say. It was going to be in print. It was like you'd suddenly become a pop star or something. Funny.

Then we took a trip to Bristol. A sort of band outing that Nick had suggested and organised. It was something that the newspaper guys would come on and get stuff for the article. And take more pictures. Bristol was Nick's manor. He'd played in a band called the 'Cortinas' who were from there. I'd never heard them but I liked the name. I wasn't keen on Bristol though. But the trip looked like a great opportunity to get pissed. And it was. We all met up in the Lock Tavern first with loads of our friends, piled on this coach and hit the road. Everyone got hammered. Really let go. I brought my sister and the Whale and a buddy of mine along. That was a mistake bringing the Whale. I could tell something was going on with her. Sometime during the trip down the M4 she'd clammed up and wouldn't talk to me. Just sat there drinking.

'What's up. Whatsamatter with you?' I asked.

'*Nothing.*'

'Oh well. Sulk if you want. But you know you're just being bloody stupid.'

I was damned if I was going to let her bring me down.

'STOP THE BUS! STOP THE BUS!' she suddenly screamed.

She leapt over me and ran down the aisle.

'STOP THIS BUS! NOW!'

The bus ground to a halt. The door swung open and she got off. We were in the middle of nowhere, somewhere near the outskirts of Bristol. I let her go. It was embarrassing. I wasn't going to run after her like some idiot with everybody watching.

I looked out the window. But there she was staggering down the middle of the road, down the white lines of a busy street. Wandering drunkenly, unsteadily from side to side. Cars swerving to avoid hitting her. Honking.

Shit! I dashed through the bus and out to get her. Dodged between the cars, grabbed her arm and dragged her to the roadside.

'What the fuck!?! You fucking idiot! You could get yourself bloody killed. What the fuck do you fucking think you're fucking doing?'

She began crying. Wouldn't speak. I changed tack. Tried to console her. I managed to get her back on the bus. Something was wrong. The bus party went on as if nothing had happened. What was it all about? I didn't understand. I didn't understand women. We hadn't argued or anything. Was there something bothering her deep down? If there was she wouldn't talk about it. I put it down to girls being crazy. Or some kind of chick test. But it worried me. Her making such a spectacle of herself like that. It wasn't cool.

We piled in this club. The Dungehole club. There weren't many people there. Just us, the Clash, and what looked like a load of students. Soul and funk music was playing. I didn't like soul and funk music. Everyone was going around happily talking and chatting but I got fed up as usual. The travelling bit is great but the arriving is a let down. Then you're obliged to socialise but you don't feel like it. But the more you don't feel like it the more you realise this pressure that you're supposed to. And so on and so on. A vicious circle. I looked around the room. Fucking phonies! I suddenly hated them all. Everyone. The Bristol lot. What were we doing there anyway? More structured university types who thought 'Wire' were really cool. Obsessed with what they thought was hip. Who'd probably never experienced a single moment of self abandonment in their entire lives. I'd had my fill of fucking university. Those people liked to identify their music on a head level. So that it represented their self image. And that image was the same as everybody else's self image. Certain things were in and certain things were out. And if you weren't in then you were out. And the end result was separation between mind and spirit. Between the imagined and the real. Did anyone *really* believe that the Clash were better than the Sex Pistols? I sunk deeper and deeper into a funk. There was no way out.

I took the Whale's hand and led her to the girl's toilet. It was understood. She checked for people. No one was in there. She beckoned me in to one of the cubicles and we quickly got at it. A bit of difficulty getting it in there. But once it slid into place the machinery began doing its stuff. And it did it hard and a bit violent. This is what she gets for trying to make a fucking fool of me, I thought! She better bloody well behave herself in future!

We rejoined the party. No one noticed we'd gone. I gave her a kiss on the cheek. Things suddenly looked better.

All in all it was a successful trip. Everyone seemed to have fun. The journalist got the stuff for his article. The photographer got his pictures. In a roadside café Kosmo had remarked to the journalist:

'See, even *SOCIALISTS* can have fun too.'

Oh dear. There it was. It had arrived. It was something I'd pushed to the back of my mind. Something I knew would come up at some point. It was on its way as sure as the sun. Politics. Everyone knew the Clash were a political band. A SOCIALIST band. Nick had begun sporting a red hammer and sickle star on his leather jacket. Was I obliged to be a *socialist* now too, as well as a wild guitarist?

The trouble was I wasn't. I wasn't anything. Not any something-*ist* anyway. Apart from maybe a *guitarist*. Not any Socialist, Communist, Activist, Maoist, Fascist, Rightist, Baptist, lobbyist, Bolshevist, pacifist, monarchist, racist, capitalist, sexist, masochist or any other kind of bollocks. People and their fucking labels! There was so much of it around at the university I went to, and at that time, if you weren't marching or angrily supporting some cause or other people thought there was something wrong with you. Like you didn't care. But I *did* care. I just thought differently. I never felt that the problems of humanity would ever be resolved by political reform however nobly they tried to tart it up. Politics *WAS* the problem! Trying to explain that to a bunch of hysterical student activists whose only desire was to get even with 'them' was futile. They were closed. Argumentative. Convinced they were right and you or everybody else was always wrong. If you believed in individualism and liberty as I did they called you a *fascist!* They were boorish. They couldn't see that it was that very attitude that was the problem. Fighting for peace. What a joke. Attacking always produced an equal or greater amount of resistance. They saw me as hopelessly idealistic. I left them to it. To their anti-this and their anti-that. My interest was in all things metaphysical and to do with philosophy and psychology and evolution. That the only real way forward was through a radical shift in thinking. You could keep hacking away at the branches but new one's would just keep growing back and things would never change. You had to chop at the root of things.

In those days I'd approach some idiot handing out leaflets for the Socialist Workers Party or something like that. They would immediately try and recruit you to some meeting or other. But when you asked reality based questions all you got back was a load of party propaganda. They didn't listen. Short on questions and long on answers. They only heard the noise in their heads. Their understanding was shallow at best. A few facts here and a few facts there and suddenly they acted like they knew it all and had all the solutions to all of mankind's problems. I felt it was *them* that didn't really care. If they did, they would go into these things far more deeply with a greater understanding. I distrusted their motives. They weren't interested in the truth. I suspected the real reason for their involvement was that it satisfied a deep seated need to *belong* to something. Filling the gaping chasm of a meaningless, empty life. What better way to avoid the lonely Sunday afternoon void than meeting up with your comrades and spending the day shouting and getting pissed? Identifying with a cause, larger and greater than themselves, one they were easily convinced was noble and humanitarian, intoxicated them with a sense of self-righteous power. All the personal conflict and anger and resistance that existed in their dull, frustrated private lives could then be vented out towards other groups they perceived as the enemy. In their minds was a simplistic equation: Capitalism=money=greed= BAD. Socialism=equality=humanitarian=GOOD.

I hated politics. I wanted Anarchy and the end of politics altogether. It was simple. No one had any claim on me and I had no claim on anyone else. I believe that people are basically good and only aggression and coercion is immoral. No one has the right to use force against anyone else except in self defence. Only government has a *legalised* monopoly on the use of aggression. Government wasn't 'left' or 'right'. Government was and is a group of individuals who have the use of guns and tanks and are violent. Government fights wars with other governments and kills millions. Government abducts children into state schools by force, indoctrinates and brainwashes them to the ways of the state and finances it all with theft. Government was and *is* evil by definition. There is no such thing as a 'good' government.

I hate that legend of Robin Hood. If that green tight wearing socialist prick came anywhere near me I'd cut his fucking balls off. And his 'merry' collective! Guy Fawkes is my hero. Now *there* was a guy with the intelligence and guts to really take it on! Of course there's Ghandi and basically anybody who can speak rationally and truthfully. After all, there is no 'society'. Or 'government'. You'd have a hard time finding it. It's just an abstraction. In Britain there are 60 million human beings living on an island who believe what they're told because it's easier to go along with the herd than it is to think for themselves.

I knew getting to a state of anarchy would be slow and was coming sometime (maybe!) and immediate action had to be taken to deal with the mess that government itself had created. But it wasn't something to get all that excited about and take personally and start blaming. For me it was a dirty business and sort of necessary. Like garbage collecting. I steered clear of it because if you got yourself involved in all that you'd inevitably start to smell.

I'd overheard Nick and Pete discussing socialist theory a bit and relating it to this and that but no overtly political talk had come up yet. Nearly a month in and Joe hadn't mentioned a word about it. Nor Paul or Bernie. I didn't believe they were all that into it really. I was grateful. I didn't really understand where it came from anyway. How the Clash had become labelled as socialists. The early songs and lyrics were always from a personal point of view. Simple statements of personal frustration, powerlessness, isolation, confusion and social commentary. Dismay at the world. That was what was good about them. They were things you could easily relate to and feel.

No socialist dogma and the like. Telling you how to 'vote'. How to put it all to rights. I guess people just fill in the missing pieces by themselves. Make the assumptions they want to make. How the hell so many could get all worked up about the rebels in Nicaragua was a mystery to me. More righteous indignation from people who knew very little about it all except what they'd read in papers and intellectual books and hadn't even *been* there. The Clash had exploited all this for their own ends. To sell records. Its function was entertainment. But people stupidly just lapped it up as reality.

Another photo session. Six hours in a studio under hot lights. Tiny movements of the hands and feet. Head movements. More clothes changes but already the novelty has worn off. Recording a tape for the soundman in the states. One last rehearsal. I reckon I've got it. Tomorrow we're off!!!

VERSE:

CALIFORNIA DREAMIN'

I stumbled out the toilet, bent down by the nearest window and pulled up the plastic shutter. I stuck my head up against the glass and gazed out. 30,000 feet. It was 1p.m. We'd been up in the air for about 3 hours. The sun had sunk back to the horizon and was stuck there, casting a thin sepia, a shadowy half light over the earth. Thousands and thousands of square miles of broken bits of ice and snow lay below. Some bits of sea. All that nothing stuff. It was majestic. Magical. No people, cities, animals or anything confusing. I was caught in time, hovering over the end of a dying world.

   I went back to my seat. Everyone in the plane had pulled their windows down and were pretending to sleep. They weren't interested in what lay outside. Maybe they were bored with it. Perhaps they weren't able to look at it. I didn't understand. I didn't understand people.

My seat was in the middle aisle next to Paul. I got out my book and got on with some reading. It was going to be a long trip to L.A.

'What's that you're reading?' he asked, flexing his hand out on some rubber grip thing. It was supposed to strengthen your guitar hand. Paul was always on show.

'Arthur C. Clarke.' I held the cover up.

His face darkened.

'What are you reading *that* for?'

'It's fucking brilliant! There's this story of this kid, right? He has super powers. He can do anything he wants. He only has to *think* something and it happens. He lives in this village and makes the rest of the world disappear. Just with his mind. Everyone has to think good thoughts or he does something bad to them. He makes animals eat themselves and all sorts of crazy shit. Mental!'

'You don't need to be reading things like that.'

I looked at his face. Paul was deadly serious.

'What? Nah. It's good. Really.'

Paul withdrew back into himself, looking straight ahead. Carried on flexing that grip. I wanted to explain something but didn't bother.

I carried on looking at the words on the page. I knew what he was thinking. That it was probably better I was reading Trotsky or something.

It bothered me a bit. I'll read what I fucking want, I thought. But you didn't want that pressure anyway. To change interests and fit in with something else. I'd been told I was in the band because of my 'attitude'. I had no attitude. I simply had no respect for authority. In whatever shape or form it came. I just wanted to be myself. I never thought of myself as a punk. A horrible word. Another label. Another haircut. Or whatever. For me, punk meant freedom. Freedom to be yourself. The whole world was doing it's best to make you like everybody else.

OUT OF CONTROL: The Last Days of The Clash

Conform. Be a number. Follow the rules. Well, fuck 'em. Being yourself and expressing your opinion seemed to be the right thing to do. I questioned a lot of stuff but my values were really only governed by what I liked. It was my own kind of aesthetic. If I enjoyed something I did it so long as it didn't hurt anyone else. But as the Clash machine began to roll it soon became apparent that wasn't enough. Be opinionated and do and say what you think as long as it fits in with our agenda. Be truthful. Yes. As long as it corresponds with *our* truth. Be wild as long as you don't cross the line.

It wasn't a band I'd joined. I began to feel like I'd joined a kind of cult.

On the way in I swapped places with someone so I could see out the seat window. As we tumbled through the thick clouds I took another swig of beer. I looked down at the can. Budwieser. I'd never seen the beer before except in the movies. I fingered every detail of the can. All the tiny writing. Made in U.S.A. A sudden wave of space and freedom and a great sense of possibilities crashed through me. FUCK, I LOVE AMERICA! I LOVE COUNTRY MUSIC!

Customs was easy and we all jumped in cabs to the hotel. I got in one with Nick and Pete. As we rolled down the streets I couldn't speak. Just looking out at everything. Every other car seemed to be a 1965 Ford Mustang. Cruising, relaxed and easy. Big spaces. Open roads. Powerful, 'don't give a shit' cool. Finsbury Park was a long way off.

'Yeah, it's really something isn't it?' said Nick.

'Yeah, amazing.'

He'd been here before. Seen it, done it sort of thing. He knew it well. I didn't care. I didn't miss a thing on that ride in.

Suddenly, this tall, young woman appeared on the pavement. Long blonde hair in the sun. Long legs. Short skirt and white stilettos swinging along. The works.

'Wow! Fucking hell! Look at that!' I yelled. 'STOP THE CAR! STOP THE CAR! STOP THE FUCKING CAR!' Everyone laughed. The driver laughed.
'No I *mean* it. STOP THE CAR!'
The driver didn't stop. He carried on, laughing. We all laughed. It was all too much.
After nearly an hour's drive we pulled up to the Holiday Inn, Hollywood and checked in.
I got my key, found my room, threw my bags on the floor. Looked around. Two big double beds. A clean bathroom with little bits of soap and things. I flopped out on one of the big beds and thought I'd better rest a bit. Jumped up and checked my reflection in the mirror. Went over to the big window and checked the view. Cars down there were ambling slowly down a long boulevard. My future was that long road, stretching out forever towards the sun. A road of limitless adventure.
Time suddenly stood still. Couldn't it move a bit faster? I emptied my bags. Put things around. Clothes in the drawers. Had a shower and changed. I was just about to get out of there and hit the bar when there was a knock at the door. I opened it. It was Kosmo.
'Here, Vince, I've got some money for you. Three hundred dollars. You'll get some more late….er…..fucking *HELL!*…………..what's *THAT!?!!!!!!*'
He looked down at one of the open drawers with a few socks and t-shirts in it.
'Are you moving in or what?' he sniggered.
'Uhm. Well. I dunno. We're here for a few days, aren't we? Whatever.'
Kosmo laughed. I wasn't sure what I'd done but whatever it was, I could see it was very stupid.
I grabbed the three hundred dollar bills and stuffed them in my pocket.
'So, what's going on?' he asked, looking me up and down.

'What do you mean?'

'The clothes. What's happened?'

I looked down at what I was wearing. A light shirt. Casual trousers. Suede shoes. I thought I looked pretty cool.

'Where's the great *Vince?* Eh? You're a *punk*. Where's your leather trousers?'

He sucked hard on his cigarette, smirking through a great cloud of smoke. Kosmo always had a fag going.

'Oh, look, I'm just getting comfortable. You know. Relaxing and that.'

'VINCE! Don't you *realise* that as soon as you walk out that door you're on *SHOW!* Remember that. You're VINCENT. You're a PUNK! Think about it.'

He turned and walked out.

I thought about it. I just waited for him to get some distance. Quickly, grabbed my cigarettes and went out.

By now it was late afternoon. The sun painting everything. It felt weird gaining eight hours but I loved the sense of dislocation you get with travelling and jet lag. I wandered down the boulevard, a bit spaced out, trying to buy some things and get some change. No one would change a hundred dollar bill. Store after store wouldn't or didn't have change. Eventually I managed to get a couple of tapes. Black Uhuru and BB King. A pair of socks. A comb. When I got back, Joe was there in the lobby, alone at the bar. He seemed happy.

'Hey Vince!' he yelled, with a new American twang. 'Wanna beer?'

'Oh, yeah, man!'

I walked over, leaned with my back against the bar and looked around waiting for the beer. There were a number of business types sitting in there looking focused and sad. Up came the beer in a big round glass. Ice cold with condensation all over it. The bartender set a little paper napkin underneath. It was just like the movies. We got to talking about movies.

'Rebel Without a Cause. Now that was IT. The defining moment,' he said, intensely leaning forward with all the presence he could muster. He was trying to teach me something incredible.

'Jimmy Dean. You know, it was *Jimmy* who really started it. Before then there was NOTHING.'

'Well, yeah, it's a great film but………'

'Now BRANDO! He was the first but it was Jimmy Dean that really got it off the ground. Truly.'

'Yeah, I like the movie but, you know, I don't rate him as an actor, man. Brando's the real deal alright but Dean? All that scrunching his face up. The pained expression. Looked a bit phoney to me. Trying too hard.'

Joe glared at me like he'd just found out I'd been molesting a 10 year old or something.

'NO! James Dean was a VERY TALENTED ACTOR! *VERY TALENTED.*'

He turned away getting another sip of beer. I could tell he was getting a bit annoyed with me.

I was on one.

'See, thing is, Joe, I think most of these icons are overrated. Marilyn Monroe. I don't get it. All those posters plastered over millions of bedroom walls. All that dumb girly appeal. Doesn't do it for me. She was FAT!'

'Marilyn was SEX ON LEGS!' he snapped back. 'She OOZED sexuality.'

The way Joe said the word 'sexuality' somehow seemed so sexless.

'Man, I just don't see it.'

'PURE SEX!'

'Nah. It's all hype.'

'PURE SEX!'

He wouldn't have it. Joe was really attached to his icons. He went on.

'And like Kerouac. Now he......'

'Who?'

'Kerouac. This guy, he wrote a book called 'On the Road'. Haven't you heard of it?'

'No. What's it about?'

'It's amazing. He travelled around, criss crossing the country in beat up ol' cars with his friend, Dean Moriarty. It's the story of his journeys. You really *HAVE* to read it.'

'What's the name?'

He quickly grabbed a napkin and scribbled the name down. Handed it to me.

'There!'

'Cool. Thanks.'

I stuffed the bit of paper in my pocket. I'd definitely check that Kerouac guy out.

The next day Nick and I were taken by our road manager to some huge guitar store. We needed guitars to play on stage. We were told we could each choose two. It didn't take long. Nick picked out two Les Paul juniors. I saw a black custom I liked the look of and a white studio version.

We both strummed a few chords and that was it. They were quickly paid for and we were out of there. No point fucking around. I had no respect for instruments. They did a job. I never understood the obsession with them. All that endless goofing off sitting around in guitar shops playing 'Stairway to Heaven'. It was stupid. It got in the way of things.

Before I knew it we were on our way out to our first show in Santa Barbara. In two cars. Joe and Bernie were up in the front one. I was in the other with Pete, Paul and Nick. We'd been given strict instructions never to refer to any concert as a 'gig'. Forthwith, any gig we played was to be called a 'show'. 'Gig' was second rate. Only losers said 'gig'.

I didn't know where Santa Barbara was. I thought it was in L.A. somewhere. The trip seemed to take hours. I wasn't used to the long driving. I quickly grew restless. Such an incredible number of cars on the freeway running in both directions. Where were they all going? Where were *we* going? We slowed down in the traffic. Speeded up. Slowed down again. The evening sun blazed over it all. The sun didn't care. But then after an hour or so we were out of that traffic and free. Moving.

There was a lot of joking and cocky bravado going on my car. Endless banter about knowing this person and this obscure this and that. The loud ego clatter. None of it interested or amused me. I tried to join in here and there. After all I reasoned, we were supposed to be a band, weren't we? The more I tried the worse it got. I'd throw in something here and there only creating confused silences. I stopped bothering with it and left them to it. Watched the pacific coast drifting past. Out there lay that great, flat, immense body of water, peaceful and serene, shimmering in the hot evening sun. Next stop Hawaii. Every now and again a large bungalow of the rich and famous came into view. What the fuck went on in those bungalows?

The Arlington in Santa Barbara was one of those crusty old theatres. With an old time vibe. It was strangely at odds with all the new housing and the wide streets and the sea drive and the glorious sunset. Walking around inside I could have been back in London. The same grubby, rank smell. Back home, those places, the Lyceum, the Music Machine, the Academy had their urban charm. But here it just looked pathetic. Just another shabby monument to human entertainment.

We quickly got down to business. Sound check. Getting sounds. Drum sound. Bass drum. Boom. Boom. Boom. Boom.

Snare please. Clash. Clash. Clash. Clash. Clash. Clash. Some tom tom. And on and on it goes. Some bass. Dah. Dah---dah-dah-dah-dah-daah. Dah—dah-dah-dah-dah-daah. Guitar please? Who? Nick playing the chords to Clash City Rockers. Over and over and over. The lead part. Then me playing London Calling. The lead. Vocals. 1-2 -3 -4. 1-2-3 -4. 1-2-3-4.1-2-3-4. Can't anyone count above 4? Where's Joe. Joe finally arrives. He's the star. We run through a couple of songs. Clash City Rockers. Nick plays lead. Then 'Brand New Cadillac'. I play the lead bit and then Joe:

'Ok. That's it.'

We're done. We go back to the dressing room and wait. And it's the same scene and ritual that wouldn't change for two more years.

In our dressing room is a long mirror with those big light bulbs around the edges like you see in films where the precocious film star puts on their make up. In front sits a long table laden with fruit. Oranges, apples, pears, grapes, a big pineapple. I never saw any of it get eaten. Ever. But there it was. Time and time again this ton of bloody fruit kept appearing for no reason whatsoever. Some sandwiches. Some nick nacks. A large bottle of Remi Martin. Next to the table sits a couple of crates of imported Heineken. I grab a bottle and start sucking. We start changing our clothes.

Bernie arrives and comes in to give us a pep talk. Such and such a number are in the audience. It's a sold out show. Raymond, our body guard, comes in and I'm suddenly aware of a noise from the open door. The hall is filling up. It's a strange unearthly deep rumbling like the sound of an approaching army. Only they haven't come to kill us. Or have they? Raymond shuts the door but the low hum from the growing crowd still penetrates the dressing room. It permeates everything and with time it gets louder and louder. That vibration fills my body. Fills my mind. I shine my boots. Nick is shining his. And Paul. Mine don't need shining but I think it helps me focus.

Raymond comes in again with a slightly nervous look. 10 minutes to SHOWTIME. He looks at me. I grin back. My heart is beginning to pound. My arms feel as light as feathers and not really parts of me anymore. In fact my whole body starts to feel outside of me. My mind though, is a placid lake of stillness. I have a strong feeling of familiarity about this. An odd feeling like I've been here and done this many times before. A few ripples pass across the lake as I mentally check a few things. Joe begins making a few 'aah- aah' noises, gets up and hunched over begins moving around. He's wearing white combat trousers. He's the old hand. Like an old time sea captain he swaggers around and shifts slowly towards the shower gargling something from a glass. He carries this 'aah-aah' thing on inside the shower only louder now. Paul jumps up and struts a bit in front of the mirror. Dancing from leg to leg. He's wearing camouflage combat trousers and a sleeveless combat shirt. Runs his hand through his hair. Pouting at the mirror.

Raymond comes in again and the noise pounding through the open door threatens to engulf me.

'Ok. You're on.'

I jump up and we head towards the door. Paul hands me a small plastic cup with a shot of the Remi in it and grins confidently at me. I'm grateful for it. The grin I mean, not the booze. Well, both actually.

'Alright, Vince?!'

'FUCKIN' A1!' I reply loudly. 'LET'S GOOOOOOOOOOO!'

Everyone has a shot in their hands. We knock them back in unison and file out the door.

We move quickly, Raymond leading us towards the stage. We pass all these people on the way. Wide eyed frozen faces stare back. Who *are* all these people? We sneak past the drums and get in behind a giant black curtain that covers the whole stage.

Some people in the audience have seen us though. Cheers multiply throughout the hall. The power of all those voices brings me fully in the moment. I'm here. My guitars are there, waiting on stands. I check the amps are switched on and the standby is off. Pick up the studio and pull it around my neck. There's a crack as I push in the jack plug. Turn the volume knob up a bit, strum the strings and to make sure there's some sound. Make sure the bass pickup volume knob is turned down and flick the pickup control there. Turn up the treble volume knob. I'm ready.

I look to my left. Joe is going through some mental paces jogging from foot to foot. We're both standing on the edge of the drum riser.

'Ready for action, boss!' I say, laughing.

Joe ignores me. He's lost in some inner space.

Kosmo's nearly finished his introduction and in the loudest raspiest Cockney voice he can muster:

'............and I'd like to welcome you. AAAAWWWLLL THE WAY FROM WEST LONDON, ENGLAND............THE

CLLLLLAAAAAAAAAASSSSSSSHHHHHHHHH!!!'

Pete is hitting the final count of four. The crowd roars. I flick the pick-up switch to the treble. The curtain shoots up. Lights blaze. I leap off the drum riser, punching out staccato chords and 'London Calling' crashes in. I find myself riding a giant wave of cheers and deafening noise. It threatens to sweep me away. But I'm good. Just there riding it. Balanced. I'm a pro. I can barely hear or think though. Shit. The chorus has arrived. Missed it. Low E chord. I'm singing the refrain. Paul arrives from nowhere next to me and we're singing it together. He disappears. I'm tottering a bit precariously after that but quickly find my balance. As Nick starts the solo I realize something's wrong. I can't hear my guitar. I edge backwards to the amps. There's no sound at all. I check all the dials. Everything *should* be working. I look at my guitar roadie, Tim but he's just staring out blankly towards the crowd. I shout to him. He sees me. I point to the amp helplessly. He slowly comes to and realises something is wrong. He runs across and begins fiddling around with leads. I carry on uselessly hitting out dead chords. I'm no longer on the wave. I'm floundering around down in the surf while the others are fast making distance without me.

'What the fuck's wrong?' I scream, helplessly.

No answer. Tim is in back of the amps now replacing the leads. Comes back round the front. It's the end of the song. Huge applause. Shit! He snaps the lead out of my guitar and replaces it with another. Still no sound. What's wrong? 'Safe European Home' starts. A new wave is crashing in. And I'm not on it. Fucking hell, get it together man! Tim is round the back again. He's figured something out because suddenly my guitar erupts back into life. Hallelujah! But where is everybody? Nick's arrived from the other side of the stage standing next to me slamming out the chords. I look at his fretboard. I can't hear Joe at all. I think we're *there*. Yes. I join back in scrambling quickly to get back on the wave. Yeah, that's it. It's going well. It's the end part. The reggae bit. That's me. I chop out the chords but the sound of screaming feedback suddenly appears, screeching over the top. It's not Jimi Hendrix. It's the amplified sound of thousands of finger nails endlessly scraping obscenely down a blackboard. I move to the front of the stage, to the left but it won't go away. I move to the right but like a turd that won't flush, it just keeps coming back. Joe's beginning to sing the end part. He's looking over at me angrily. But as the song picks up and I hit the louder chords the feedback seems to disappear. Slowing down at the end and all together we crash- end the sound, holding......................BANG-AH!   Stop. Relief! The crowd screams. The song's over but my guitar carries on howling like some demented animal. I switch it off and it stops.

Run to the amp to adjust the treble and volume setting but the next wave's already begun and the others are all on it and moving away again without me. Oh God! In my confusion I don't even remember what song I'm supposed to be playing! I run to my set list. Shit! It's 'Know Your Rights'! The wave's crested but it's easy to get back on. There's only one chord in that song after all. I'm aware of a sick feeling in the pit of my stomach spreading out through my arms and legs. The song ends to incredible cheers. Joe announces:

'Thank You. Thank you. I'd like to welcome you......welcome you now ....HEY! *HEY!* give me some LAAAAIGHT! Do me the honour of welcoming ....over here................. Mr VINCE WHITE on the GUITAAAAAAAAAR!!!'

I hold my arm stupidly in the air. Isn't that what you're supposed to do? I'm expecting boo's and hisses but amazingly I get a massive cheer. Cool whistles. But I feel a fraud. An imposter. I've done nothing but fuck up so far.

'And on the other side. Mr. Nick Shepperd. Another guitar.' More cheers.

'And one more at the back of the stage. Pete Howard on the drums. Are you ready for WAAAAR???!!!!!'

Pete starts a funky intro and we're off. In the middle my guitar cuts out again. Tim gets it going again a bit quicker this time. Paul and Nick are all over the stage. I try moving around but with all the chords to remember at the same time, it's too difficult. I decide to remain in the same spot and play the songs as best as I can remember them. Through howls of feedback and my guitar constantly cutting out I somehow make it to the end of the set and through the encore. Deafening applause. Raymond hands me a white towel as I head off. He's smiling and encouraging but I'm bad. I know I've screwed it. We gather back in the dressing room.

Bernie comes in but doesn't say too much. He turns to Nick.
'Well, done.'

He says nothing to me. Everyone's joking. Pete is laughing. Nobody looks or speaks to me. That sick hole in my stomach remains. I change my clothes and soon it's time to move out and meet the 'people'. We troop outside to a group of a couple of dozen or so fans. They want autographs. I sit down in a chair and bits of paper get thrust at me. They don't even ask. It's just expected. I start signing my new name. To who? Sarah? Who? Vicki. Keep on rocking Vicki! From Vince x. I'm chain drinking Heineken. Raymond brings them up to me one after the other. Soon that sick feeling gets replaced with a warm careless glow. Fuck it. Fuck 'em. Fuck it all. I'm painfully aware of an incredible self loathing but I've no idea what to do with it. A couple of young girls come up and compliment me on my performance but it only seems to make matters worse. I do my best to keep up a solid front and try not to disappoint anyone. Someone looks down at me brimming full of excitement and tells me the new Clash is AWESOME DUDE! I look up at him and fake a smile.

'Thanks,' I say, confidently scrawling away.

When the party's over we move out to the parking lot for the drive back. On the way to the car Joe says to me he doesn't understand why I didn't move around much on stage. He thinks I'm a pretty wild guy and got so much energy. What happened? He doesn't get it. He's not mean. Just sort of disappointed.

I get in the car with Bernie and Joe and we drive back to the hotel. Nothing much is said. A few words here and there. It was a good crowd. The support, Los Lobos went down well. Something about the promoter. I think secretly though, they're all thinking about me. What an obvious bloody mistake they've made gambling on this spiky haired unknown wannabe. I steel myself, preparing to be given my running orders at any moment.

'Look, Vince, we really don't think this is gonna work out. I know you're disappointed but we have to be realistic about this.' Or some such thing. They still haven't come when we finally pull in back at the hotel. Hardly a word has been said to me. I realise I'm still in with a chance. Tomorrow we leave for San Francisco.

It takes less than an hour to fly there and we book into the Sheraton. I throw my clothes on the bed opposite and lay down, trying to relax and think it out. Nothing has prepared me for this. I'd played live before. In bands. The biggest being the back room at the George Robey in Finsbury Park to about 10 people. Playing a few small clubs and pubs hadn't helped in the slightest. I'm painfully aware of being out of my depth and more than a bit overwhelmed. I don't know what to do. All I know is I've got to do something. The Santa Barbara experience had taught me one important lesson. That it didn't matter how prepared you were beforehand, *nothing* could prepare you for that moment when the curtain went up. *Everything* changed. You moved into some other dimension. Like an alternative universe where normal laws of reality didn't apply anymore. At sound check you had it all down of course. The chords, the backing singing, the arrangements. The sound. You had it all in your head. You got it just right so you could hear yourself, the drums, singing, Nick's guitar, Joe's vocal. Your vocal in the monitor. Then with a full hall and everything on full tilt it all went out the window. In the moment it all meshed into one giant thing of screaming people, guitar chords and drums and adrenalin and surprises. And the surprises weren't usually good ones. I needed a new set of ears. Performance ears. Where could I get them? I didn't have the time to grow them. I needed something fast. What I needed was a bloody miracle.

That night we went out to a Cuban night club. Paul, me, Nick and Pete. It was Paul's idea. He was into latin music. I was drinking beer, slumped in a chair. Still stinging. Still thinking.
  'Hey, Vince! Whatsup?!' he said, grinning at me.

'Oh. You know. I'm pissed off about last night. I fucked up. I feel I let the side down.'

He looked at me like I was mad to even think about it.

'Look, Vince,' he said, 'when we started I couldn't even *play*. None of us could, really. I had to put markers on the guitar neck so I'd know where the notes were. It was mayhem. Chaos. Don't worry about it!' he laughed.

I finished my beer. The waitress came over with more. Paul spoke politely to her. She came back with a full tray of tequila shots. We began knocking them back one after the other. I ordered another beer. I looked over at Nick. He was talking loudly to Pete. He was confident. He'd done good. He'd set a high standard.

Paul and I carried on talking. I began to feel better. What was I worrying about? That was my fucking trouble. I thought too much. But in that moment I was humbled. I looked at Paul. I hadn't given him much credit. I didn't think he was intelligent in the abstract thought kind of way. But I knew only too well that 'intelligent' people were often the stupidest. The 'intelligent' types I'd known at university could get the grades but you couldn't rely on them help you do something as simple as put up a tent. I prided myself in being 'intelligent'. But all my thinking seemed to do was create an even bigger mess for myself. I couldn't see the wood for the trees. Even when I did resolve some question it just opened doors to more questions until you got lost in it all and became frozen. His attitude was an example. I began to understand something. That none of it really mattered. You just got on with it. You let it go and let it happen. And what will be will be. Sort of anyway. Nothing seemed to bother Paul. Things happened and he just gracefully rolled with it. And suddenly it didn't bother me anymore. I remembered that bit in the Clash film 'Rude Boy' where he steals money in the taxi from the girl. I liked that moment.

'What about Rude Boy? What happened there?'

'It's terrible. A terrible film. We didn't want it released but we didn't have any choice. We signed something. They put it out anyway.'
'Nah! It's not all that bad. The live stuff in it was great.'
'I hate it. When it was released none of us went to see it. It's awful. Depressing.'
'I liked that bit with you in the back of the cab. That was funny.'
He smiled. We got drunker. Paul had some advice for me.
'When I go out on stage, Vince, I imagine I'm Billy the Kid. That's it. I'm Billy the Kid. Taking it on. All guns blazing. That's all you need, Vince. Just see yourself as something.'

We left Nick and Pete talking and wandered on to the dance floor. There were no hit hot young sexy chicks there to play with. Just ugly, fat women doing a kind of funky lambada type thing. We began dancing with them. Getting all the sexy moves going with them. Laughing our stupid heads off. They began laughing too. It was so ridiculous. And of course it was. Because nothing really mattered anyway.

The next day four of us drove out to Mill Valley. It was a beautiful, sunny day. Went shopping around the market and the record stores. Bought some vinyl. Crossed the Golden Gate Bridge and up into the hills. Hung out in a log cabin up there amongst the trees. It was owned by a couple who knew the band. It was beautiful up there. A bit hippy and peaceful and as a punk you weren't supposed to like that kind of thing. All I could think was it was such a contrast to my grubby little bedsit and all the noise and filth and madness of Finsbury Park. One of the rooms was especially reserved for frogs. Or was it ducks? I can't remember. Toy ones. All different colours. There must have been a thousand different toy frogs or ducks in there. It was the girl's thing. It was a beautiful home. It looked to me like they had plenty of money to spare. I dreamt of being rich too and living in a place like that. With the sun cascading through the trees into a little wooden room like that overflowing with toys. Living the good life.

We drove back for the soundcheck. Joe was in a funny, serious mood. He'd been told that the ousted members, Mick Jones and Topper Headon had formed a new band and were calling it the Clash. What was going to happen? He didn't say much about it. I didn't know what to think. But it was time for me to stop thinking and just get on with things.

The Civic Auditorium in San Fransico was a lot bigger. I think there were around 40,000 people at that show. As the hall filled up straight away you could sense the size of the audience. I stood at the side of the stage and watched Los Lobos do their thing. They were good. They were different. I don't think the crowd knew what to make of them. They were waiting for us.

The same ritual in the dressing room. I sneaked a few extra Remi's hoping no one would notice. And then another. And another. Then the ritual last one we all drank when Raymond came in and called:

'SHOWTIME!'

Back behind that black curtain again. Restless, stomping expectancy out there. Of course you couldn't see it. But you felt it in your bones. Joe there next to me in his dark Ray-bans holding that decrepit Telecaster. Hunched over head down, breathing deeply. Muttering. Something dark and monstrous was in there pacing around. Trapped and restless getting ready to leap out. Feeding time. I got myself ready. For something. This time I'm gonna do it. Just do it. No idea what. Just DO *IT*. This is war.

Suddenly, the curtain shoots up and that intense hot white light slams right into me. I leap off the drum riser and there we are again. Airborne. Back in the sky to face the enemy with only two hours of flying behind me. I pull the joy stick right back and shoot straight up. I know I can do it. Enemy at 8 o'clock! I throw the stick hard to the left and swoop down hurling a salvo of burning bullets. I've hit a wing. I miss the main target. The fuel tanks. But it was close. No worry. I've plenty of ammunition. What was that? The rapid, dull sound of bullets tear through my fuselage. Some clanking of metal on metal. Smoke. I'm shaken but I'm OK. Shit! That was close! I was still for too long. That's the problem. Gotta keep moving! Stationary targets are vulnerable. I instinctively pull the stick hard back and to the right. I bank swiftly out of trouble. Out of the corner of my eye I see Nick. He has the enemy in sights. Firing. He scores a direct hit and I watch the target fall from the sky. I turn to look forward. The target looms in front of me. I jam my thumb on the firing button maniacally shooting cannons. Swoop past and roll back. The target goes down in a plume of smoke. A hit! Yes!

I see Joe and swoop down next to him. He sees me and nods. He's on target. I fall back to help Pete who's gunning down a stationary target. I start spraying the target incessantly. We both are. Back and forth. Back and forth. It's just a matter of time before it gives up the ghost and falls. Stick back. High and far and drop. I've no idea where I'll fall. But that's it! No idea. Just keep moving! Another target appears and I'm shooting. I clip it. It's wounded but still flying. I think I'll turn back and finish……it……off…...but out of nowhere I realise I'm under attack from above and behind. The sickly sound of death screams all around. Smoke rising. I begin to panic. I throw the stick forward and start falling. Pull to the left. Bullets shatter my windscreen. I can't see a thing. Icy fear. Dropping. Somehow I manage to pull out of the drop, rising up with the team and enemy blurring all around me. I begin shooting aimlessly. All over the shop. Fuck, I'm losing it. Get a fucking *grip* man! In desperation I pull hard to the left and clear. I quickly check my equipment. A strange buzzing noise. But there's no time to waste. I bank hard back into the fray. Another target. Another salvo. Another hit! Then another. I'm back on the wave. A surge of confidence and aggressive power is coursing through every fibre. I'm there. Fluid motion. It's happening without me. My hands and feet and brain and all begin to synchronise in effortless control. I swoop up next to Paul. Flying in formation. We look quickly at each other. I smile. There's no grin from Paul now. No joy. Just grim determination. There's a job to be done. We bank left and right. I remember something about the sun. Dive from the sun and the enemy can't see you coming. I soar high and fall. As I do I see Nick on target again. All guns blazing. I see another target. Head in for the kill. Suddenly I realize I'm under attack from behind but forget about it and concentrate on the score. Fuck it! I pile on the pressure determined to get a hit. The target goes up in smoke. I quickly pull left. But it's too late. Smoke streams from my engine. But I'm still flying. I've another kill. And now the battle is over. Thunderous applause. All five of us regroup and swoop back over with three victory rolls. We return to base. Victorious.

Back in the dressing room I survey the damage. My right hand is covered in blood. There's blood spattered about my shirt and arm. I've torn open the soft skin behind the nail of my right forefinger and it's still bleeding. The little finger of my right hand is badly swollen. I can't move it and it's throbbing painfully. I hadn't been aware of it until now. I realise I must've hit it on the guitar body somewhere doing those arm twirls. I go up to the mirror. Shit! There's blood on my face too. Ray looks at me and laughs. I wash it off with the stage towel.

Bernie comes in and he's pleased. He tells me I did good. He says everyone did good. The show went down well. There's a quiet confidence in the room. Joe comes over and looks down at my bloody hand.

'What happened?'
'Oh. I dunno. The strings I guess. Hitting them too hard.'
He pauses for a moment, reflecting.
'You know, I used to do that all the time in the early days. My finger bled after every show. I met Pete Townsend after a Who show. His hand was fucked like that too. Worse.'
'Yeah. But the small finger's in a really bad way.'
I hold up the side of my hand.
'Oh, you're alright,' he snorts and walks off to get a drink.
Despite the pain I'm good. I know I dropped a lot of chords and made a lot of mistakes but I think I've pulled it off.

We drive out the next day for a show in Stockton. At the soundcheck I pulled out my guitars. They were caked with bits of dry blood. I got them cleaned up with a cloth. I knew I couldn't go on like that. My little finger had swollen gigantic and turned black. It was hard to play with it. I got some bandage and wrapped it around the next finger and put a plaster over the forefinger. It was painful but it was enough to be able to play. That night you did it all. Everybody did. The feeling, the emotion and getting it done. But the crowd weren't there with it. And the more you pulled out all the stops the less it happened. I learnt then that there wasn't much relation whatsoever between an audience reaction and what happened on stage. You thought you'd played like shit and people loved it. You pulled out all the stops to nothing. Sometimes it all gelled. Sometimes it didn't. It was mysterious. It worked inside and outside of you. You were engaged but somehow had to stay detached at the same time. In it but not of it. Odd.

We flew back to L.A. For the show at the Long Beach Auditorium. Bernie and Kosmo set this up to us as the big one. We had to pull this one off. It was important. Joe was doing some radio promotion for it in his hotel room. Coming out of my room I walked past his. The door was slightly ajar. I listened for a moment. I could hear Joe yelling at the top of his voice. I could hardly believe my ears.

'Yeah. Yeah. YEAH, YEAH!! Get yourselves DOWN there. We're gonna kick it up and shake it down and all you PILL POPPERS and all you SHOWSTOPPERS ………we want you there to take the floor and break it down and get with the *real* sound of REBEL ROCK!'

And so on and so on. In this awful accent without a trace of irony. He sounded like some demented Americanised version of Del Boy. Without the humour. I was shocked. I didn't recognize him. I didn't like it at all. I didn't get it. Surely we didn't have to stoop to that kind of cheap stuff. Couldn't the music just speak for itself? Wasn't it enough? Wasn't it better to have some air of mystery about things? Let people make up their own minds? Rebel rock! What the fuck was *that*? *Rebel rock?* A soap powder slogan. It does what it says on the tin. It was insulting and degrading. To people's intelligence. To us and everyone who came to the shows. Surely people weren't that stupid? Even Americans! But maybe they were and he felt he had to play up to it. Suddenly, I felt a million miles away from the white man in the Hammersmith Palais. What had happened? Was this *really* the same guy who wrote 'I'm So Bored With The U.S.A.'? *'CAPITOL RADIO'?!!* Did he have no fucking integrity? What was going on?

I never got the chance to find out. Joe was mostly off doing interviews and other promotion stuff during the day. It wasn't just that but you felt he was beginning to separate from the rest of the band. Back in London we'd all been rehearsing together and hanging out together as a band but now it was us three new guys and Paul or just us new three together most of the time. It looked deliberate. Things were evolving and being set up by Bernie as a kind of Joe Strummer and his Clashers. You only saw him on stage or at a band meeting. At soundcheck he'd turn up at the last minute and clear off after checking his vocal and running through a couple of songs. After a show he'd be out with us but that was drinking time and off somewhere else talking to fans. Nothing serious ever got talked about then anyway and if it did it was forgotten the next day. He'd become aloof and distant and you felt you were there just to do your job. Of course there were the band 'meetings'. But they weren't a place you felt too safe airing your views. I'm cringing now just thinking about them.

We got summoned to a meeting. Bernie informed us that Mick Jones and Topper had got a band together and were calling it the Clash. Jones was going to sue for the name. There could be two bands called the Clash out on the road! Bernie and Joe were in a militant and very serious mood. An injunction or something might be issued on the name. Would we be prepared to carry on under a different name? We all agreed we would in that case. The news created a sense of solidarity. It brought us together in that 'us against them' kind of way. It wasn't good news but at least it lifted some of the pressure away from me. I'd begun dreading these meetings. Every one had begun turning into a joyless, depressing affair where you were constantly on edge, ready to have some aspect of your personality under attack. My selfish, lone operator tag had persisted across the Atlantic. But now it wasn't just me who was getting it. Sometimes it would be Nick. Subtle references to him being a 'not-happening' person. Sometimes Pete. He was 'mollycoddled'. A baby. Paul, of course, was exempt from all this. In Bernie's eyes Paul could do no wrong. He was 'working class.' Us 'new' guys weren't. And being working class gave Paul a kind of street understanding of life, Nick, Pete and I could never understand. It was demoralising. Joe would pipe in here and there and support Bernie's offensive. But when someone else was getting it you were just glad it wasn't you at that time. Of course you got built up a bit too. Not too much though. For example, when Nick was getting it I might be appreciated for being full of creative positive ideas. Speaking up. Being a risk taker or something. But already, I'd had to become more guarded and careful of everything I said. Any open expression of excitement or happiness got ruthlessly shot down. If you weren't pissed off and angry then something had to be wrong. No one seemed happy unless they were inflicting pain of some kind.

But being more closed and guarded only reinforced my lone operator tag. It was a vicious circle. By playing us off one against the other, Bernie maintained control and dominance. I didn't understand things like that at the time. He went too far with all that. All he really achieved was a tense, hostile and suspicious atmosphere. It's hard to see how that would've helped anything. And slowly that atmosphere began seeping into you without your even realising it.

The long beach show went well. Not great but good. My hand was killing me but I didn't feel it during the show. Only afterwards. During each show I got carried away and forgot about it and after each show I watched it getting a little worse. The nail on my forefinger was virtually non existent now and my little finger throbbed constantly.

After that we had a couple of days off. I hoped it would give my hand time to heal up. I wandered about Hollywood by myself. To clear my head and try to make sense of things. Get some peace of mind. I bought a couple of books. One was 'How to Win Friends and Influence People', a famous self help book by Dale Carnegie. I was looking for something that might help improve relations with Bernie and the rest of the band. I didn't want to be seen as a selfish, lone operator. It sucked. I wanted to be accepted and find a way of relating better. I should have returned it to the shop and demanded my money back all the fucking good it did. Smile. Show sincere appreciation. Begin in a friendly way. Avoid an argument. That stuff might work with normal people under normal circumstances. Nothing about this situation was normal. I seemed to have more success when I turned these things on their head and did the exact opposite: snarl, take the piss, be a cunt and a wind up! But I couldn't be like that 24/7.

That evening we drove up to the Griffith Observatory in the Hollywood hills. Up near where that big fat Hollywood sign sits. Joe, Paul, Malcolm Mclaren and me. Malcolm Mclaren, the great manager of the Sex Pistols. Malcolm was opening the Clash shows with his break beat thing. I'd seen him around in the hotel lobby a couple of times. He seemed shy and reserved and nothing like the monster I'd been led to believe. It was odd to watch Bernie fawning around him though. Bernie appeared so excited to be with his mentor. He underwent a complete change of character. He even smiled and laughed a bit. I never saw Bernie smile or laugh. And Mclaren sat back regally, paying little attention all his supplicating. So there they were together. The big and the smaller Machiavellians. The little and large of punk rock management.

Joe was in his element up there at the observatory. Of course it was the scene of the famous knife fight in 'Rebel Without a Cause' and he went on quite a bit about it. I didn't care about all that. I was more interested in the sunset. It was superb. You saw the whole of LA from up there. Things always look better from high up. A great sprawling checkerboard mass of white buildings under a yellow mist with the sun. It looked beautiful but I'd been told that when it rained that mist turned into a corrosive acid. It was eating away the city.

The tour continued and we went on to play Santa Monica, Fresno, Santa Cruz and back to Santa Barbara. As it progressed my airborne sorties began improving. I was making fewer mistakes and scoring more hits. I was closing the gap with Nick. Off stage things were a different matter. I'd picked up a flu bug. It knocked me out. Bernie then fired our road manager. He fired the soundman. It was to be a regular thing. People were always getting fired although you never found out why. At soundcheck or rehearsals Bernie turned my amplifiers down so they were barely audible. It was impossible to play. You couldn't hear a thing when the drums started. It was frustrating. I got pissed off with him. Why couldn't he mind his own fucking business? There wasn't a single aspect of things he didn't have his finger in. He stormed out.

'You're ALL A BUNCH OF SHIT!' he screamed.

We went on without him. It was OK after he left. But you knew he'd be back.

But it was all of us this time. Not just me. It got us all down. It got to everyone. It was a constant battle to stay positive. Only the excitement and promise of playing live kept me going. I could feel myself tightening up inside like a spring. Tighter and tighter. As the days went by I got more and more pissed off. I guess that was happening to all of us. I often wondered if it was being done deliberately. Making us all uptight like that so we'd deliver a better performance on the night. Become more 'happening' people. Something to fight against. I didn't think it helped me. It did build up a sort of energy but it was dark and negative and destructive. It didn't feel right.

Backstage, getting ready to go on at Santa Monica, Joe began to uncoil.

'Well, I'm looking at *Vince* over there and I reckon *HE* would make a great *POPSTAR*, don't you think?' he sneered, nodding at Nick. He knew Nick and me had a bit of competition going. Nick laughed. Pete stayed silent, smiling.

That spring tightened a little more.

'Yeah. Vince. I reckon you'd make a great POPSTAR alright.'

'What are you having a fucking go at me for? Just fucking leave it.'

I went back to polishing my boots.

'All I'm just *saying* is I think you have the makings of a great POPSTAR!' he sniggered, knowingly.

'Well, it takes one to know one don't you think?. You're full of shit Joe. If anyone wants to be a popstar it's *YOU*, Mr Joe up your arse FUCKING STRUMMER.'

Joe laughed but he wasn't. I went on.

'What about 'Bankrobber? Eh? Are you trying to tell me that wasn't a cynical attempt to try and get that top ten hit? A third rate sing-along Three Blind fucking Mice nursery rhyme. Maybe you're not a popstar Joe, but it's not for the want of fucking trying is it?'

He leapt out of his seat angrily and loomed above me.

'I'll have you know I was in Portobello Road and these two black women, real earthy ghetto women came up to me and told me it was the *best* record they'd *ever* heard. *They knew what that record was about!* So don't *you* try and tell me otherwise.'

He was angry and losing it. But not really. The diplomat in him still had control.

'I don't give a fuck about what some black women said. Don't give me that shit. It was dull. Pop sensibility masquerading as 'real'. You wanted a hit record. It's *YOU, YOU CUNT* who wants to be a fucking pop star!'

He had nothing more to say. Walked off. He was angry. But you never felt that Joe was *really* angry. Like he might take a pop at you or something. It was always from a distance. I didn't really care about 'Bankrobber' or popstars. I was just sick of being picked on. Nick came over. Doing the compassionate bit.

'What are you saying? Why are you doing this? There's no point to it. We're going on in a minute. What do you think you're trying to do?'

I had nothing to say to him. I was tight lipped and burning. Nick looked at me with a mixture of hate and pity.

'Vince. I really don't UNDERSTAND YOU!'

I had nothing more to say. Nick walked off. We went back to getting ready. I felt better letting off some steam. I was sick of being pushed around. Told what to think. How to behave. Know my place. Being in this great band was proving difficult in ways I'd never anticipated.

A couple more shows and it was over. We flew back to London. No sooner had the plane touched the tarmac and we were off again around Britain.

CHORUS:

SAFE EUROPEAN TOILET

Our first European show is in Glasgow. We drive up from London by coach. It takes nearly a day to get there. The venue is called Barrowlands. As the hall fills up I get nervous. There's no stage pit which is that bit of separation between the audience and the stage where the camera people and the security sit. I sneak out every once in a while to check it out and it I'm worried. There's a kind of atmosphere going on here that makes the U.S. gigs look like a picnic under a rainbow. A totally different mood. It's the atmosphere of suppressed violence. You can only hope that people are gonna be *with* you. There were a lot of Mick Jones fans out there. You just knew. Every now and again something seems to erupt in out there in the dark crowd and beer and bottles start flying for no apparent reason. Some fist fighting. I'm uneasy. It's all black and white. It looks fucking dangerous. My imagination goes wild thinking of what might happen. I tell Raymond but he just laughs his usual laugh. There's nothing to worry about. But I'm not convinced.

When we begin playing it's not like anything I've done or will do before or after. I never saw anything like it. Or rather *felt* anything like it at any other show. But you just got in there and started swimming with the tide. You trusted. It was one of the most exhilarating shows I played with the Clash. And it was all down to the audience. Their energy. Just bordering on complete destruction. But there was a good thing in there too. It's so hard to describe in words. A bit like when you had a play fight at school but you knew it could always turn serious in a moment. But when I realised that I wasn't going to be killed I really got into it. I came away from that show with a lot of respect for Glaswegians. I felt they were really in the right place. I'll never forget it. You can go on about social deprivation and all that but I don't know. There was just a spirit there that seemed authentic and true and unlike so many other places we played. They really laid it on the line. And it inspired you. Maybe it was the sense of real danger. You stepped out over that line with them. I wasn't from a socially deprived background, supposedly. But I understood desperation. Desperation is a state of mind. Where nothing makes sense and there's just pointlessness in being alive. You could have that in a council tenement or on luxury yacht. Of course when it was all over you'd go back to the same old shit. I'd done it before many times myself going to see bands. But in that moment you were released from something. You touched a source of some kind where nothing mattered and life made total sense for a couple of hours. I'd get more of that feeling in England and Ireland but nowhere else. Later I asked Joe about it.

'What is it? Why are things so different in Britain? The shows are so different. To Europe and America.'

'Yeah, I thought about it a lot. You see, we're an island, Vince. It's history. Hundreds of years of fighting invaders. It makes the people violent. It's innate. That violence, it seeps into the culture. It's part of the mindset. America is new and Europe is just lines on a map that change. Our borders are the sea. It's been instilled into us over the generations. It's suppressed but it's there anyway. I think it's developed like that.'

It made sense.

'Yeah, and I reckon that's why we play better rock'n'roll than those fuckers, too!'

'Yeah, I think so.'

It was a bit silly. But you got into it and all patriotic thinking about it. Britain was great. The rest of the world were a bunch of amateurs. They didn't get it. I felt proud to be British but at the same time I knew it wasn't right or sensible to think like that.

And on to Manchester, Leicester, Bristol.

I read the press from the shows. It was either extremely good or extremely bad. Some loved the 'return to basics'. Some would rather hear the band's later stuff like 'Overpowered By Funk' and some sort of progression from that. It was a confusing time. For everybody. People either wanted something new or they loved what they knew. I liked what we were doing and the new songs: 'Dictator', 'Three Card Trick' and 'Are You Ready For War'. It seemed the right thing to do and I felt good playing them. It was still a time of big expectations though. People were wondering: 'What would be the next big thing after punk?'

But there was nowhere to go. Except do more of the same and explore different themes. Trying to evolve and be shocking or whatever for the sake of it, just for the sake of the 'new' thing always ended up being contrived. Or boring. Or avante garde. Like in the art world. When that urinal went in an art gallery it was shocking. Is it art or isn't it art? Is it taking the piss? But that day spelled the end of the art world. And nearly a hundred years later it's still the same thing. Tracy Emin's bed. The shark. A pile of bricks. Or whatever. And the same question. Is it art or not? But really it's just the same thing. The same question. The same joke. But it's not funny anymore. It's boring. But I guess people had become spoilt. Gorged on the excess of punk and all the progress of music of the previous three decades continually evolving to new and better and different things. But punk was like a kind of watershed. The tide could only recede from there. I understood the naysayers. But to me and so many I met after shows it was simply the spirit that was important. Not style. The obsessive need to keep changing that for the sake of it was a dead end. There were still things to say and punk rock was the best way to do it.

We went on, playing Manchester, Leicester and Bristol. At this time, Joe got the news his father had died. He didn't show much emotion about it and it didn't stop the tour. Nick and Pete seemed concerned and worried if he was 'hurting'. I found it hard to sympathise. I had nothing to relate it to. I hated my father. The sooner my father died the better as far as I was concerned. I knew I'd have bumped the fucker off myself if I wasn't so afraid of going to jail.

On to Europe. Norway and Sweden.

After the show in Stockholm we end up in a bar somewhere. I had trouble at the bar waiting to get served. These giant Neanderthal long blonde haired thugs began rugby barging me trying to get to their beer. One by one they would come up to the bar and would literally shove you to one side. The Viking mentality. I wasn't about to take them on so I guessed it was my problem. The English politeness thing. I wasn't used to that kind of behaviour. But you had to remember you weren't in England and it was just their way of doing things.

The band were on full form in there. Joe, Kosmo and Nick really taking the piss out of everything and everybody so that anyone within half a mile could hear. It was embarrassing. I drowned one lager after another. One guy pulled away from his small group and walked over. He'd had enough.

'You people.......who do you think you are? I'm so sick of listening to you. It's shit what you're about. You're so ARROGANT!'

Kosmo looked at him and turned to me.

'ARROGANT! Well...........now that sounds pretty good to me, huh, Vince?!.......I LIKE the sound of *THAT!*' he laughed.

I didn't say anything. I looked at the guy. It had taken some balls for him to come over and tell the Clash what he thought of them. I didn't think arrogance was a good thing. I felt bad for him.

'You people are no good,' he mumbled and walked off.

I was with him on that one.

Later we meet up with Bernie and his girlfriend, Wendy in a restaurant. It's dark in there. We're all there for dinner. Tour manager, promoter, Kosmo, Raymond and everyone to do with the band. The verbal sarcastic sparring starts. Around and across the table. Attack and counter attack. Forming allies. United front attacking. Looking for the weak spot. Deflecting this and that. Sarcastic laughter. Then a quiet spell. Then a bit friendly but before you know it you're lulled into a false sense of security. Weakness. Another attack. Counter attack. Laughing. Ignoring. Eye contact. Attack from the other side. Shot again. Hurt. Don't show it. Think of something to hit back. I can't think anymore. That's enough. I give up. You win. Pointless. Misery. Silence. Withdraw. The *WALL.*

I want to run away but there's nowhere to go. Just drink. Drink. Drink. Drink.

The empty banter continues without me. Can't anyone be *genuine* just for once? Give it all a rest?

Bernie's on the other side of the table, thankfully, in one corner. He's far away from me. I'm in no mood now to deal with him or anything. He's talking to the promoter. It's all big and important stuff. Raymond laughs his big friendly laugh. But you think even *he's* just playing out his role like everybody else. There's an undercurrent of something miserable. Nothing is real. I wish I were a million miles away. I'm the big new Clash guitarist who's supposed to have it all but really has nothing. I'm isolated. Lonely. I hate everybody and everything. Wendy is sitting next to me. She suddenly turns to me.

'Hi, I'm Wendy,' she says. 'You're quiet. What's up? You were great tonight. It was a brilliant show.'

'Really? Did you think so? I wasn't too sure. Bernie wasn't too pleased. Or Joe.'

'No! You were great! What's up?'

'Oh, I dunno. Things. I find it hard to get with it sometimes. Just the way it is I suppose.'

She went on to tell me about herself. She was from Detroit, U.S.A. She'd had some problems in her life. It seemed like Bernie had saved her from something. Picked her off the street and cleaned her up and that. I suspected it was drugs or some such thing.

'So, you're like a bit of a stray dog then? Bernie took pity on you, you poor thing. Can you bark?'

She laughed and punched me on the arm.

'Noooooo!'

'Go on. I bet you can. I bet you got a good bark.'

'WOOOOOF!'

'There. I knew it.'

We ate dinner. I had some chicken. My misery began to melt away. All the black leather and shirts and faces and sarcastic laughter and the big important this and that and the verbal bombs just disappeared. Suddenly they weren't there. I couldn't see any of it anymore.

I looked at Wendy. She was warm and sweet. She seemed to understand. All that bleached blonde hair and soft skin. Like a ray of light in the darkness. I felt I'd suddenly found a friend. I was sick in the head. My head had resolved itself into only two distinct states. I was either a worm not fit to crawl in the filthiest mud or else I was the biggest axe wielding superhuman giant adored by everyone I met. Nothing in between. But here was someone who wasn't undermining my every word or staring at me in stupid wide eyed adoration.

'What's that?' she asked.

'Oh, it's a bullet belt. My ammunition.'

'*Ammunition?*'

'Yeah. It's a metaphorical concept you see. A psychological defence strategy that recognizes the Jungian warrior archetype in physical form and provides the assurance that the individual can destroy any enemy he desires. It's also an aesthetic concept that explores universal function and resolves paraliminal tension!'

'Oh, I *see*,' she laughed, ' I think it's sexy.'

'Here. Try it on. See what you think.'

I pulled off the belt. Put it around her. Connected it up. She laughed.

'Oooooh. Now I can take on the world!'

'Yeah. You sure can.'

'I gotta go to the ladies room. Won't be long.'

She gets up and walks away. I watch her swinging off towards the exit. Wearing my belt. I lean back and look back around the table. Bernie is locked into serious discussion of some kind. Everyone is. Head stuff. There's nothing for me here. What I want has just moved away. I realise I need to go to the toilet too. I get up and follow Wendy's path towards the toilets. I see the gents door. I see the ladies door. Wendy is in there somewhere. I push open the ladies door and walk in. No one in there. One of the cubicles is locked shut. I tap on it.

'Who's that?'
'It's me.'
'Hold on.'

I hear some noise. Some movement and then the door opens. It's her. I push inside and smile. A seconds pause. She doesn't say anything. I don't say anything. Then that millions of years old machinery begins to work its thing. Effortlessly. Synchronised. Meant.

When it's over I come back to reality and try to assess the situation.

'Oh, look. I'll go out first. You follow in a bit. If anyone says anything just say we went for a walk. OK?'

'OK'

We must have been in there longer than I thought. As I come out Pete, Nick and Raymond are standing there in the exit foyer, watching me. Shit. I thought everyone would still be at the dining table.

'Where've you *been*,' says Raymond, frantically. 'We're leaving. Bernie's going crazy. He's outside with Kosmo looking for.......where's Wendy?'

I try to go on nonchalantly pretending like nothing's wrong but I can't think of anything to say.

'Oh. I just.........well, ok.......'

Just then Wendy appears from behind me.

Raymond is now more frantic than ever.

It's suddenly very obvious to everyone what's happened. Raymond really doesn't want to believe it.

I turn to Wendy.

'Look. The story is we just went out for a walk. That's the story. Now you *STICK TO IT*. OK?'

'Yeah, ok.'

Wendy goes outside to try and find Bernie. It begins to dawn on me now what I've done. But there's nothing I can do now except see what happens. Nick, Pete and Raymond stand there for a moment looking at me trying to decide what to think. I look at them. I can see their confused brains spinning around like the wheels in a fruit machine. I wonder where they'll land.

Pete is the first to speak. He suddenly speaks up.

'Vince! Fucking BRILLIANT! Fucking *BRILLIANT!*' he screams. 'That is the most BRILLIANT thing you've EVER DONE!'

Wow! 3 lemons!

He erupts in stitches.

'Aaaaaah! That is so *BRILLIANT!*'

It's all he can say. He's desperately trying to contain himself. He twists from side to side laughing in strange, jerky movements. He's ecstatic and speechless. I want to laugh as well and relieve some of the tension but I don't. I look at Nick.

He's come up 2 cherries and a bell.

Half and half. He doesn't say anything. He hasn't decided what he should think.

Raymond? He doesn't look so impressed. I think I can see where he's landed. Down on the moral side of things. A bar, a plum and a lemon. I've done a bad thing. Maybe he's right. But his attitude only seems reinforce this rising sense of sheer outrage in me. I've become demonic. All werewolf chaotic and released. There's a full moon outside. There's blood all over my teeth and it's dripping from my mouth.

Bernie comes back and asks me where I've been. 'I was out,' I say nonchalantly. Went for a walk. Bernie, Joe and Paul get in a cab with Wendy. I get in one with Nick, Kosmo and Pete. We drive back to the hotel. I stay silent. There's nothing to say. A big part of me is intensely happy for some unknown reason.

Back in my room I calm down a bit and reflect on things. Well, that's it, I reckon to myself, I'll never get away with *that*. Not a chance in hell. No more screaming fans and expensive restaurants for me. Jetting around the world. I've screwed it. It's back to Finsbury Park and the blue labels. Oh well. *Whatever.*

But the next day it's like nothing happened. It's incredible. I can't believe it. I hear that Bernie's got violent and beat poor Wendy about. She's still got my bullet belt. I'm confused and feel responsible for all the wrong reasons. I hope she's OK. The tour continues on to Düsseldorf. I try to forget about it all and it's quite easy actually. No one says another word about it.

The show was good. But no one comes back stage afterwards. Only a about four people. Kosmo tells me it's the German mentality.

'We go to zeeee show. We drink zeeeee beer. We enjoy zeeee show. We go to zeeeee home!' he laughs, 'Stupid fucking Germans!'

And on it goes. Brussels. Paris is cancelled because of a lorry strike. No one can get in or out of there. Switzerland. What a dreary place. Long grey overcoats and hats. Old people. Everyone looks like an escaped Nazi war criminal. Can't wait to get out of there. Milan. Paris. Edinburgh. Then all this touring begins to blur into one seamless event thing. Everyday becomes hotel check-in room sound-check meal room meal backstage get ready *SHOW* encore backstage autographs bar drink meal drink club hotel fans drink bed wake-up call bus passport plane bus hotel check-in room soundcheck meal. Blackburn. Liverpool. Portsmouth. London.

Five shows have been set up at the Brixton Academy. Three and then a trip to Ireland and back for the last two. I spend the day pissing around home. There's nothing to do really and you got to save your energy so I wander around Finsbury Park and spit at the pigeons. It's not a punk thing. I just like to see if I can hit them with gob. I'm not respectful or disrespectful of nature. I'm completely ambivalent. I love it and it also disgusts me. It's just there. I haven't hurt anything. But there's a couple there who don't like it and walk away angrily mumbling something under their breath. Fuck 'em, I think, they're probably going home to eat a chicken anyway.

I go home and put some clothes in a bag and I leave my Finsbury Park bed-sit and travel on the underground to each of the shows. I put the Whale and Sammy on the guest list. It's easy for me. It's a direct journey on the Victoria line from Finsbury Park to Brixton. Getting near Brixton the train starts filling up with spiky hair and leather jackets. No one recognises me. It's funny sitting there watching and listening. They chat excitedly about this and that and the Clash without the slightest idea that it's the guy sitting opposite them they're going to be watching in a couple of hours. When I get to the Academy there are long queues at the front door and the ticket office. I'm completely anonymous and I like it. I go to the back stage entrance. I knock on the door and the security opens it. He doesn't believe I'm in the band and due to play that night. He tells me to piss off. He slams the door. I knock again.

'Look. Just get Raymond. Or Kosmo. Don't *fuck me around*. OK?'

There's a weird attitude in my voice I've never noticed before. A bit petulant and full of it. I'm a somebody now. Don't fuck with me.

Raymond comes to the door and I'm let in. He shows me to the dressing room and I get ready. It's the same old thing. The washing gets dumped on the floor and we all pick out our bits. Pants and socks and shirts. It's the same thing but it isn't. This is London. And London is different. I'm well aware how critical and judgemental it is. But I've plenty of flying time behind me now and I'm confident. We all are.

The show starts and everything goes well until the spitting starts. Showers of gob start flying through the air smacking all over me. Joe's getting it too. Everyone is. It hits you in the face. On your arms. A giant piece of phlegm strikes the guitar neck. It sits there, hanging on the strings. A real big green glob. I'm

playing the siren note thing in 'Tommy Gun' but when it's finished I have to move my left hand down the guitar neck and right into it. My hand moves across the neck stroking someone's cold gob about. More spit storms. The song ends but the shower continues. I remember the pigeons. It's the revenge of the pigeons. Then I hear:
    'You're SHIT! YOU! Fuck off! Bring back Mick Jones!'
    I see the culprit. He's looking at me. I whip off the guitar and throw it on the ground. I've had enough.
    'I see you, you CUNT. You got a problem then get up here. I want you, you FUCK. GET UP HERE. *NOW!*'
    The bastard just laughs. Doesn't move.
    'GET UP HERE YOU CHICKEN SHIT! I WANT YOU! LET'S SEE WHAT YOU'RE REALLY MADE OF.'
    More spit. It's all in my hair. I'm really losing it. Joe sees the trouble and quickly comes over and whispers in my ear.
    'Leave it, Vince. Remember. The *wise man rises above it!*'
    I pick up the guitar and ………….. 'We are the Clash' starts. More spit storms.
    Joe stops the show and tries to get it all to stop. Pleading with those at the front. We go on but it never stops. Where can it all come from? I don't see how anyone can have so much gob to offer. There's been nothing like it anywhere else. We group back in the dressing room.
    'Oh maaan! That did me in. All that spitting. What's *that* all about?' I ask Joe.
    'It's the Damned,' he moans. '*They* started it. In the beginning they started spitting at someone in the audience they were pissed off with. But this guy in the audience, he spat back. Then the whole audience started to spit back. It went on from there. It became a 'thing'. It caught on. *They're* responsible.'
    'What can you do?'
    'Nothing. I hate them for that.'

OUT OF CONTROL: The Last Days of The Clash

Two more shows at the Academy. More spitting. There'd been a bit in Scotland and other places but nothing like this. But you just had to get used to it. I didn't understand it though. Why anyone felt the need to do it. It had been going on a long time for the Clash. Perhaps it was a sign of affection. Joe had picked up hepatitis somewhere on tour and reckoned it was from someone spitting into his mouth.

The next day I had a day off and hung out in the pub with some of my old mates. It was a bit weird. Being on the move all the time, flying here and there doing shows and whatever had changed my sense of reality. I was moving faster. Mentally and physically things were moving at a different pace. I didn't know how to relax anymore. My boredom threshold had become incredibly low. I was aware of a separation from my friends. Not that I thought I was better than them or anything. They just appeared to talk slowly and didn't have anything interesting to say. I didn't want to appear different and full of it but it was difficult. I just wanted to get back on the road. The good thing about being on the move was there were far fewer band meetings too. There was less opportunity for Bernie to keep putting his oar in and piss me off. And the distraction of touring allowed more time to pass after the Wendy incident. So it was just playing and drinking and travelling and playing and drinking. And more drinking.

The next day we flew to Belfast, Northern Ireland and drove to the hotel. The streets outside were full of armoured cars, tanks and army personnel. I had no idea it would be like that. There it all was sitting in the street with normal people all walking around doing their shopping and stuff. It was bizarre. Of course you knew there was trouble in Northern Ireland, you'd seen it enough on the news. But seeing all that machinery and armoured power actually face to face in the street was ugly and intimidating. The hotel was surrounded with barbed wire and there were armed security at the gate. You had to show identification when you went in or out. Kosmo told me we were staying in the most bombed hotel in Europe. I wondered if a bomb might be set off with me in it. But that night we played a good show. Spitting there as well. But I was happy to get out when I got called the next morning to drive to Dublin. It was a beautiful day. Bright and sunny. The lush Irish countryside rolled past and endlessly green and it was suddenly hard to believe in all the troubles. Small villages floated past the window and the peace and softness of it all affected you. We stopped for Guinness in a little pub. We each got a pint. The bartender made little shamrocks in each of the heads with the pump. For a brief moment there was peace. Peace in your head. And everyone knew it and felt it too. Guards were dropped and it was almost like we'd suddenly become friends.

The first night was insane. And it was Barrowlands all over again. There was some trouble in the audience. There was a lot of fighting going on before the show. We'd begun using radio mikes for our guitars on this tour. They were new inventions. They meant you could run all about the stage without tripping over guitar leads. They were great. You could do all kinds of stupid stuff. But I got carried away with the freedom of it and fell off the stage and into crowd. When the security pulled me back out of there I discovered my radio mike was missing. These things were expensive and I had no replacement. I played the rest of the show with a normal lead.

Backstage I found out what the trouble was. It was the ticket prices. About six guys were back there, disgruntled and pissed off. All real punks. Orange hair. Leather biker jackets. Thin and wiry and full of it. They began yelling at Joe.

'You're taking the fucking piss Joe. Who do you fucking think you are?'

Then one of them abruptly leapt forward and smacked him hard in the face. Raymond was quickly there. Paul, Nick and me. We stood in between. But it was more a show of things than anything. These guys went on and on grinding their axe. It seemed the ticket price was about half as much again as the English shows. Why? The Clash was a punk band. Why was the Clash ripping them off? Was the Clash a super band now or something? Were we too big for our boots.

I watched them. Their faces excited and torn at the same time. Here they were in front of Joe, their hero. To see this band that meant so much to them. The band that matters. With all those lyrics that spoke directly to their hearts. They were in love. And they'd been betrayed. It was agonising to watch. It was like their woman had come home early in the morning with the stink of betrayal on her face. Why? Where have you *been*, you bitch?

Joe went through a ritual I saw him perform many times. He was concerned. Saying a bit here and there but just letting them speak. Diplomatically letting them get it out of their system. He had no real explanation for the high prices. Like a marshal arts expert he patiently deflected each verbal blow one by one until they simply became exhausted. He put up no resistance whatsoever. Told them exactly what they wanted to hear. Then their faces suddenly changed. They began smiling. They began laughing. Joe hugged them. And it was all resolved without any real explanation whatsoever. I guess those in love will believe what they want to believe. And these guys became putty in his hands. Their hero was reinstated in their minds. Their image was intact. One of them said he'd look around and see if he could find my radio mike. The next day it miraculously turned up. That's politics for you.

I didn't get it though. Why *were* the tickets half as much again? Later I felt the need to find out.

'Joe. I think those guys had a point. I mean, why are the tickets so expensive?'

'Vince. These guys just need to have a go. Don't worry about it. Our tickets are comparable with everyone else who plays here.'

'Yeah, but…….'

He turned and began talking to someone else.

I didn't feel he gave a shit about it. I don't think the punters did either in the end. It was all just a big game of emotions and the whole point was irrelevant really. What *was* the point, anyway?

We flew back for the last two Brixton shows. The spitting hadn't stopped but by now I was getting used to it. You just got on with it. During the last show I heard someone keep shouting my name. I saw this face yelling out amongst a sea of faces. It took me a while before I recognised my friend from school I hadn't seen in years. The mate I used to meet up with every Saturday afternoon to practise guitar together. I was so happy to see a familiar face. An old friend. We shook hands and then he slipped back into that sea of faces. I never saw him again.

Towards the end of the show people began jumping onto the stage. Someone would get up and start jumping around before Raymond would encourage them to jump back in again. But as more and more began jumping on it got harder to send them back. Maybe it was a bit staged. A bit allowed. You never knew. But anyway, the whole stage ended up full of dancing bodies. You just went on playing and suddenly it wasn't a show anymore. It was a party. And everyone was invited. The last songs were usually the early ones. 'I'm So Bored'. 'Janie Jones'. 'Garageland'. They were the easiest to play and the most fun. And to me they were still the most relevant. It was what worked.

The reviews weren't so up for it. All those intellectual types saw 'back to basics' as a reactionary move. They wanted progress. But what the Clash was doing then was what people wanted to hear. People didn't go home disappointed. That's what mattered. Maybe music could never change the world. But it could empower you. You came away from a Clash show with a sense of something. You didn't intellectualise about it. But you were enhanced in some way. You went back into the meaningless of living a bit stronger. I never expected revolution but thought you might feel a bit better about living. More self actualised. It wasn't some massive sweeping change but it was a force in the right direction. It was better than nothing.

We had four days of practise. A three month tour of the U.S.A. had been set up

MID 8:

I'M SO BORED WITH THE U.S.A.

We had five days of solid rehearsal before we left for Nashville and a long tour of the U.S.A. We weren't getting a day's break. It was non stop. We were working on a new song: 'In the Pouring Rain'. 'In It had a more plaintive feel than the other newer stuff and I liked it. We played around with it coming up with different arrangements. A bit of a reggae style. Then more straight ahead. Different speeds. Joe turned up here and there. He was already turning up less and less to rehearsals. I don't think it was just that he couldn't be bothered but more the fact that he was extremely self conscious about his voice. I thought he had great voice but he couldn't hit any high notes. He wasn't really a *singer* singer, Joe. I think it bothered him a bit. He seemed more comfortable singing in front of 40,000 people than in front of 4.

Just before leaving I met up with my friends from the King's Cross warehouse in a dingy pub in Mornington Crescent. Most pubs were pretty dingy back then, but that was OK. You could feel relaxed in them. But this one wasn't just dingy it was plain rough. In there were all the hard core gypsy drinkers, drug addicts and all the dregs of Somerstown. And us. I was happy to get away from the band for a bit. Not to have my every word scrutinized. Always on edge, never knowing what the prevailing mood would be that day. Preparing for the insidious character attacks of one form or another. It was Harry's leaving drink. He was moving on and I was happy for him. I came with the Whale. It was great to see my old friends. They were excited to see me. I knew they wouldn't want to hear about all the shit I was having to deal with so I kept to all the good stuff. How great it all was. That's what they wanted to hear. I kicked back and played it cool and gave it to them, bathing in my new found celebrity status. Playing the rock star.

Over on another table was a group of girls sitting near us. About our age. Tough types. One of them got up quickly and came over and just stood there. Killing stare, hands on hips. She began shouting at the Whale.

'You, you fucking blood clot. What are you looking at? Eh?'

The Whale ignored her.

'I see you, you fucking looking at me, bitch. What you fucking want, eh? You want fucking shit?'

'Look. I think you've made a mistake,' I said, getting up quickly, trying to defuse things, 'we're just here for quiet drink, my mate here is..............'

The woman just leapt over the table at the Whale and the two of them were at it, screaming and tearing and hair pulling and slapping and weak girl punches. In a split second Ken and Waz were in there pulling the woman off. I grabbed the Whale and held her back. The other women got up from their table and began to move over, shouting. They wanted the Whale. I dragged her out of there, everyone yelling and crazy and out onto the street. Began looking for a cab. There's one! I wave at the yellow light. It pulls up and I throw her into it. The girls were coming out of the pub now and they want blood. I caught sight of Ben.

'We're out of here, my friend! Speak when I get back.'

'Have a good one!' he yelled.

The cab pulled away. The Whale began crying.

'What was *that* all about?' I asked.

More crying.

'Were you giving her the eye or something? What were you *doing*?'

'NO! It was *her*. Fucking black bitch. I'll *kill* her.'

I looked at her pretty face streaming with tears. She wasn't a fighter. I couldn't imagine her killing anyone. She had trouble opening a bag of crisps. We'd never had trouble like this before. Where was all this stuff coming from?

Back home she calmed down. I cracked open a beer and gave it to her. Opened one for myself.

'I'm going back there. I tell you. I'm gonna *kill* that bitch.'

She began to get up. I put my hands on her shoulders.

'LEAVE IT! You can't win with those people. They're ignorant. Don't you get it, stupid? They got nothing to lose. They'll fucking kill you.'

'I don't care. I'm not taking that shit.'

I didn't really believe she'd do anything. I didn't know how it all started. I didn't really know whose fault it was. But you had to play a bit of a game in these situations. The caring, considerate bit. Play with the drama of it all. I'd already picked up a tip from Joe. If you did the truth thing all the time you often came unstuck, badly.

I put my arm around her.

'Look. I'm going away. Promise me you'll leave it? *Promise me?*'

'Ok.'

I got up and went to the toilet. Our toilet was in the hallway outside and up the stairs. It was a communal one. We shared the house with another six bedsits. Fuck, some rockstar I was. When I got back I found the Whale lying out on the bed, eyes closed. I sat next to her. Drank some more beer. Then I went on with one of my monologues. She's better than that. Sometimes it's better to walk away. Violence just breeds more violence, don't you see? She's a great girl and I love her. Hand on shoulder. Stroking hair. Look, I don't need all this trouble now. I'm off to the U.S. tomorrow. Don't you think I can really do without all this fucking drama? I have enough of my own already dealing with Bernie and all the rest of it. And I really think.........

I notice a bottle of painkillers on the bedside table. I pick them up. It's empty. Oh fuck. NO!

I pick her head up and begin shaking it.

'What have you done? Did you take *all* these pills?'

No answer. She mumbles something. Shit.

I throw her head back down and run outside. I stop, go back and lock the door in just case she disappears for some reason. I run downstairs, pick up the house phone and dial 999. Which service? Ambulance. Quickly, please! The woman on the phone is so fucking slow. What's your name? Where do you live? What's her name? I want an ambulance NOW! Don't you realise? It's a matter of life and death! More slow, measured questions. Eventually, I'm told the ambulance is on its way.

The ambulance arrives. Two orderlies come up to our room and put the Whale on a stretcher.

'What's happened?' one of them asks me.

'I think she's taken an overdose.'

The ambulance man looks at me like I'm a complete piece of shit.

They carry her down the stairs and she's lifted into the ambulance. I move forward to get in too.

'No, you can't come.'

The orderly slams the door shut.

I want to know why I can't go with her but he won't tell me. Says I can make my own way to the hospital if I want to see her. The Whittington. He scowls a bit and moves away. He knows my type. I'm to blame for everything.

When I get there the Whale's had her stomach pumped. She's white and a bit pathetic lying there on that stretcher. She smiles feebly. But she'll be OK. She's not going to die. I'm relieved but pissed off with her at the same time. I hang around for a few hours trying to be as nice as possible and then go home. She'll be let out in the morning.

Next morning I nearly miss the flight. It's not the events of the night or the hangover. It's the clocks. They've gone forward an hour. I didn't realise. I scramble down to the Piccadilly line. It's gonna be close. I sit there, squirming in my seat as the train slowly ambles along towards Heathrow. Stopping. Starting. It doesn't care. It has all the time in the world. Northfields. Boston Manor. Stop. Start. Osterley. And on. The closer we get to Heathrow the slower it seems to go. I keep looking at my watch. But it's no good. I pray to God I make it in time. At last the train pulls in. I rush past the ticket collector who yells at me but I keep on running up and over to the check-in desk. Raymond is there.

'Where've you *been?*' he asks, nervously.

'The fucking clocks!'

His face breaks out into that big grin. Nothing fazes Raymond. Last call.

'Come on!'

We skip and run and walk and run and hop to the plane and laughing and get there just in time. I find my seat and the plane taxis out to the runway. The engines scream up to the higher pitch and we start rumbling forward. Moving faster. Shaking all over the place.

I look around and begin to relax. The plane is full. Nick and Pete are sitting relaxed and joke with me. Joe's reading the inflight magazine as usual. Paul has his ghetto blaster. Raymond grins that big grin again at me but I can see he's covering up. He hates flying. For some reason being on a plane with the band again gives me an odd sense of normality. The vibration shuddering through the plane suddenly stops. We're in the air. I look outside and watch the ground slipping away. I'm happy to be leaving. Breathing pure oxygen again. The little meals they serve up. Little bottles of champagne and wine. Getting away from all the madness of the night before. Being on the move. Fucking rock'n'roll. Fucking AMERICA here we come!

Some people on the plane want our autographs. There's been some debate about it in the Clash camp. Whether we should give them or not. I don't mind. It's fun. It makes you feel important. But Nick and Pete aren't happy with it. They're making a thing of it like it's not politically correct or something. Joe is scratching his head. In the end he's decided that we should. And so we scrawl our names out to the parents of some kids who want them. I'm happy to be doing it. Of course they're excited and happy to be getting them.

It's eight hours to Chicago and then a connecting flight to Nashville. Book in. The following morning I'm up too early and go have breakfast. Pete is there too. We have breakfast together. We're really excited to be back in the States again. I have eggs over easy with hash browns. And they know how to cook an egg in the U.S. Such a relief from the hard broken flat bubbly old smell oil greased things that you get slapped in front of you all the way from Shepherds Bush to Bethnal Green. It's the little things in life that really count.

After, I go for a walkabout with Pete. To check things out. It's already around 10a.m. but out there on the street there's no one.

I'M SO BORED WITH THE U.S.A.

It's deathly quiet. Not a soul around. Long blocks of wide empty streets and dreary red brown dull generic buildings. The occasional car drifts past. There's a shop front with some guitars in it and we try and get a bit excited about it. But it's all a bit dead. We can't believe we're walking around the streets here in the great home of country music and rock'n'roll.

We expected…..what? …..*something?* I guess our heads are still full of the noise of London and so we wander back to the hotel. Later that day we do a T.V. interview for channel 4 and the whole machinery has started again. Joe begins going on about this and that with us lot posing around behind him in the background. Listening to him makes sense. He goes on about the sad state of pop music and there's no effort and don't buy a ticket to the machine show and where's the meaning and it's all overindulgent and punk rock is here like a blow torch to sweep it a blow torch to sweep it all away and it's more relevant now than ever and he says all the right things and I believe him and chip in my bit but fuck, we're in America and I keep feeling that vast emptiness that lies outside the studio. Thousands of miles of empty spaces. I can feel it soaking up his words and spitting them up and out and into the wind. Out there the whole urban punk rock city music thing suddenly seems meaningless. I wonder how Americans in all these hick towns from coast to coast, all some three and a half thousand miles across of Nowheresvilles can relate to the claustrophobic sound of London's Soho and Portobello Road. But they do. And so we carry on. Fuck it. I don't care. I'm gonna enjoy myself either way. I dig the U.S.

That evening we watch ourselves on the telly back in the hotel bar. On the television screen it all becomes real. The authority of the interviewer. The big rock band from England here to show

how it's done. The excited faces. I drink beer and laugh. I'm on the telly.

The next day we go to see the Country Music Hall of Fame. There's footage of the early Elvis and others in there. Check out his big gold Cadillac car with T.V. and bar in it. Some footage and songs of Carl Perkins. Nick tells me he was the *real* rock'n'roller before Elvis. Oh yeah? Yeah, man! He wrote Blue Suede Shoes! It's good fun but secretly I know I'd rather be listening to Motorhead. It all looks too showy. Trying to fill up that big outdoors. And the outdoors is winning. I find it all a bit tawdry and dumb Roy Rodgers. All that 50's stuff. But hell, it's rock'n'roll and I'm supposed to like it so I try to look for the good in it and try to join in and be interested. But it's hard. Everyone is wearing army dog tags now except me. It bothers me a bit for some reason. I feel conspicuous for not wearing them but no one has said anything. For some reason I don't want to and so I don't. I want to be involved but I really don't want to pretend something that isn't. It's an old thing from 'Combat Rock' and this is new. I'm aware of a sense of separation but I don't know what the hell to do about it.

We get to some shops and Nick and Paul buy a couple of guitars. Paul buys a semi acoustic Gibson bass and proceeds to carry it about everywhere with him. He's always at it, picking away. Posing.

And we're off! Nashville rocks well for the first one. Then Knoxville, the University of Tennessee.

'We Are The Clash' and 'Glue Zombie' get dropped. 'Dictator' and 'This Is England' crop up here and there. I'm glad 'We Are the Clash' is missing. It's nothing to do with the title. The song just feels lumpen with a nursery rhyme singalong chorus that doesn't do it for me. I feel stupid singing it. 'Three Card Trick' is my favourite of the newer songs. It rocks. It has spirit. Nothing like the version that ended up on the final recording. It's a full on onslaught reminiscent of the Clash's second album 'Give 'em Enough Rope' and we play it every night. Together with 'In the Pouring Rain'.

  More problems with equipment. Guitars cutting out. Fourteen hour drive to Orlando, Florida and already I'm knackered. More shopping. And so it goes. Miami. Atlanta. Drive hotel shopping photo session meal soundcheck meal SHOW signing party drinking hotel drinking sleep drive TV hotel meal. With bits in here and there. Nothing memorable. Drunken talk. More shopping and eating. It's a blur.

  Life on the road and touring quickly loses its romance for me. Although for Joe, apparently it's everything romantic. The whole three month tour has to be taken by Greyhound bus. No flying is allowed. It's been structured that way so we have a down to earth real travelling experience. We're not allowed to be pampered rock stars. But for me it gets essentially boring. All the long hours driving between shows are simply filled up with eating and shopping. Breakfast at the hotel. No sooner does the bus hit the road than we're stopping for a few sandwiches and bits. Then later a Denny's or steak bar somewhere around lunchtime. Joe won't eat meat or dairy. It makes him fill up with mucus and he reckons it's bad for his singing. So he just eats fish and rabbit food. Salads.

  At the venues we do the soundcheck and the cooks have prepared an elaborate meal for us and the road crew. Eating it kills a bit more time. Then back to the hotel. More food. The whole band and Bernie and Kosmo sit around and we all have a three course dinner. The only time we stop eating is to play a concert. After the show someone orders pizza. We eat that. Then more drinking. I'm stuffed. But that's all there is to do. I skip the odd meal here and there and try to discipline things a bit but what do you do with all that TIME? The day exists for two hours of playing. 24 hours in the day. That leaves 22. 4 to 6 hours of sleep a night. That leaves 16 to 18 hours of hanging around, waiting. There's nowhere you can go and nothing to do. It becomes like sitting in the dole office all day trying and waiting to get your giro. Going on stage was the release from it all. Like when you got that slip of paper and got out of there and ran to the post office and you were out in the street and free. Cash in time!

We go on crisscrossing the East. Columbia, Chappel Hill, Washington, Poughkeepsie, Albany, Portland, Worcester. The reviews are pretty good. The general consensus seems to be that the new band are re-ignited and they welcome what is a return to the basic primal sound of the original Clash. Many of the long-time fans reckon it's an improvement over some of the more recent shows. For many there was energy and conviction where two years ago there had been boredom. But Joe was pushing the political thing hard for me. At a lot of these shows fans would climb up on stage during the encores. They'd get gently returned. Then more would climb up. Sometimes the security would get a bit carried away.

At some point Joe lost it. He stops the show and suddenly announces: 'You people gotta realise some HUMANITY. Human beings gotta be treated like HUMAN BEINGS even in this *FASCIST* country.'

I heard a lot of boos. Not many cheered. Then: 'to all the women in the audience with the hope that a new anti-sexist, anti-racist human being is emerging.'

We began the 'Sex Mad Roar'.

I thought it was out of order. Individuals weren't responsible for the way their government acted. I loved the U.S.A. and I'd have felt insulted if I was American. I suppose a lot of fans were into social politics and wanted to hear all that. It was a rocking show for 9000 people and I suppose in the end you just get ignited by all the confrontation. But was there any real conviction here or was it all just being used as a selling point? I was confused. The lines were completely blurred. You couldn't talk about it with anyone. Everything had become a great game of semantics and I was already sick of talking. It got you nowhere. It could be seen as anything you wanted to see. I never really knew whether Joe was really convinced of it all either. Did he have some other angle? Perhaps it was so confused in his own mind and he just let it go where it wanted to. I doubted his sincerity and then again I didn't. But the fact is with art you can get away with anything. Poetic license. Any artist can hide behind it all and just call it provocative. You could just see it as that. But seeing it like that diluted the intensity of a 'band that matters' that relies on the reality of it's convictions to be a 'band that matters'. And those that took the band seriously were inevitably disappointed with the hypocrisy. I suspended my disbelief and just enjoyed loud guitar which is what I think most people did.

There were TV screens were up at every show showing God knows what behind me. Night after night I jumped around in front of them. I never saw what was up there but I heard about it. Carnage, bits of films, war, bloodshed. Whatever. Nobody in the audience could really see any of that stuff. Only the press who were close enough. If there had been one big screen then everybody could have seen it. Bernie said to one interviewer: 'The small TV's were used in place of one giant screen because the Clash *refuse* to employ anything that could not be in the normal workers home.'

Normal workers home! It hadn't been debated with me! None of us new guys knew there were even going to be TV screens up there until we started playing. But off stage none of this socialist stuff was ever mentioned in the Clash camp. It suited me. I wasn't very social anyway. I didn't give a shit. I just wanted to play music.

Off stage was where politics became a real. Band politics. An indoctrination sinister 'mind control' there's *something going on I don't know what it is* feeling I'd had before began getting me down more and more. A sort of complicity, like everyone was agreeing to something I didn't understand or didn't want to. It was there whether Bernie was around or not. I put it all down to my own paranoiac nature and ignored it. But as the tour rolled on and it became more and more insistent I began to wonder if it wasn't just my imagination anymore. That it was being designed deliberately. It weirded me out. There were no rules laid down in pen and ink but there they were and as time went on you became more aware of them. Everything was under scrutiny. What you wore, the music you listened to, what you said, the books you read and your opinion about this and that. Of course nothing was said in clear, simple English of what was expected. That was what any normal employer would do. Things were stated and implied and it was assumed that you would go along with the game. It couldn't be seen but it was there, nevertheless, like a solid block of ice lying under the surface of everything. I don't know if Nick and Pete were aware of it. Maybe they were and just rolled with it and played the game thinking that it was to be expected. I had a lot of difficulty with it. It contradicted my sense of punk and what it was all supposed to be about. For me, rock'n'roll or punk or whatever you want to call it is about freedom. I had little freedom. All the hallmarks of being in a cult were there. A strict music policy on the bus had developed. Practically nothing other than 50's rock'n'roll was allowed to be played. Maybe some jazz or soul.

Joe had proudly announced to one interviewer: 'We only listen to American music pre-1970's. Nothing English.'
I hated the word 'we'. 'WE.' A disgusting little word that collectivist-fascists use to get people conform to their way of thinking and their interests.

I'M SO BORED WITH THE U.S.A.

Day after day for nearly three months I was subjected to this enforced musical diet on the bus. It drove me nuts. No punk or rock. Which was the only music I ever really listened to. The only exception allowed was the Sex Pistols. But you just couldn't keep playing 'Never Mind the Bollocks' non stop for 3 months. It was a problem. Sometimes I would rebel. I was sick of it. Bob Dylan's greatest hits was playing. His voice irritated the fuck out of me. I had a tape of 'Inflammable Material', the first album by Stiff Little Fingers. I loved that album. It rocked. I walked down to the front of the bus, pulled out Dylan, stuck the Fingers in the machine and turned it up loud. Went back and sat down. The incendiary guitar began exploding out of the speakers at full volume. Suspect Device. It meant something to me. It was alright. It was the sound of freedom.

I got about 20 seconds of it. Yells and moans around the bus.

'Get it OFF!'

'Rubbish!'

'Terrible!'

Joe got up angrily and pressed it out. He sat back down in his seat and the cool sounds of Miles Davis began filtering through.

'Fucking fascists!' I yelled, laughing. Laughing but not really. But how could you fight it? It was democracy in action. Everyone believes in democracy. Isn't that the civilised way to go? But I wasn't a big fan of democracy. With democracy there is always a loser. The majority wins and the minority loses. The majority of people for me were stupid. And stupid people could easily be told what to think and do by one or two. With democracy you voted first and took orders after. With Fascism you just took orders and didn't even have to bother voting. Socialists forced you to comply with some ideology or other. It was the same old shit in the end whichever way you looked at it.

Paul came over and handed me my tape. He sat down. He was very concerned.

'Why do you want to listen to this?'

'I like it.'
'This band are just a pale imitation of us. It's second rate. It has nothing to say. It doesn't add anything.'
'They write about the situation in Northern Ireland. The Clash hasn't written anything about that, has it?'
'Yeah. Well I see your point. But it's *still* second rate.'
'Well, I like it.'
He didn't say any more. Got up and went back to his seat.
I put the tape into my Walkman.

'DON'T *BELIEVE THEM!* DON'T *BELIEVE THEM!* DON'T *BELIEVE A WORD THEY SAY!*................!!!!!!!.'

None of the irony of my situation was lost on me. I withdrew even further. I was aware of something I'd felt so many times before, growing up. Behave. Tow the line. Comply. Do what you're told even if we're not telling you what that is. You just gotta figure it out what we want for yourself. And woe betides you if you don't. What a joke.

I looked up the aisle of the bus where Joe sat. Always near the front and to the left. Head buried in the newspaper. He'd become totally aloof and separate from everyone. He was hard and indifferent a lot of the time. Sometimes he would warm and be what I felt was his real self. But that hard attitude he had reminded me of the sort of attitude I noticed a lot of upper class people have. A bit suspicious and calculating. Furtive. Removed and above it all.

'Fucking phoney!' I thought.
Nick and Pete and Paul were laughing together about something. I really hated them. It was all so wrong.

I was really isolated. And trapped. I was supposed to get along with things but I couldn't. But feeling squeezed and crushed only added fuel to my performance each night. Playing and singing songs about oppression and alienation fitted only too well. When I was playing on stage, I was free.

I had a tape of one of the early Hawkwind albums called 'Space Ritual' in my tape box. It was hippy music. The complete opposite of everything the Clash and punk was supposed to stand for. I put it in my Walkman and turned it up as loud as it would go. I knew everyone would hate it if they could hear it. It wasn't 'correct'. For that reason I enjoyed it even more. The spaced out electronic rock guitar of 'Brainstorm' began exploding in between my ears. I gazed out the bus window and watched it all drift by. Texaco garages, fields of grass, motels, hypermarkets. Small factories. People processing this and that. This and that. To think that someone actually got an idea and managed to get all excited about it and up and out of bed in the morning and begin to make it and market it! All that responsibility. Maybe that was my problem. I wasn't good on responsibility. I remembered the 'Dianetics' place in Tottenham Court Road. They had told me that. It was the home of Scientology. They always had someone out front of that place trying to recruit people and they offered you a free personality test. I thought I would take that test out of curiosity. I went in there and answered a ton of questions about what I would do in such and such situation. What I liked. My feelings about this or that. They kept me hanging around and it took hours to get the result. Eventually it was given to me in an envelope. I took out the paper. It was a graph of columns. Each column corresponding to personality characteristics. Happiness. Energy. Confidence and so on. Mine looked pretty good. All the points were up in the top part of the graph in the white part of it except one. There my point sat in the darkest area near the bottom. The top of that column was labelled: 'Responsibility'. While I was looking at it a guy in a suit came up and told me I had a good graph but I really should enrol on one of the programs to correct this one shady area of my character. I said I'd think about it. I quickly got the hell out of there.

And on and on. There it all was passing by. The great United States of America. Miles and miles of synchronised bland nothingness. I began to realise that perhaps all my love of the U.S.A. was just something I'd constructed in my head. Something entirely vague to do with fast cars, cool chicks, free sex, the wild west, cowboys, space exploration, freedom and the like.

Plumes of smoke over some large building. In there, there were bosses and owners employing people. They were busy at it. Making it. Packaging it. Distributing it. Soap bars, pens, tap washers, sissors, razors, sheet glass, rubber gloves, hair grips, diapers, nails, hammers to hit them, nuts and bolts. How in the hell could it all happen? All the people in those places and their lives being lived which are the only ones they'll ever get and getting on with it and turning around the machinery everywhere so you could go out and buy what you needed to exist and write letters to employers and fix up you hair beforehand and make the telephone call and drive home and do your washing and make a cup of tea and watch the television and feed the dog. I'd done it too. It was happening the world over. A world upside down.

But soon I was happy and content. Relaxed in my own inner outer space. My head was where no one could fuck with it. For the time being, anyway.

We pulled into New York. It was exciting to watch the skyline approach. Those great concrete towers. The Big Apple! We drove through Harlem. On a street corner I watched a cop twirling his baton. Like a super cool circus performer. There it went round and round and round his arm. Everyone thought it was cool. It was the ghetto wasn't it? The Clash liked ghettos. It was supposed to be romantic in the 'real' sense. I didn't like the look of it all one bit and was happy when we were out of there and booked into the Gramercy Park hotel. The Gramercy was the hip place where all the big rock stars stayed. I didn't like hip places.

We drove out and played a show on Long Island. Then back and out to some hip club. The entrance to the club was a long corridor and on one side were these large glass windows looking into house rooms. A bedroom. A kitchen. Lounge. In each room were one or two people living and pretending it was like their normal life or something. One snotty looking girl was sitting on the edge of a bed filing her fingernails. Someone else was cooking up something in the kitchen. It was all very arty. We went straight in past the long queue. All of us. Kosmo, Pete, Nick, Paul, Joe and promoter and promoter and someone else and whoever else. A quick word and we're in. I arrived on the dance floor. All around were these giant soap boxes. HUGE soap boxes the size of garages. Hundreds of people. All the hip and beautiful were there. Dancing and laughing and posing. Their cigarettes pointing towards the ceiling. Models. The rich. The famous. What was I doing there? I needed a drink. Already the novelty had worn off. I decided to get a round in for everyone.

'What do you want?' I shouted to Kosmo above the din.
'Beer!'
'And what about…….'
'Just get beers Vince! For everyone!'
'Ok, come to the bar and give me a hand.'
I ordered seven beers.
The first one came up. I started sucking from the bottle.
The barman said something. I casually tossed him a hundred dollar bill. Got my change and a little ticket in a small metal tray. I picked it up and left a couple of dollars in the tray. Handed three of the beers to Kosmo. I looked at the ticket.

'Fucking hell, Kos! 65 dollars! Can you believe it?'
'You wanna *play* you gotta *pay*, Vince!' he shouted, smugly laughing.
'Yeah, but that's a fucking joke, man.'
I grabbed the rest of the beers and got back to the others. Shit. What a rip off!

I stand there beer in hand. You can't talk. You gotta shout. Pounding beat. The new hip hop sounds. I hate hip hop. And rap and all that bollocks. Time is passing and there's no relief from it all. Except the toilet. And a razorblade.
Then some guy to do with the club comes up to me. The club is called Area or Aria or something. All I know is it's full of hot air. *He's* full of hot air. He's so very happy that the Clash are in his club. He offers me some cocaine.
'Thanks, but no thanks, man. I'm strictly a beer man.'
He seems slightly surprised I've declined. Cocaine is what rock stars do. He comes back with some beers. Hands one to me and everyone. We shout a bit about nothing and then he moves off.
Fucking twat!
Joe is talking loudly and animatedly with a couple of fans. It's nauseating to watch. Their faces are the same as ever. Wide eyed, keen and awestruck. Kosmo is talking to Nick. Everyone's in animated conversation. I'm standing alone. Bored.
Little squeals and pearls of blonde hair and twists and turns and tight arse in jeans I'm so cool with tits a glance excited hand to drink to mouth and more looking and suddenly she bumps into me all accident-like.
'Alright?' I say.
Wheeling around in sudden surprise which is no surprise really and kind of expected and looking all modelly self satisfied and dumb shiny eyes but hard. Unforgiving.
She begins to talk.
'Are you guys…….'

'Do you *put OUT*?'
'What?' she says, laughing.
'You know? Do you *FUCK?*'
She thinks excited possibilities challenge danger interested and but......
'Well, that's hardly a way to start......'
'OK THEN. FUCK OFF!'
I walk away. I've had enough of it. Pay for another beer. Get a chaser. A double. Fuck the expense. Toss another hundred dollar bill. Why all this anger and hatred in me? I dunno you dummy don't know. I'm back. Pete has found himself a nice looking girl so very pretty and he's all nice boy talking to her. Good for him but the dance modern sound of hip hop trendy central begins to make me wish I had a machine gun. Kosmo gets them in. More beer. Beer. Beer. Beer. Steer. Steer clear. Clear. Clear out. Fear. Beer. Beer. Bear. Bare. Bare it. Bare it *ALL UP THE ARSE y*ou shallow cunts!

I wander around in a daze. Hit the toilet. I puke. Hard shiny bowl all real and solid. Humming humming air conditioned shell hell. Another retch and I'll be OK. It's a clear headed logical decision. Scientific! Just one more and I'm sure I'll be OK. One for the road.

PLURGHAAAAAAAAAAGH! AAAUUUUGH! UUUCK! Uuuuck!.

I'm done. Press the button, leaning over the basin watching the rush clean away the debris. I stand up. Pull yourself together, man! OK! I'm good! Out of the cubicle and check the mirror. YES! I'm a rock star! Then back into the fray dear brothers and sisters and more pretending and talking and drinking and meaning and walking and soul bearing and to whom? Someone. Someone else. And some others. I've known them all my life of course.

It's early morning when I find myself back outside on the streets and Pete is there with me. Everyone else left long ago. It's dull grey pissed early April New York morning and we decide to go see the Statue of Liberty. We're excited. Yeah, man! Let's do it! A couple of fans are with us and they want to come too. Girls. Where did *they* come from? But it's Sunday and there's nothing doing. It doesn't start till 9am anyway and so we just go for breakfast with them. Weird tired dislocated talk but Pete's happy. He's scored with the pretty girl. She's a model. He's got her number. I've had enough. I leave them to it and make my way back to the hotel and crawl into bed and sleep till 2.

I'm suddenly woken up by a knock at the door. I pull on my leather trousers and open it. Standing there is this gorgeous looking woman. Long dark slinky hair. Jeans and breasts in a tight fitting white shirt. She's taller than me. Wow!

'HI!' she says.

'Hello!'

I let her in. She sits in the chair. We begin to talk. It seems we met at the club but I don't remember a fucking thing. She's a model for some swanky magazine.

'Wanna drink?' I ask.

'Uhm. Yeah. Have you got any O.J.?'

'Yeah.'

I go to the mini bar and pour myself whisky and knock it straight down. Pour her some juice. Get a beer. I go back and sit on the edge of the bed. Hand her the juice.

'What's a nice girl like you doing in a place like this, then?'

'I have a couple of days off. So I thought I'd come up and see you.'

'Yeah? What's your name again?'

'Emily.'

I try a few more stupid comments. I wasn't much of a ladies man. If seduction is like fishing, as they say, my only approach skill was to get a boat, a ton of dynamite, sail out there, lob it over the side and blow the fuckers out the water. Of course, I could get a lot of fish that way. But then I'd wonder, stupidly, why most of the women I ended up with were slightly damaged in one way or other.

I grabbed her hand. Pulled her onto the bed with me. I put my arm around her and kissed. She didn't resist. Just no feeling. Tense. Just motions. I pulled back and looked at her. She really was beautiful. I guessed I needed to do a bit of talking first. Maybe she was a nice girl and all that. So I just go on about things. Mix it all up a bit. A bit rude. A bit nice and considerate. A funny story. Something interesting. No response. A bit more rude. Ruder. Cruder. But *nothing.* No laughter. There's nothing there. I lean over her. She's pneumatic. Everything in the right places. The curves and lengths and skin all right. The eyes you see popping out at you from deodorant posters. But it just wasn't happening.

I gave up and flopped back on the bed, staring at the ceiling, saying nothing. She lay there next to me. I began to hope she would leave. But she didn't. We just lay there, like that, not saying a word. All that beauty and fucking nothing. I'd had enough. I jumped up.

'Look, Emily. I got a photosession to do. I'll give you a call, later. Leave me your number.'

She wrote it down. Got her bag and left. A pause at the door with that deodorant smile. I watch all that super figure and hair and eyes swing out and disappear off back into the concrete hallways of New York. I close the door behind her. I knew I'd never call her. Christ! More con. What was wrong with everything?

There actually *was* a photo session later that day. More hanging around and slight movements. Look good. Look cool. It's boring but I don't care one way or the other. Wasn't it better than sticking blue labels back in King's Cross? Back to the hotel. Sleep. I wake up at midnight. I'm wide awake. What to do? My head is firing on all cylinders. It's all dressed up with no place to go. New York is the city that never sleeps so I go out and wander the streets a bit. Wander in some coffee place somewhere. Everyone in there looks like an extra from 'One Flew Over the Cuckoos Nest'. Or 'Taxi Driver'. It occurs to me that they might all be actors, doing it all on purpose for some reason. One guy in there is jerking his head strangely and his eyes are darting about. And there's another all dressed respectable in a suit but he's mumbling something to himself. Just won't stop mumbling. A strange tarted up woman. But is she really a woman? A real freak show. I go back to the hotel with a take away. At 4.30a.m. I manage to get to sleep.

The next morning I get a call from Wendy.

'Hi Vince, it's Wendy.'

'How're you doing? What's happening?'

'Oh, I'm going shopping. Wanna come?'

'Oh *yeah!* Uhm. I dunno. Where's Bernie?'

'He's out of town. Come on! I'll show you round.'

I'm not sure I should. Nick and Pete say she's trouble. Everyone says Wendy's a bit of a wild child and I've been seriously warned to stay clear. I can't see it. She seems warm and sweet to me. But I don't want any more trouble with Bernie. I got plenty. But I'm lonely and bored. So we meet up and walk around. I don't know where I am but by all the look of all the loonie types hanging around I guess it's a downtown area of some sort. We go in some trendy boutiques trying on clothes. It's a laugh. I try on some stupid hats. She buys something. We go have pizza. I drink beer. I take the piss. She laughs at my jokes. I'm aware of the fact that I'm really having a great time. I look at her. She looks great all punky blonde mowhawk cool and I realise she's probably the only *real* person I've met since leaving London. But I know I gotta keep a lid on it. She's my manager's girlfriend after all.

'So how's things with Bernie? Is it all sorted out? I heard he knocked you about a bit.'

'No. It's fine. He's working hard getting things sorted for the new album. Negotiating.'

It was strange hearing her talk about him like that. Like he was a regular sort of dude or something. Busy working away like normal people do. Didn't she see it?

'Well. I'm glad to hear it. That was a narrow squeak.'

'Yeah,' she laughed.

To her everything was normal and going along just fine. I saw nothing normal about any of it. I kissed her goodbye and went back to my hotel room. It was good seeing her though. It was a breath of fresh air. That afternoon I lay about on my bed restless and began reading some of the newspaper articles. It was the same thing over and over. Why are we touring without a record out? Wasn't it an unusual thing to be doing?

Joe: 'We're just going out and playing for the hell of it. We all have a common goal now, we want to become a *real* band.'

Or the reason for sacking Mick Jones:

'He thought it was still the '60's; he wasn't aware that things change. Mick was totally into the 'star' image trip. He once told me that he used to lay in his room and dream of becoming this big star and he couldn't accept the fact that The Clash wasn't going to become the dream he had in his bedroom.'

I lay back on the bed thinking that in fact the Clash wasn't the dream I'd imagined either.

'Mick was also into emotionally blackmailing the rest of the band, he'd start doing things like calling up an hour before a show and saying, 'Well, I just might not show up. He was destructive to..........' And on and on.

And at the end: *'That's* why I think it's much better that we're *meshing* with one another now. It's good for us to become a band first and then go into the recording studio.'
Another one.
'We don't want to be strangers when we do the new album. But by the end of this tour, we're gonna know each other inside out.'
And again: 'Mick changed,' says Kosmo, who operates the Clash's propaganda ministry, 'Mick seemed unenthusiastic about the group. He didn't seem to trust the people he was working with.'
I was with him on that one too.
Another article went on about Jones' reluctance to share songwriting credit and revenues with the other band members, in the spirit of the group's avowed socialist policy.
I wondered if I would ever see any money. My wage had risen from £150 a week to $500 a week for this tour. It seemed like a lot of money compared to the warehouse job but it was difficult. I had to watch my hotel tab. I was running up huge telephone bills. The Whale and I were back on. I was calling her a lot, desperate to hear a warm, normal voice. The hotel mini bar and drinks. After the tour it would go back to £150 a week.
I threw the article away. Pulled open another beer. I picked up my book. I was reading Edgar Allen Poe. Tales of mystery and imagination. I liked Poe. He was a real nutcase. I reckon he never voted for shit.

As the tour routine rolled on, homesickness begins to set in for most of us. Especially Paul. He wants to go home. So do I. The tour bus arrives at some college campus and there they all are running up excited to see their heroes. Bland long haired stupid kids in white plain clothes and shorts and curly hair DUMB, DUMB, DUMB.

'Hey you guys! You guys are fucking great! We been with you all the way since Combat Rock, man!' they shouted excitedly.

Paul and I had bought some water pistols. Pump-action things we'd bought at a truck stop. They had a range of about 30 yards. We were ready. As the bus stopped and they got nearer we began furiously attacking them from the open windows at the top of the bus. An unstoppable water onslaught. I thought they'd get pissed off. But amazingly they didn't. They just carried on laughing. Like they *enjoyed* being abused.

'We wanna go home! Fuck you!' yelled Paul, laughing, letting go another spray.

'Hey! HEY! *HEY!* What are you *doing?* We *love* you guys!'

'Get a fucking life, you wankers!' I yell, frantically pumping away.

We drove on leaving them soaked and still laughing and shouting at us. Clash fans. What a bunch of fucking idiots they all were.

Another Holiday Inn. Another two beds telephone TV air conditioned menu card sanitised prison cell. I lay on one of the beds gazing at the ceiling. The money trust socialist principled band thing kept playing on my mind. $500. The rate of exchange was around $1.65 to the pound. So I was getting around £300 a week for this. I liked being on the road despite the boredom. It was fun a lot of the time. I loved the shows but it was also fucking hard work. I was lonely. All that band *meshing* stuff was bollocks. Homesickness. I missed my girlfriend. I missed my friends. I was tired and sick. Sick of being stuck on a bus for ten hours a day. Lack of sleep. The unrelenting sarcasm. I'm a guitarist in the fucking *Clash* for fuck's sake. Playing anything from 3000 to 10000 people a night. Five or six nights a week. Some people had been complaining about the ticket prices. They were around $15 a head. It was a lot for a socialist band to charge. And when you added it up it was a lot of money for each show. And the merchandise. T shirts. Posters. I didn't really care about money but surely what I was doing was worth more than £300 a week? Nothing had been said by Bernie, Joe or anyone about money. But it began to bother me and I wanted to know what was happening.

I went for a stroll. Nick and Pete were alone in the hotel lobby. All three of us were on the same wage. I went and sat with them. They carried on talking, ignoring me. I interrupted their conversation. It was something that had to be dealt with.

'Look, I'm not happy about the money thing. What do you think?'

'What do you mean? What money thing,' said Pete. Nick said nothing. He rarely had anything to say to me. *He* was the real Clash's guitarist. Unfortunately for him, so was I.

'Well. Nothing's been said about it. It just doesn't seem right to me just getting only $500 a week. Busting our arses like this 34 hours a day. 11 days a week. I know we're not the original band and that but.......you know......the *roadies,* my guitar *roadie* is on *three grand a week* plus expenses. They're earning tons more than us. We're making this tour *happen* aren't we? And the money from just t-shirts alone…..'

I could see both of them were immediately uncomfortable. They didn't want to go there.

'Yeah, I see what you mean,' said Pete. 'But what the hell are you suggesting?'

'Look, I'm hungry, I'm gonna get something to eat. Let's meet in my room in a couple of hours and talk it over. I looked at my watch. Say 3 o'clock?'

They both agreed.

I went and had an excited lunch. If the three of us became a united front in this area then we could sort something out. It would bring us together too. We might even become friends! Here was an opportunity for us to pull together. To assert some control over things and be more than just wage slaves to the

Clash machine. To have some power in things and stop being victimised and being replacement puppets. We are the Clash! I couldn't do it alone. Us newbie's were playing with a marked deck. If we only pooled our resources we'd have a decent hand. It was our only hope. We could at least deal with things openly and find out where we stood. I laughed to myself. All that bloody socialist rhetoric. *This* was fucking socialism in *action!* Up the workers!

3 o'clock rolled around but neither Nick or Pete showed up. Half an hour later I tried ringing their rooms. No answer. I was bitterly disappointed. I knew then that any solidarity between the new Clash members was doomed. Everyone was watching their own arse. And worse than that word would probably get back to Bernie that I was causing trouble in the ranks. Fuck. I'd be in for it. I was the lone operator again.

Despite it all I decided to take it on. I approached Bernie in the hotel lift as soon as I saw he was alone.

'Bernie, what's happening about my money?'

'What do you mean?'

'Well, nothing has been said about it.'

'What money? What are you talking about?'

'Well, money for all this,' I said, sweeping my hand out.

'What's the matter? You're getting $500. Isn't that enough? How much do you *need?*'

'Well, it's enough to get by but what I mean is when will we see any *proper* money?'

'What do you want money for?' he asked.

Suddenly I felt bad for asking. What *did* I want money for? Money was an ugly thing. You didn't talk about money. Only those greedy Capitalists worried about money.

'Well, I'm just living in a single bedsit, sharing it with my girlfriend for one thing.'

'Vince. You're on the road now. I don't think you should be worrying yourself about it. I think you should focus your attention where it's required. Like learning to improve your skills. Did you know that some of the band are not happy with you? You've got a problem. I suggest you sort it out.'

With that he moved off and the matter had been dealt with. Later that day there was a band meeting. I thought I'd be in for it after all that. We're all sitting there quietly nervous, fingering bits of clothing and smoking. But it was Pete's turn to get it this time.

'So. What *ARE* you going to do about it?' said Bernie.

'What am I going to do about what?' said Pete.

'I'm getting complaints. The rhythm is wooden. It seems to me you're not taking your job very seriously. If you're not serious then it means you're not taking *me* seriously. And that's a problem.'

'Problem' was Bernie's favourite word. And you knew what it meant. His favourite saying was 'look, if you've got a problem there's only one solution. Get *RID* of the problem.'

'We've been elected to do a job here,' began Joe, 'it requires commitment. I'm not convinced. I'm not sure you're fully committed to this.'

'Yes, of course I'm committed!' Pete blurted. You could see he was getting flustered.

'What do you *expect* from me?'

'Well for one thing it's realising what you're about. Giving your all. Nick is delivering. Look, even Vince is raising his game now. You treat this like you're on a fucking holiday and I'm afraid it's not good enough,' said Bernie.

I had no idea what it was all about. I had no problem with Pete's drumming. I thought his drumming was good. I wanted to support him but I knew he didn't want my support and so I didn't give any. Nick remained quiet.

'Well. Look, this is the way I play. If there's something you want from me then you have to *tell* me.'

'I *am* telling you. You gotta shape up. I'm only prepared to work with people who have a *professional* attitude. I'm only prepared to work with people who want to work *with* me. If you don't wanna work *with* me then you've no reason being here.'

Pete jumped up. Hot and petulant.

'Oh! Ok then. I QUIT! If I'm not good enough then get someone who is. I'm not taking this shit!'

Pete stormed out the room. He slammed the door. Bernie began laughing.

'Well. Can we find another drummer for the rest of the tour? Shouldn't be a problem, eh Joe?'

'No. I shouldn't think so,' Joe replied.

The mafia meeting was over. I went back to my room. I was pleased Pete had stood up for himself. The big guys were riding roughshod over us. I wondered what would happen that night. We had a show to play.

Later Pete appeared and we did the show and carried on. Bernie had gone to his room and talked him back round without too much of a problem apparently.

Show after show and the same thing each night. In my hotel room I would practise a bit of guitar and play along with one of the band's early recordings. Working out something different for solos. To find some different colour to things. Something original. The same songs we were playing every night. 'Garageland'. 'White Man In The Hammersmith Palais'. 'Spanish Bombs'. 'Complete Control'. I'd had to *insist* on playing 'Complete Control'. Joe didn't want to play it. It was one of Mick Jones' songs and Joe wanted to keep his songs out of the set. But if I insisted on playing a song Joe would usually give in. Not only was it my favourite Clash song but in my mind probably one of the greatest songs of all time. It said it all. It was all about how people and things and institutions tried to control you. Misunderstood you and tried to crush your spirit. It gave me a lift to play it. It was so relevant. I sighed. I found it hard listening to the early Clash songs. They meant so much to me. It was class. The early band had been so much class. It all seemed like light years away. What was once a lean tight hungry outfit was now a lumbering giant. A big fat cat slowly gorging it's way through all the stadiums across the U.S.A. Drunk with success and sick with ambition it had overreached itself. I'd seen some video of our performances and had been suddenly struck by something. How *old* Joe had become. I felt he was more than a bit jaded. Christ! It wasn't *that* long ago I'd watched him in 'Rude Boy' with all the fucked up teeth putting his all and out into 'Police and Theives'. The mental movements and soul baring. Youthful and dynamic. Urgent. He wasn't the same person. Now he was sporting a mowhawk. Deep orange hair and a white suit all under the spotlight and cabaret entertaining with in an 'Out Of Control' t-shirt. The solo star. Slowly moving around if at all. Us all running around him like demented monkeys. He was stiff. What had happened? No doubt Bernie was working on him. Contriving this and that. Every night he was there with his hand over one ear making this contorted grimace like he meant it, man. It was weird to watch. He'd become a bit of a caricature of something. Why couldn't things just work themselves out naturally? So things just went on like that and you knew something wasn't quite right. You didn't know what was to be done.

Despite everything the shows were good. There was a lot there. I felt it. The reviews continued to be good. All of it continued to get me fired up night after night. But as the tour continued on through New York State and into Canada and playing six high energy shows in a row, night after night and all the travelling in between and sleepless nights, the pressure begins to show. You got blasé. Going through the motions a bit. You begin trying to conserve your energy. The show starts with 'London Calling',

'Safe European Home', 'War', 'Know Your Rights', 'Three Card Trick' and by then you're already exhausted. Something easier starts like the 'The Magnificent 7', slow and rhythmically dancey and then you sit back a bit and your mind starts thinking of other things. I like the look of that girl at the front. I hope she comes backstage. Things like that.

I wasn't bothered about groupies in the beginning. I had the Whale back at home. I loved her. Most of the girls that came backstage weren't all that good anyway. They were a bit chubby or a rough looking. It was mostly guys who came backstage at a Clash show with their boring conversation and political talk. Structured, intellectual types. You got tired of hearing the same old thing again and again and felt deflated and had to be courteous and try to pretend you were interested. Sometimes Raymond would come up to me and said some girl over there wanted my hotel room number. Did I want her?

'Nah. It's alright.'

It was all way too forward for me. It didn't like it. But as things went along you began going for it. It filled in TIME. Each night after a show I was down. Even after the very good ones. *Especially* after a good one. We all were. Joe had the explanation for why we all sat back in the dressing room after a show like that, dripping with sweat, like a bunch of suicide cases.

'I've thought about it. The reason we get depressed is to do with *energy*. We give everything to the performance and after it there's nothing left. When all your energy has gone the result is depression.'

'Are you sure?'

'Yes.'

So after each show you'd have to go out and meet fans feeling like shit. You wanted that high you had before, like when you were playing. There were only two things that could lift you back up a bit. Booze. Or drugs. Or a girl. But I didn't do drugs.

They scared me. I knew I didn't have the constitution for them. With girls it was mostly the same thing. Someone to pass the Time with. A bit of company. Someone to hold onto. The warmth of flesh.

Until the twins arrived. The twins were called Kim and Shania. Maybe they weren't *actually* twins but they said they were. They looked like twins. Real wild cards. Can't remember where it was. Another Holiday Inn somewhere. Both were about 23. Dark long hair and tall and slim with loads of make up and eyeliner. Goths. Which was unusual to see in America at that time. They appeared at my hotel door out of the blue one evening. I had the curtains drawn. I was in bed. I made the mistake of letting them in and as soon as they were in there they were straight into my mini bar. Picking out whisky miniatures. Vodka. Drinking them straight from the bottle.
  'Hey! Go easy on that stuff. I gotta *pay* for all that you know?'
  'Don't worry, Vince! There's LOADS in here!'
  'There won't be the way you're fucking going at it.'
  They annoyed me. Americans were way too forward for my liking.
  'Do you want one?'
  I reached down by the bed. I had a small bottle of whisky down there. I lifted it up proudly and grinned.
  'Oh! You CHEAT! Give me some!'
  One of them ran over and went to grab the bottle. I pulled it back.
  'Get away! This is *mine!*'
  'Oh! PLEEEASE!'
  'Only if you give me a kiss.'
  She leaned over and planted a big one.
  'Me too! I want one!'
  I kissed the other. Gave her the bottle and turned over and put on some music. Led Zeppelin's 'Physical Graffitti'.

They began dancing.

'Hey! You're supposed to be *Clash* fans. You *can't do that!* This music's not politically correct. You'll get me fired! Behave yourselves!'

'We like it!'

I went over and joined them. I took a another swig of the whisky. Silly moves. Slow moves. I pulled back and thought I better say something.

'*Look*. We need some actors for the new Clash video. You guys ever made out before?'

'Of course we have.'

'I don't believe you. Come on. Lemme see.'

Kim and Shania began kissing.

'Uhm. Yeah. That's a good start.'

I put my head in between theirs. A sexy three-way kiss. I leaned back.

'That's *good, OK*. But I'm not sure it's *enough*. I don't think the boys will go for it.'

'Why *NOT!* We're good.'

'M.T.V. won't show it. You're not working hard enough. You need to put a bit more into it. Get the ratings. Know what I mean?'

They began putting more into it.

'Good. That's more like it.'

I walked away and around a bit and left them to it. Went and lay back down on the bed. I'd never had a threesome before. And here they were. Twins! Wow! What were you supposed to do? How did it work? I took another pull of the whisky. Kim came over. Or was it Shania? You couldn't tell.

'I think you're cute.'

We began kissing and got to it. Then the other one. Their clothes quickly peeled off. And there it was. Nothing like the porno movies of course. Just moving and going from one to the other. A bit with one and then the other.

It was a fest. But after you made it with both you got bored. Reality began to bite in again. I needed more drink. I went to the mini bar and got another beer.

Then for some unknown reason I begin to break things. I pick up an ashtray and throw it at a wall. I'm woken up by the noise of the shattering glass. They both look at me a bit nervously. Where is this going?

'Oh come on! It's *fun!*' I reassure them.

I go over and pull the telephone from its socket. Throw it into a corner of the room. Go to the window and pull it wide. I look down. My room is about four stories up. There's a swimming pool down there below. Then I'm at the bed, grabbing pillows and running back and they're flying out the window. I look out. They're off floating out there somewhere.

'Come on!'

They're quickly at it with me. Going mad. Everything begins to exit through the window. Everything that isn't tied down. Coat hangers, the bible, lampshades, the bed sheets. .

I get the standing lamp. It's a long gold plated thing. Hang it out the window.

'Hey! Look at *me* girls……..I'm *fishing!*'

'What! There's no *fish* out there!'

'Yes there is! Down in that pool. Look, I'm gonna get that stuff back out of there!'

I lean back and start singing.

'Goin' fishing…….there's a sign upon my door!'

'You're mad!'

. I've suddenly had enough of fishing. I slowly ease my fishing rod out the window and with a final cool push it's off and out into space. Run back in to see what else there is. The twins have the other bed stuff and are stuffing them out the window. Peals of crazy, stupid laughter. More stuff. Glasses, a tray. One of them begins pulling at the curtain. She can't get it off. I come over to help.

'Like this, idiot!'
With a big manly pull it's off.
'Stupid Americans! That's the *English* way to do it.'
I give it to her all business like. It's out the window with a girly grunt. Now I'm on a holy mission. All three of us are on a holy mission. I walk over to the T.V. pick it up and walk back with it pulling the lead out of the socket.
'NO! STOP! YOU CAN'T!'
I've got it on the window sill.
'Here goes! Ready?'
'NOOO!'
With a massive shove it's off and out there crashing down into the pool.
'YEAH!'
I looked around. Empty bottles smashed. Broken glass everywhere. Stained walls. One of the girl's is at the mini bar. It's Shania. She's trying to move it.
'Vince. Help! It's too heavy.'
'Leave the mini bar.'
'What's next?'
'I dunno. Use your bloody imagination. If you've *got* any.'
Kim gets one of the chairs balanced on the windowsill ready to go when there's a sudden knock at the door.
Bang! Bang!
Oh shit. I freeze.
BANG! BANG!BANG! BANG! Louder this time.
I run over and quickly turn the music down.
'Sssshhhhhh!' I warn them.
BANG! BANG! BANG! BANG!
I go over to the door and listen. Some mumbled sounds coming from out there.
'YES?' I say.
'SIR! What is *going on?* We've had some complaints from the other guests. About the noise. We can't…..'

'Oh, I'm *sorry*. Look, I've turned it down.'

'SIR! Would you *please* open the door?'

I quickly try and make myself look a bit presentable. Put on a shirt, button it up.

Hide the bottle. I'm not opening that fucking door.

'Ok, I'll turn it down some more.'

I go to the twins put my finger over my mouth and whisper.

'Keep quiet…..keep outa…..'

'SIR! WILL YOU *PLEASE* OPEN THIS DOOR! IF YOU DON'T OPEN THIS DOOR I'LL HAVE TO CALL THE POLICE.'

More banging.

I half open the door and stand there blocking the view.

'What *IS* the bloody problem?' I shout. 'I've turned it down. Whatsamatter with you people?'

'We've been having a number of complaints from guests. People are trying to sleep.'

'Ok. Ok. We'll be quiet. Don't worry.'

'Thank you sir. If there's anymore trouble I'll have to call the police.'

'Ok. There won't be any more trouble.'

With that he leaves.

I look at the twins. I jump in between them and roll around on the bed. Howls of laughter. It was a close shave.

'Ok. We better stop. Who wants a drink?'

At some point I pass out. There's another knock at the door. I look at my watch. It's 7.40 a.m. I go and open the door. It's Raymond. He looks at me. I look at him. He's in a bad mood.

'Twenty minutes.'

'Ok. I'm there.'

I shut the door. Go back and look around the room. The twins have gone. The beds are lying at odd angles. The window is wide open and you can hear the depressing sound of cars out there on the highway. People off in the half grey morning light driving to work. Getting up in the morning and dealing with the difficulty of life and honestly earning money to feed their children and just being decent and doing their best in this god awful sad life. A terrible sense of guilt descends over me. Plates of half eaten food are scattered around. Cigarette butts burnt into the carpet. Ash. Broken glass is everywhere. The mini bar is on one side. Half the room is missing. As I get up to get my things together there's another knock at the door. It doesn't wait for an answer. A key goes into the lock and it just opens. It's the maid. She walks in with some sheets and stuff. I hear a helicopter buzzing overhead. It's probably a police one, I think. The maid doesn't look at me. Just politely moves around starting to clean up.

I pack my things as quickly as possible. I don't feel too good. There are little white sparks darting menacingly at the edges of my vision.

'Oh, uhm, I'm sorry for the mess,' I say.

She doesn't reply. Just gets on with it.

I get out of there quickly. God, I'm in a bad way.

Later that day we're in the next town. There's another band meeting. Another Holiday Inn. The band and Kosmo sit around. Bernie is standing to one side quietly menacing.

'Well, if you're gonna destroy a hotel room you gotta know, Vince. It's YOU who has to PAY,' begins Kosmo. 'It's all very well playing the rockstar. But all that stuff with the Who. *Think* about it. Who do you think *actually* pays in the end, Eh? It's not the hotel. See, *they* don't care. It's YOU! The *band* has to pay.'

'Yeah. I see your point.'

Bernie and Joe remain serious and quiet. Nick and Pete are silent. Kosmo went on.

'It's like if Joe incites trouble at a show. It's happened before. The seats get torn apart at a venue. Who do you think *pays*?'

'I think....'
'It comes out of *YOUR* wages.'
I was hungover. The reprimanded schoolboy. I really didn't give a shit. They could take it out of my wages if they wanted to. I didn't have any.
'Yeah. I see what you mean,' I remark, feebly.
'Think about it.'

The ship sails on through Canada. Montreal, Ottawa, Kitchener and back into the U.S. Bernie's disappeared again. He's gone back to England for some reason or other. We arrive in Detroit. We play the Fox Theatre there. Detroit is Wendy's home town. She calls me up after the show and we go off to a party somewhere to meet some of her friends. I'm happy to see a friend. We get a cab there and walk into someone's house. It's real dark in there with people standing around holding drinks and it's just like being at party back home. Normal. The furniture's been cleared out leaving dim, empty rooms. Punk music's playing. Five or six people are dancing. A Clash song comes on. I'm introduced to some of Wendy's friends and they're cool but I don't really want to talk to more strangers about the Clash. It's the same thing over and over. Pretending to keep everybody happy. Being social. It's all too draining. We find a quiet place sitting down on the floor and talk.

'That was a fantastic show tonight. What did you think?' she says.
'Yeah. It was good I suppose.'
'You *suppose?*'
'Well. It was another show wasn't it? Joe's barmy army. Bernie's hit men. Another day, another dollar. For someone else.'
I take a pull from my beer bottle and begin peeling the label off.
'Whatsamatter?'

I'M SO BORED WITH THE U.S.A.

'I can't really get with it Wendy. I mean I love the music and everything. But …….I just feel pissed off the whole time. Playing is great. But you know…...Joe's on another planet, Pete and Nick ……...I don't even *like* them, frankly. They're stuck up and boring. I have no connection with them. It's obvious they don't like me. And Bernie and Kosmo, well, I can't *relate* to all that clever, clever shit they go on about. I think it's all bullshit. It makes no sense. It's all diversions and smokescreens and for what? Paul is cool. But he's dumb. He rolls along with things and he's got his image and that but I don't think he's got a fucking clue what's going on. He's lucky. He doesn't think……I don't think………..'

'Just *forget* about it. Enjoy the ride! What are you going on about? You're on tour with the Clash! Enjoy it! Don't make so much of it.'

'I *DO* enjoy the ride. But it's all confusing. It's hard to enjoy the ride when you feel boxed in the time. It's crap. And the ride's great at the same time. Oh, well, I dunno, whatever.'

I pulled another big slug of my beer thinking I better stop being such a downer. But as usual, it was hard to control things. To do and say what was in yours and others best interests. Something just happened and you had to let it all out regardless. Fuck it.

'It's ALL FUCKING BOLLOCKS! Don't you see, Wendy? It's an endless stream of fucking SHIT! People piling shit upon each other. Heaping it over and over and over. And it goes where? NOWHERE! You try and try your hardest to so something but there's always something else that comes along to fuck it up. And even if you *get* something precious you want………well, ……...you *think* you want……… it turns out to be nothing in the end, anyway. And even if it's good you get bored with it quickly enough. And so you move on to the next thing. And then the next thing. We're driven along, baby. By nature. Like mules! Packhorses! And all around you are people doing the same thing struggling and sucking the blood out of each other and *you* to get something they *think* they want and for what? NOTHING! Nobody really cares whether you're successful and happy! They just think about themselves. Ok, so you try to and relax and what? Let it all go. Like all the spiritual thing? Find the answer. Oh, yes! I'll be good! I'll eat the right food and sit crossed legged and think about my navel and treat others right and be righteous and good and that and what happens? You get fucked over! You can't make it that way because people think you're weak. They suck you dry. And you gotta get along with the fuckers whether you like it or not. So, OK, yeah, let's go to the mountains. Get away from it all. Live in a cave, right? How long would you last? Come on! How long? What do you think? About a fucking week, I reckon, before you're bored out of your fucking skull! So what can you do? Kosmo says he's a *realist*, right? What does realism *mean*? Surely that means giving up your ideals for the way things are, yeah? So how do you *feel*... knowing you're *doing* that*?* Making *do*. Just getting by with reality? IT'S SHIT! I tell you, it's SHIT! It happens one way or another. But of course you know none of this is the way to go so what do you do? What? Be a *cunt*? Manipulate things and people and have power and get rich? It's awful. Appalling. Money doesn't mean anything really. We know that. So what? Become a punk? Pick up a guitar? Be an artist? As soon as you do anything you're back in the same ball park. Criticism. They tear your soul out with all their logical filthy mind fuck scrutiny and hang it out to dry. But then in a hundred years you're an icon. But then you're dust. So what's the point? I tell you, it's ALL HOPELESS! Don't you see? Life is just pain of all kinds. It's endless. Within and without. I'm telling you Wendy, *THERE'S NO FUCKING ESCAPE!'*

Wendy laughed.

'You can have some fun with it anyway.'

I quickly switched gears. Girls weren't illogical as they all say. They were logical because they were more adaptive to the stupidity of things. Flexible. It was men who were stupid. With their stupid rationality, trying to figure out the impossible.

'Yeah, the more the better!'

'I'll drink to that!'

We clinked our bottles.

It was good letting off a bit of steam. I suddenly felt better. Wendy looked incredibly good sitting there in the half light. Beautiful. So relaxed and cool. My manager's girlfriend.

'Look, I'm bored here, Wendy. Let's go back to the hotel and hang out. Have some more drinks.'

'O.K.'

We got a cab back. I was always like that with parties. You were excited to be going to them but as soon as you arrived you couldn't wait to leave. I had to keep moving.

We went up to her room. It was Bernie's room really. But he wasn't around, was he? Fuck him!

'Bloody hell! This room is massive. A lot bigger than mine. Fucking hell!'

'What do you want? Beer? Whisky?'

'Beer'll do. Ok, give me a shot too.'

I drank the whisky down and put it all out of my mind. Wendy lay out on the bed. Wendy looked so good lying there. Like in a poster or something. I wanted her. And so there we were. At it again. There was something a bit tarty about her. I always like that in a girl. Something soft you could violate. The rudeness of it all. She was a great fuck. But when it was over you came suddenly back to earth and it was that same old thing again. We lay there smoking.

'Do you *like* me, Vince.'

'Of course I like you. You're brilliant. You're the only friend I got right now.'

'Only a friend?'

'Well, you know what I mean. You're really cool. You're the only person I can talk to..........*And* you're bloody sexy,' I added, trying to steer things a bit away from something. Wendy took my hand and held it tightly. Something was wrong. The booze was wearing off. I became acutely aware of the fact that I was lying in my manager's double hotel bed with his girlfriend. I began to imagine he might appear at any moment. Maybe he was in that big closet waiting to spring out. I thought of the Whale back at home.

'Look, Wendy, I'm not feeling too cool with this.'

'It's *fine*. Bernie's not due back till tomorrow.'

I began to get up. She tried to pull me back down with her. I let her, lay back and tried to relax. She took my hand.

I jumped up quickly.

'Look, I'm going back to my room. I can't do this. Not here, for fuck's sake.'

I had to get out. I put my clothes on. Wendy looked up at me, sadly. I was a terrible mess. I liked mess. But not this kind.

'I'm sorry, Wendy. I really don't understand what's wrong with me. I'll see you later.'

I went over and gave her a quick kiss and ran out of there.

I got back to my room. I was only back a few minutes when my phone rang.

'Hello?'

'Hi, it's me.'

'Yeah?'

'Vince.................. I think................. I LOVE YOU.'

'Well................... I can't say I blame you, Wendy. I'd feel the same way if I was you.'

'It's *TRUE*.'

I didn't know what to say so I said nothing. There was an awkward silence.

'I'm tired, Wendy. I gotta sleep. Speak soon. Goodnight.'

'Goodnight, Vince,' she said, quietly.

I put the phone down. I put my head down onto the stiff, starched pillows. What was I doing? It was all out of control. What was wrong with me?

With a big effort I tried to pull the starched sheets around me. It was hard. Those sheets were so tightly pinched under the mattress. Even when I thought I'd got them loose it wasn't enough. So I got up, walked around and yanked them hard from the bottom end of the bed. Soon I had those sheets loose and easy. I got back into bed and pulled them tightly around me. Rolled them between my legs. I tried to sleep. Why were hotel beds made like that? Everything was so tight-arsed. Even in bed they had you working at it.

But we had two days off now and the band was going nowhere. *I* was going nowhere. I caught a cab and went to the Detroit zoo. Everyone else was going somewhere else, to some exhibition or art gallery or something. No one invited me along. I felt a little rejected but I was happy I wasn't invited. I needed to be by myself. Exhibitions bored me. The band bored me. Art bored me. I was tired of pretending. I was happy to be alone. I couldn't band mesh. I couldn't care fucking less to tell the truth. So I wandered around that zoo, alone with my camera, taking pictures of all the trapped animals under a grey sky. Those animals didn't look at all too happy being stuck in their cages. I didn't like zoos either. I sympathised with the poor fuckers. I was trapped too, after all. So it went on like that, me and the giraffes, the lions, the gazelles, some rat looking things that kept popping out of the ground and up on their hind legs looking around stupidly. What they were looking for God only knows. It was all so pointless and sad. Human beings had put them in there. And human beings had put human beings in the big human zoo. We were all in it together, trapped one way or another. For no reason whatsoever. I began to imagine I was on the African plains with my spear ten thousand years ago with these animals. All free on some desert plains somewhere. I knew that would be better life. Simple stuff. Working with nature as it had made things. Kill or be killed. Just physical necessities. No constant mental stress torture. That's how I imagined it anyway. Technology, information, industry hadn't improved anything. We were all getting screwed by it.

Later that evening I'm in the hotel bar. I'm getting drunk. Everything becomes alright when you're drinking. I even manage some band meshing. And the band meshes with me for a while. I'm sitting with Joe at the bar and he's in confidential mood. He's got a napkin from the bar and he's scribbling.

'What you writing?' I ask him.

'Vince. I've *decided*,' he says, turning to me, 'The new album is gonna be under the name 'Clash by Night'.

'Clash by Night? Why not the Clash?'

'Yeah. See, that way we can escape Mick's injunction over the name. Otherwise we could be tied up in court over the record. And it won't get released.'

'Oh, I see.'

'And the album's gonna be called 'Out Of Control.'

Out of Control? It seemed appropriate. He had it all scribbled out on that napkin. He showed it to me. I looked at it. He'd sketched some strange picture of a street in the dark with figures and the name in bold capitals.

'Sounds good, man.'

'And we're gonna get this album out by the end of the year. We've *got* to, Vince.

See, we've gotta get in the studio as soon as possible and bang it out raw.'

'Brilliant! I think it would be amazing to do it like that, you know and really .....'

'*Why* do you think we're really touring like this? With nothing to release? We need to finance the recording. We need to shape up the songs in front of an audience. That's the ONLY WAY. That's the ONLY WAY to get some *reality* into things. I don't wanna make the same mistakes we made in the past, Vince. 156 tracks of studio self-indulgence. Plinkety plink compress this and that with some high flying producer. We have to stick to what we were good at in the beginning. Rebel rock can rule! This way we're getting the audience feedback. When this tour's finished those songs will be shaped up and we'll be ready to just go in there and shoot straight from the hip. No messing about.'

'I love the sound of that and do you think……..'

'And the money from this album will be split equally. We're all in this together, OK?'

'OK.'

I sat back and thought about it. Clash by Night. A raw, exciting album like the first. With *me* playing guitar. It would be so brilliant. Nick and I would work out our differences. We both had different things to offer. Different styles. He was good at the technical stuff. I would put in the wild screamy stuff. Wow! People wouldn't know what hit them! And we would all share equally. That was the way to do it.

'It's the right way to go Joe. I'm sure of it.'

All my misery about things disappeared hearing Joe speak. Things would work themselves out now, I was sure of it. We were going to make a brilliant album. Joe wandered off and I got talking to some girl, full of renewed confidence.

On we went. Dayton, Ohio. Michegan. Back to Ohio.

Nothing really eventful ever seems to happen. Then one morning we're all sitting in the bus waiting to leave the hotel but no Paul. Where is the cunt? No one knows. We have to just sit there and wait for him. An hour goes by. Two hours. Then he turns up and we move off. I'm a bit pissed off with him keeping us waiting like that. Playing the rock star. But as we roll on I notice something strange about his face. About an hour into the ride I see his face has gone all red. It gets redder and redder. His neck too.

'What the fuck's going on with you?' I laugh.

Paul says nothing. Raymond whispers in my ear.

'Paul caught a dose. He's been in the clinic,' he laughs. 'It's the effect of the pills they gave him.'

'Oh! Fucking hell!'

For hours Paul's face is like that. A beetroot. Well, who would have thought it? You never saw Paul with a girl. He was a right dark horse sometimes.

Milwakee. St. Paul. Des Moines. And Chigaco.

Chicago. What a name! What a place! You get fired up by a place when you feel something. An atmosphere. And you know immediately you're somewhere special. Especially after all the dull hick towns with no personality your sorry arse has been dragged through. After the show we have a day off. I can't wait to explore. But I'm exhausted and end up in bed all day. But that evening the great blues axeman, Buddy Guy is playing in his club. It's gonna be good, I know it. And blues music seemed to be a point of connection for me and Joe. It was the only music I was passionate about that seemed to be accepted. On the road I'd picked up some John Lee Hooker in a truck stop. Put it in my Ghetto blaster and was walking around playing it outside the stop. Joe had rushed up. Pulled the tape out and put it in *his* blaster!

'Hey! What are you fucking doing? Give it back.'

'This is IT!' he exclaimed, moving off with my tape. He began playing it loud by himself by the edge of the road. I watched him. He had both hands in pockets, hunched over and swaying and nodding slowly to the beat like Bob Dylan on the cover of one of his albums. He was going at it like it was the first time he's ever heard any music. It looked a bit odd all that theatrics of his. I could never tell how much was real and how much was put on with Joe. I was a bit annoyed he'd grabbed my tape like that but I wasn't in the habit of spoiling anyone's fun. I walked over, curious.

'Vince!' he exclaimed, 'This is where it all comes from. This is *my roots.   *Rock'n'roll! *Everything!!!*'

'Yeah?'

He was so lost in it and absorbed, enjoying himself I walked off and left him to it.

Buddy's club is on the South Side of Chigaco which is a dangerous place for white people to go. But our tour manager has sorted it out for us. We all bundle in cabs and get there safely. Nick, Pete, Joe, Kosmo and me. It's dark outside and you can't see too much but you know it's all dodgy out there. Run down buildings and little signs over stores that don't read properly. Buddy's joint is a small place. Basic décor and little tables and chairs set out like an East End London café. I'm excited beyond belief. We're in there early and I sit near the front next to Joe and the place begins filling up. Only black people come in. We're the only white people in there. I feel privileged to be there. I begin going on to Joe about it all. I love the blues. I'm twisting in my seat. Buddy is one of my heroes and all that. This is IT, man! The First Time I Met the Blues! Joe plays along with my excitement but I know he's not really getting it the same way. He's a bit cool and reserved. I'm aware of being a bit intense and over the top but I don't care. I reckon it's wrong to put the brakes on things just for the sake of being cool. I look over at Nick and Pete. They're chatting. I've a lump in my throat. Wow! It's all too much.

Suddenly Buddy shows and he's up there and begins to do his stuff. It's the stuff of life. It hits the spot. It builds slowly. The set, I mean. I watch his fingers running around the fretboard picking each note with his intense precise style. I'm suddenly a bit ashamed of my lack of technique. But I'm gonna improve!

But it doesn't matter! It's just the intensity that counts. It's all the same, the blues, the 12 bar progression but it's what I *need* to hear now going round and round and starting and finishing and soothing and rising and falling predictably like the waves of the sea. And that's what it IS! The sea of Time that has sculpted the human mind experience with this music over aeons back way back when to who knows when into the dark beginnings of everything and I know this is IT! A rising sense of completeness in things begins. More and more. Round and round. Bigger and bigger it climbs. Never endingly getting better and better. Guitar solos swirl across the room and through my head and shouts appear from women in the audience and that's just the way it's supposed to be.
  'Yeah! Yeah! Go Buddy! Go!'
  'YEAH!!!!!' I shout.
  Over to one side is an old guy nodding and black wrinkled face and here it's *his* music and no 60's revival in his brain but just what it is and that is his fundamental but right now it's my fundamental too and so what if I'm white? I *get it* and that's all that matters.
  Junior Wells comes on to massive applause after a couple of songs with a little bag of harmonicas and starts blowing.
  Yeah! Yeah! Yeah!
  It's the particular moment in Time that counts. It's the memory of the moment that keeps you moving through life and keeping on going. 80% of living is pure drudgery and boredom. 19% is barely average, OK. 1% is feeling good. And a fraction of a fraction of a percent is ecstasy. And this was it.
  I pray it will never stop. But of course it does. When it's over Buddy's relaxing at the bar. I go over to see him. I arrive in front of him but I'm speechless. I've no idea what to say. But it doesn't matter because everything's been said already. I ask him for his autograph! I'd never got anyone's autograph before. It

always seemed like a silly thing to do. He writes his name on a small piece of card. I put it in my pocket.
Buddy is the perfect gentlemen and leads us all out onto the street when the taxis had arrived. He's anxious for our safety.
'You white folks gotta be careful, you don't want to be walking around here!'
I looked at his face. He wasn't joking. We all shook hands. Got in the cars and drove back to the hotel. I took out my piece of card and looked at his autograph. Wow! What a night!

A new film about a rock band on tour was on release called 'Spinal Tap'. The following evening all the band go to see it. Together with our tour manager and Kosmo. Our tour manager gets the tickets and we pile into the cinema together and sit down. The film starts and we begin watching our present moment existence unfold on the screen right there in front of us. Every little bit. Down to the smallest detail. The band that matters was no different. Spinal Clash would have made an even better film. It would have to be a black comedy though and it would require some skill to make.

On to Davenport, St. Louis and Kansas City. Every show is the same now, the same set with minor changes. Bernie arrives back from England. He stands proudly in the centre aisle of the bus holding up a copy of the Sun newspaper. He knows we're all tired and homesick and the sight of that paper will raise our spirits and give us the feeling of home. In a way it does. I could die for a Lamb Madras and some Pilou rice. A plate of baked beans on toast and a real cup of tea. I miss the pub and a pint of lager. But I hate that paper. I hate all newspapers but especially that one. It's stupid and panders to the lowest common denominator. The stupid masses. It's the paper that supports Margaret Thatcher and it's right wing. But it's also the paper that the Clash are affiliated with. The 'Bizarre' entertainment column in that paper has officially been allowed to represent news of the Clash. I don't get it at all. A band with pronounced left wing ideals consenting to being represented by a right wing, fascist newspaper. Not that I cared about left wing ideals either. But the inconsistencies were irritating. It was pointless to challenge it. Joe always had an answer for everything. It was the most widely read rag in Britain. We have to use the *system* to get our *message* across to the *most* people. We use the system to undermine it from within. Or something like that. The only real act of integrity the Clash ever stuck with was not to appear on Top Of the Pops. And in the hard world of politics and entertainment one act of integrity will cover up for thousands of rotten ones. It's the one noble gesture that people remember.

And Bernie's brought me a present from England. It's a rubber t-shirt with large metal ring holes running down both sides of the front it. It looks like rubber fetish wear. It looks gay. Kosmo wants me to try it on. I look at it in horror.

'You've got to be kidding. Are you taking the piss?'

Kosmo looks a bit disappointed and hurt. Apparently it's been styled especially for me.

'No fucking way I'm wearing that.'

Nick takes it and tries to put it on. There's a big zip along the side to do it up. With a bit of difficulty he finally gets into it. He stands up, laughing. Luckily it's all turned into a bit of a joke but for a moment there I was worried. What the hell were they thinking of?

By now the bus has become our home. Bits of trinkets and things picked up here and there are stuck all over the walls. A big 'REBEL PUNK' sign has been painted up at the back. A picture of Jesus. Bits of '50's memorabilia. Nick and Paul are becoming inseparable. Like newly wed couple they cling to each other and follow each other around everywhere. Sitting together and playing together. We've hit a patch of snow. All around us it lies out there. The bus stops for something and everyone runs out into it throwing snowballs and laughing. It's all good fun and woops! And Wow! I GOT YOU! And playing which is no playing at all but real put on and phoney. We're rock stars but we still know how to have fun and be 'child-like' sort of thing. Hateful. I can't do it. Join in that is. I stay in my seat and sulk and leave them to it. There's something bad going on which disgusts me to the bone. I know that isolating myself is a bad move. When you're isolated you're an easy target. But all the same it's impossible to pretend. What seemed to start out as a band now resembles a medieval court. With Joe as the king figure head and Bernie as the Macheavellian seat of power. And the game is the game of courtiers. Seek allies. Don't upset your masters. Be honest but only selectively. Don't look too perfect or too intelligent or you'll arouse resentment. Challenge your superiors but not too much. You must let them feel superior, don't offend them, and keep the truth hidden. Step on those beneath you. Pretend, pretend, pretend. But that's how courts work. And cults. It's all about manipulation and power. The very kind of thing I thought punk music was there to expose. And what to do? Speak the truth? But the truth is way too harsh and unpleasant for most people. Out there are all the believers in the 'band that matters'. Buying their tickets to concerts where they imagine they'll find something real to believe in inside all of the madness. Some truth. Some integrity. A cause, a new faith which is really the old faith that music can change things. Vague words full of promises. And it matters not a jot whether it all adds up. Not to the band. And not to the thousands in the audience. The masses too, only want a fantasy version of truth after all. Even if it only comes in the form of a romanticised version of the ghetto. Those first few days of speaking my mind when I joined and being respected for it seem like another time. Now it only arouses anger and disgust. So be it. Just shut your mouth up Vince and get on with it.

The ship sails on and into Denver and there are only a couple of dates left on this tour now. We're playing at Red Rocks which U2 made famous in one of their videos. In fact back in the hotel lobby we're all sitting there watching the TV and U2 are up there on the TV waving their stupid flag. They're doing well in the U.S. They have that rocky, echoey sound that seems to fit with all the wide open spaces and a singer with a powerful voice. He can hit all the high notes.

'They're ripping us OFF!' yells Bernie, annoyed. 'Look, even the drummer has a 50's haircut. They've taken what we're about and repackaging it. It's disgusting.'

Joe quietly nods in agreement. Everyone is silent watching it. I know I'm supposed to hate it. I'm not that bothered about U2 one way or the other but they got a big sound and whether you like it or not it's pretty impressive.

It's a bad omen. We drive up to the venue in a bus. It's a long drive up there and when we pile out it's suddenly a lot colder and windy. We're up in the mountains. The air is thin. Our support is Joe Ely. He's a country rock type and delivers a good performance. But something isn't right. When we go on to play the wind gets up and starts throwing the sound off the stage. The audience seem like miles away. There's a space of fifty yards or so of some metal structure between the stage and the first row of people. Joe jumps off the stage and onto it and runs up towards the crowd. Nick and Paul follow. I move up too but I can't hear my guitar. Bernie is at the mixing desk. He's got my guitar sound so low in the out front mix. He controls the sound. Two soundmen have been fired already on this tour. I imagine they've disagreed with him over something. No one lasts too long who disagrees with Bernie. I also suspect he's getting his revenge on me for Wendy. It's frustrating. Without much coming out of the main speakers it's impossible to hear what I'm doing that far in front away from my amps and monitors. The further forward I move the less I hear. Soon I can't hear anything. I can only hear Nick's guitar. I'm hitting chords without sound. I'm a punk puppet up there. A moving punk mannequin in leather trousers. Just something to look at. I realise that I'm nothing more than a monkey pilot. With no control of the capsule. Blasted into space with millions watching. There's really no real reason for me being there at all. I decide to move back to the stage where I can hear my guitar from the amplifiers. In order to hear what I'm doing I have to stay right at the back through the whole set while everyone else is up at the audience barrier. I have no contact with anyone at all now except Pete who just glares at me every time I get up on the drum riser. There are several thousand people in the audience across the stage and it begins to rain. I'm crushed. Humiliated. I make it through the set trying to put my best into it. But it's hopeless. But the show must go on as they say. It steams off like a runaway freight train to the end of the line and I can only watch it steaming ahead, helplessly.

Backstage we group ready for the encore. I look at the band. No one looks at me. I don't seem to exist. I'm a complete loser. A non entity. A target with nowhere to run. Joe is up and ready. It's time to move. I contemplate just staying there and not bothering but decide against it. Suddenly, we're back on the stage. I turn to Pete waiting for the count. He looks at me.

'What's the matter with *YOU? YOU FUCKING CUNT!*' he snarls, viciously.

I tear off my guitar and get up on the drum riser.

'WHAT DID YOU CALL ME?'

He looks away with a sneer.

It's too much. Before I even realise it I'm diving headlong over the drum kit and smacking him hard in the face. It takes him completely by surprise. *I'm* taken by surprise. But already Raymond and another security are there dragging me off. My fists are flying around hitting nothing. I desperately want to kill him. To destroy him. To destroy everything.

'You're MAD! You're fucking INSANE!' shouts Pete, behind the security men. He looks pretty shaken.
I collect myself, coolly pick up my guitar. That felt good. It's pissing down. What's the next song?
'White Riot' starts. Hell, it's strange the way things seem to fit. I'm happy when all the backstage signing and crap is all over. Some of the fans noticed the trouble but they haven't seen anything really. I want to get drunk. Back at the hotel there's a party. The band are still ignoring me but I get talking to Joe Ely, our support. He's got one of those southern country accents. A good 'ol boy. Right away I realise I've found a like mind and I warm up a bit.
'Ok, Vince, let's get ourselves one of those purty girls. What d'ya think?'
'What purty girls, man? Where?'
'Over there.'
He slyly points to a corner of the room. Sitting there were two *women*. I mean they must have been at least 30 years old. Not really my type but El is loose and easy and friendly. He's a dude. Oh, what the hell?
'Let's do it.'
We go over and begin talking. They're wearing high heels and got those tight skirts on. But they look a bit like secretaries. I wasn't convinced.
'Hello!' says Ely.
'Hi!'
'We're getting restless. Me and my friend Vincent here reckon you might be able to entertain us.'
'Entertain *YOU!* That's not *our* job.'
They both laugh.
It turns out one of them is an accountant. The other is a high flying something or other. I end up with the accountant on the balcony. I'm kissing her and feeling her up and I can tell she's keen but it seems like she wants a relationship or something.

I can't get with it.

'Look, El. Let's get out of here and find some *proper* chicks!'

'Anything you say, dude.'

We each take a bottle of wine and wander off around the hotel getting drunker and drunker. Down the long corridors looking for fun. But there's nothing to be found. No music anywhere. No girls. We can't go back to the party so we end up in my room playing music.

'What are you putting on dude?' he asks.

'Look, it's AC/DC. But for fuck's sake don't tell the band OK? I'll get shit for it.'

'Highway to Hell' begins its diabolic lament to the road.

El produces a small bottle of bourbon from somewhere and hands it to me. I take a gulp.

He leaps up on one of the beds and starts playing air guitar! He's got his country cowboy hat on and he's yelling.

'YEEEEEEHAAAAAA!'

I get on the other and there we are at it, playing air guitar like fools. It's good being a fool. But then you get a bit too released from it all again and before you know it the trouble starts again. Breaking things. El doesn't miss a beat and he's suddenly at it too. Upturning things. Pissing out the window. Trays and chairs are flying around the room. I take a lamp and smash it against the wall. There's an incredible anger inside me. Before it was fun. Now there's something mean going on. The switch has flipped from light to dark. It's time to stop. Something is wrong here. Whatever it is it's not nice. It scares me. I regain some self control.

'Fuck it, Joe, let's get out of here. We need some action!'

Ely follows me outside and we swagger drunkenly down the corridor. He puts his arm around me.

'See trouble is, Vince, we need *pussy*. Quality pussy, OK? No pork chops. Just PRIME, DUDE!'

'Yeah. But where, my friend? Let's check the party again. I'm gonna show that secretary a thing or two.'
So we wander back up there but it's all over. The girls have left. No band. Nearly everyone has left. All there is to do now is to keep drinking. But the drink isn't working anymore. There's no conversation. No possibilities. No hope. Just the pointless desire to keep moving forward relentlessly like a pair of gamblers who just don't know when to quit. It's pathetic. There's no dignity. But I never cared for dignity or anything else for that matter. I want kicks. The whisky gets finished. I look through the room and can't find any more booze. It really is the end of the line. I get up and shake Joe Ely's hand.
'Man. I gotta sleep. I hope we'll meet again.
He hands me a card with his number on it.
'Sure. You come look me up sometime.'
He gives me a big hug. With that I'm out of there. Joe Ely is cool. A real fun dude. I hope we'll hook up again under better circumstances.

Next day starts a three day trip across the West to Eugene. I'm dreading it. I enjoyed my time with Ely. Now I have three days stuck on that fucking bus with those tight stuck up fucks that are supposed to be my friends. Who needs it? In the morning I'm in the lobby with the others waiting for Strummer. He suddenly appears in leather jacket and stands proud. Straight away I notice something strange about him.
'OK. OK. OK! Are we ready? Are we READY? Are we READY? Let's get this thing *TOGETHER*. Have we got ………..hey…….hey…..HEY! Where's KOSMO?'
He looks around not really looking at anybody in particular but moving around in jerky movements. He's really pepped up. It's a lot of incredible positive energy for so early in the morning. He's suddenly become a holiday camp compere. Or the speaker at a self help seminar. A sort of punk Tony Robbins. Bizarre. I

wonder secretly whether he's been taking drugs to get himself out of his room. I look at Paul. Kosmo. But no one else seems to have noticed anything odd. We all get on the bus. We've a long way to go. I slouch in my seat put on my walkman and kick back for the ride.

The bus moves off through Colorado. The sun is out and it's real hot. The snow capped Rockies stand up powerfully in the distance against a clear blue sky. The sort of sight that can make you almost believe that there really is a God. It's a real sight for sore eyes and a hangover. And on the bus it's business as usual only now as we move off through Colorado and into Utah the landscape completely changes. Small towns give way to empty long roads that fly off towards the horizon and shimmer in the sun. The Wild West! It's like we've entered another country. The atmosphere in the bus changes too and becomes warm and friendly. I begin to relax. It's all good! We stop somewhere on route and go walkabout. We're on the trail of the old Wild West pioneers and off the main road there's some evidence of that trail left in the dust. We wander around with our cameras. We've all got them now. We're out there for half an hour or so snapping pictures, trying to imagine what it was like back then. But something's bothering me. I walk up to Joe. He's in a good mood. It seems like a good time to deal with it.

'Joe, look. I've got a problem. I nearly died up there at that last show. There's none of my guitar in the mix. I can't hear what I'm playing. The sound is……..'

He stopped and led me to one side, away from the others, listening attentively. I went on.

'Like when I play a guitar solo it can't be heard. It wasn't like that before. Bernie's mixing me out, now. He's squeezing me. It's stupid. The solos I play in 'Complete Control', 'Tommy Gun' and the others are important to hear. It's stupid to just hear the rhythm guitar in those parts. And Paul's bass too. You can hardly hear that either. The mix is just…..'

'Paul can't play,' he began, quietly. 'The engineer has to mix his bass deep as he can so the notes aren't distinct. That's the way it is. We have to do the best with..........'
'But *I can play!* It's……....'
'Vince, don't worry about it.'

I wanted to get to the bottom of it but we were back at the bus now and every one was getting back on. It was time to move. I'd sort it out later. Later as the sun went down we stopped again. Streaks of flames, red and orange lay from one side of the sky to the other. Not a soul in sight. But that unusual warmth in the group camp stays for some reason. Where did that come from? We're a band again. It's funny how the environment can affect you. All the beauty of that landscape seeps inside of you without your realising it and changes things. Or is it the emptiness of it all that brings people closer? But the ugliness of things does the same thing if you're not careful. And you begin to wonder how much control you have over anything really. Or whether you just think you do.

We're on the last stretch coming towards Salt Lake City. Coasting down the road from the mountains under power of gravity.

I'm reading a new book I've picked up en route. Something by Norman Mailer. Joe leaves his seat at the front for the first time on this entire trip and comes back and sits next to me. He wants a friendly chat. He looks at the book and is impressed. He goes on about Mailer. Mailer is such an important writer and an influential this and that and about the history of all things modern literature. I'm just happy to have a point of connection. To have some rapport with our singer. Joe has a way of getting my confidence and making me forget how things really are. After a few minutes Joe got up and left. I went back to that book. I didn't know who Mailer was when I bought it and his fame or anything. I bought it for the cover. It had a picture of pyramids on the front that looked cool. I went back to it. I read a sentence. Then another. And then another. A whole page would go through my head before I realised not a bit of it had stuck there. I reread it again. I tried again and again. It was impossibly dull and tedious, that book. I never got past chapter one. I threw the bloody thing away in disgust and never looked at it again.

Down off that long road and into the city. Into the hotel and straight to the bar. We're the Clash pioneers off the lonely dusty trail. Punk prospectors and we need our drink. The first beer goes straight down but suddenly the bar is closing. It's only 11p.m. We beg and cajole the barmaid to stay open a while longer. We're not ready to give up.

'I'm sorry sir. It's against the law.'

Even Joe and his awesome diplomatic skills can't sway her. The manager arrives. He wont have it either so we wander out into the street looking for a bar. There's nothing out there. It's a ghost town. The city of the dead. We walk around the dark streets but it's a lost cause so eventually we give up and go back to our rooms and go to sleep early. Those religious types had settled this town. Mormons. Those religious pioneers had got here first long ago and screwed things arse tight for everybody right from the beginning. 200 years later and those screws were still arse tight. You knew they'd never come loose. It was all for our own good of course.

The next day and it's another 12 hour slog up the interstate through Idaho and to Pendleton, Oregon. These long trips wear you out and even the all that great scenery gets boring after a while. And the propaganda machine. Another tape is removed by Joe from the player. It's one of Pete's. Brian Eno. Our driver has had enough of it.

'I KNOW what you're doing,' our driver suddenly yells at Joe. 'I've been watching you. You and Bernie, you're trying to BRAINWASH these kids into your system. It ain't right.'

'Yeah, and SO WHAT? So what if we are? No one is forcing them to be here. If they don't like it they can leave at anytime.' Our driver mumbles something. Joe sits down, we carry on. But I'm happy. At least someone else has spoken up for what's going on. It's not all my imagination. They won't get *my* mind, I think.

We stop at a small town in the middle of nowhere. All anyone can think is beer. We go in this little bar filled with a dozen country types. It's like in the movies with cowboy hats, pool tables, fashions still left over from God knows when. Time has stood still and there's no outside world. Country music on the juke box. As weird as it all seems to me I realise we must look even weirder to them. Like invaders from another planet walking in there in all our leather and funky hats and shirts. The place falls silent. We get our beers and try to relax. The atmosphere is tense.

One of the group around the pool table suddenly saunters over.
'So, where you folks from?' he begins all friendly-like.
'We're a rock band from London, England.,' says Joe.
'I knew's you's was musicians. Didn't I say, Rick?' he shouts back at his friend, pleased with himself,. 'The ways yous all dressed and all. I guess you ain't playing round *here*. Where you headed?'
'We're on our way to Eugene. We got a show there tomorrow night.'
'Hell Rick! These guys playing in Eugene tomorrow. They's from England.'
Rick comes over.
'What you boys drinking?' asks Joe.
And there it is all the tension settled and Joe and Paul and Nick and Kosmo and Pete all talking the dullest conversation imaginable with the hicks from the sticks but its all diplomatic and friendly now after all. I can't keep up with small talk. I get

I'M SO BORED WITH THE U.S.A.

bored right off the bat with it. It amazes me how Joe can just keep going at it endlessly humouring people. He can go for hours. He's in his element. I find myself at the bar ordering more beer. I'm nicely jingled now. There's a country lady on the bar stool next to me.
'Hey! How're you doing?' I ask her. 'What's been happening in Pendleton? Seen any U.F.O.'s lately?'
'WHAT?' she laughs, ' Noooo! Nothing much happens around here. Where you from?'
'London. Nothing much happens there either to tell the truth. It's dull and grey and noisy and everyone walks around looking miserable as sin.'
'England! I'd LOVE to go to England. London. The smog! I love smog!'
'NO! There's no ....oh, never mind, what's your name?'
'Sandy. And this is my best friend, Patty,' she says introducing her friend on the next stool.
'Hello, Patty. You girls like a drink?'
And on it goes. And jingled becomes jongled and before I know it and I'm touching Sandy's hair at the back of her neck and she's touching my shirt and then I'm kissing the country lady full on the lips. I lean back and look at her. She's wearing a blue top and skirt and shoes the fashion of which I can't seem place in Time. It could be the 50's or the 60's or the 70's or the 80's. But she has lovely blonde hair and a cute smile.
I'm ready to go in for another kiss when something black and nervous is suddenly whispering in my ear and pulling at my arm. It's Kosmo.
'Vince. We got to get out of here. NOW!'
'What? Why? I'm having fun. What's the problem?'
'That girl you're talking to? See, her husband's just gone back home to get his rifle.
The guys here say we got trouble. We got to get out quickly.'
'What? I don't believe..........'

I looked hard at him. He wasn't messing.
The rest of the band are all standing up and getting ready to move out. I'm up quickly.
'Sorry Sandy. But it looks like we gotta go.'
Sandy looks at me.
'Bye Vince. Come back anytime.'
'Yeah.'
Everyone's running to the bus. No one wants any trouble. Especially me. He's getting his gun! Fucking hell! I grab my biker jacket and run.
'You got to be careful out here, in these places, Vince. It's not the same,' says Kosmo, laughing now we're back in the safety of the bus.
'Yeah, right. See what you mean.'
The show in Eugene is good. We play a blinding version of 'Straight To Hell'. Onto Seattle. 'In the Pouring Rain' is back in the set. One of our best versions. The tour has wound right down now. Over the border into Canada for one last uneventful show in Vancouver. And it's over. All thirty odd dates of it. Everyone is subdued sitting in the airport. We all want to get home. We're all tired. The pressure is off. I'm so looking forward to getting home. I've bought a few presents wandering around the market in Seattle. Some duty free too. Airplane. Flight. Drink. Eat. Sleep. Heathrow and suddenly it's grey, dreary cloudy English morning when we arrive. We slouch around until our luggage comes through. One by one we move off. We don't even say goodbye to each other. I check a new guitar I bought through customs and get a cab back to Finsbury Park with Pete. We hardly speak on the long journey under grey skies in bleak late morning now traffic in the familiar but strangely unfamiliar rise and fall of the black cab diesel engine clock ticking over and stopping and starting. Years later we pull up outside my place in Finsbury Park Road. I get my things.
'See ya Pete! Later!'

'Ok, Vince.'

I have my key and climb the stairs to my bedsit. Open the door and stand there. My sister and the Whale are sitting at the little table.

SOLO:

WHO PUT THAT HEAD IN MY BED?

I stand there just staring. A casual glance goes in my direction. The Whale and Sammy go back to talking between themselves. I blow.
 'You FUCKERS! Is that ALL YOU CAN DO? Just fucking *SIT* THERE? YOU FUCKERS! I been half way around the world for THREE months and WORKING and getting my poor arse SCREWED HALF WAY OFF TO INFINITY BY ALL THOSE CUNTS OUT THERE and this…….THIS is the kind of reception I get? BOLLOCKS SHIT ARSE FUCKING SHIT BOLLOCKS!'
 I slump down on the bed. The Whale comes over.
 'But Baby. I wasn't sure if………'

'Sure if WHAT? WHAT? *WHAT?* Oh, FUCK BOTH OF YOU! Everyone's a CUNT! I know it now. Including YOU TWO!'

'OH BABY, I'm REALLY HAPPY TO SEE YOU! REALLY!'

The Whale suddenly jumps over me putting her arms around me.

'Well, it's about time you started showing it, don't you think,' I say pulling away, angrily. 'What is all this for? Eh? You think all this stuff is fun and games? Eh? Punk rock star? You think it's all glamour and roses? What's the point? I tell you. What's the point anyway if you got nothing to come back to?'

She's hugging me frantically now.

'I'VE MISSED YOU. OH, I'M SO HAPPY YOU'RE BACK!'

'Don't be stupid Vince. Of course we're happy to see you,' Sammy chimes in.

'OK, then let's celibrate. Where's the wine?' I say.

'We haven't got any. Don't worry. I'll go to the off license.'

'Good. And hurry up about it!'

That wine arrives and my sister disappears and soon the Whale and I are back in bed and I unexpectedly land in heaven. Heaven comes in the form of her and a £12 a week bedsit. Leaves rustling outside the sash window. A humming fridge. A packet of cigarettes. Nowhere to go. Nothing to do. No one to be. I fall asleep in a jingly wine haze and each time I wake up in a warm bath of bliss. Another screw. Another bottle of wine. A curry take away. A beautiful girlfriend. Perhaps Bernie was right, after all. What the fuck *did* I want money for?

Later, Sammy's back and we're going to the pub to meet my mates. I'm putting on some nice strides.

'Oh, look! Vince. You've put on weight!'

'What? Nah. Not me. No chance.'

'Yes you have, Vince. You got LOVE HANDLES!'

'You girls need your eyes testing. I'm 100% pure meat HUNK! LOOK, no fat on that!'
I begin swinging my cock out of my fly.
'Put it away! Put it away!'
'Disgusting!'
We go to the pub. Oh dear, they both think I've put on weight. I decide it's not possible and put it out of my mind. The Whale never asks me if I've been faithful to her. I'm immensely grateful. I know I would've lied and I hate lying. But sometimes you just have to.

But it's not long before jet lag leaves me and my strength returns. The novelty of being back home with loved ones wears off and I crash. Like a cartoon roadrunner I've reached the end of the road, over the cliff edge, legs frantically spinning in momentum with no more tarmac. There's nowhere to go but down. I try in vain to keep things going but it's Tuesday.

I meet some friends in the pub.
'Look, there's this club in the West End we've got to go to! They got this band playing. Let's go. Come on! Let's do it!'
'Uhm. No, I can't. I got no money.'
'I got to go to work tomorrow.'
'I've promised to baby-sit.'
'Maybe at the weekend we can do something.'
'But it's TONIGHT! It won't be on at the weekend. Life is NOW! Don't you *see?* We have to do it NOW! The weekend is fucking three days away.'
'Nah. I can't. My cat needs a manicure.'

And that's how it goes. Even the Whale has to go to work. She's selling advertising space for the Guardian newspaper. Working part time in the Lock Tavern. Shit. What to do? I got time and a bit of money left over. Too much time. I want kicks. I know I gotta slow down but I can't. And don't want to. In the three months I've been away no one's done anything new except buy a new ash pan and brush. It's frustrating. They think I'm being arrogant.

'It's alright for you, rock star. But we got to deal with reality.'

'Yeah, but come on. Just tonight. It'll be GREAT. It's a real show. With go-go dancers.'

They walk away and I'm left alone. It's a problem that just seems to get worse. I begin going out alone but it's the same thing everywhere. I wander around the West End streets trying to fill in Time. Going in guitar shops and buying things. But there's no escape from it. The heads I see everywhere are only filled with necessities and dullness. Millions of miserable heads enclosed in the mediocrity that the drudgery of life insists upon. You can't beat it. A week later I'm sitting indoors most of the time watching TV too, reading, playing guitar and cooking. I take up some fitness training to try and shed those extra pounds.

With no tour lined up it's just pointless rehearsals for me, Nick and Pete. Joe is nowhere to be seen. Or Paul. Not that I'm bothered. Joe's tireless propaganda speeches bore me. The whole thing bores me. The Clash is a corporation. We're business partners but somehow I'm more like the company janitor sweeping floors with my guitar broom. Like those jobs where you're supposed to believe in the company's mission statement even when you're operating at that level and you always have to look busy and enthusiastic. It's stupid. I'm not even making any money. I have no say in anything and no touring to distract me. I'm beginning to flounder.

And worse of all Bernie begins turning up more and more at rehearsals, standing there in those half grey shoes of his walking around delivering spiteful verbal tirades at the three of us making sure we realise how inadequate we are. How tenuous our position is. How we need to become more 'happening'.

'When you we're invited Vince, asked to play a part in this, I expected ....some kind of ....*decision* on your part. That you would take a certain………..road…………away from that fucking liberal provincial mentality of yours……….and realise and take advantage of what's on offer……………..and it just isn't happening…………..'

'LOOK! I'm busting my arse! I'm doing my best!'

'It's not good enough. You see, all three of you are…….where are you coming from? What is this? A holiday? Just another rock'n'roll band? Is that what it is? Just Rock'n'Roll? I listened to Raw Power the other day. The Stooges. I don't know. Is that what it's all about? Banging bums together on stage?'

I laughed and caught myself.

'This is no laughing matter, *look* at you, Vince,' he spat, 'How WEAK YOU ARE.'

'I'm not fucking weak.'

'Yes you are. Paul. Well, he has a connection. Being working class he has an idea. You guys just ……your liberal mentality……..want to play it safe………and that attitude of yours is just disgusting. It's a problem.'

I gave up trying to justify myself. I didn't feel I ought to. He could think what he fucking wanted. But time after time Bernie would arrive and keep knocking you down as hard as he liked and there didn't seem much to stop him. I tried to build a thick wall in my brain against it. Somehow that wall was never strong enough and it kept tumbling down.

Bernie's next move was to set us tasks. Nick, Pete and me. Tests of some kind that you could only guess at whatever for. The first takes the form of each one of us new guys to arrange a new song each. Nick's is 'In the Pouring Rain.' I can't remember what Pete's was. I've chosen the song which was to become 'Do It Now'.

I got the chord sheets but since most of the chord structure is boring I simply *change the chords!* Except the beginning part. The signature. That bit's OK. I turn it into something I like which is in a way reminiscent of earlier Clash songs. A bit more full on and rocky. Some simple lead parts to go around it. I'm excited. We're given a week or so to do the recordings. I can do anything I want with my arrangement and tell Nick and Pete exactly what I want and they have to do it. No arguments. Freedom! I get mine recorded in less than an hour. Pete is great on the drums and really bring it together. I'm completely happy with the result. There's no singing or anything, just instrumental stuff. Nick and Pete do theirs. I do whatever they want on theirs. The final results are handed over to Bernie.

We have a meeting a few days later to discuss the results. I don't care what anyone thinks of mine. I know it's good. I don't care much for Nick and Pete's efforts. They sound wimpy.

'I've listened to all the songs and ………well, I have to say I'm not impressed by any of them,' says Bernie at the meeting. 'When you decide to make a thing……..when you make a definite *decision* there has to be ……….a symptom…….that symptom……what is it? It's unrecognizable from it's original form……………….if you think *that* can separate from it's meaning then you're mistaken. All it can ever possibly lead to is something……derivative…….mediocrity. And that's what we have here. But I suppose of the three then I would say…… that Vince's effort wins ……..by default.'

As usual, I had no idea what he was on about but I was sure when Joe heard it he would be interested. It ROCKED!

But Joe didn't show up. Or Paul. Summer '84 just rolled on interminably and us three punk stooges were just left to it. Just happy when a day would go by without our manager showing up. We were as bored as anyone can be. And out there on the hot summer streets things were changing. I was convinced that the world had finally ended. There was no fanfare. No Big Brother watching us. No room 101. There was no bomb. They hadn't needed to drop the bomb. Somehow it had all just happened by itself. Cars were beginning to look the same.

People began to look the same. All that struggle and talk of freedom and now we'd got it everybody just began imitating everybody else. Values and ideals had decayed and become derelict. Music was being made by machines. Punk had turned from something light and hip and individual into a green mowhawk haircut, a studded leather jacket and a bottle of cider. RELAX T-shirts were everywhere. For me there was fuck all to *relax* about especially as nothing can make me feel more tense and tired than doing nothing. Day after day we'd turn up to the rehearsal space in Chalk Farm dutifully banging away. Weeks and weeks passed. At some point Joe turned up and gave us some more chord sheets for new songs. They were just chord arrangements we were supposed to learn and come up with ideas for. But we had no lyrics or the vocal melody or even the remotest idea what the songs were supposed to be about. Just chords. I decided to forget it all and just focus on my guitar playing.

Then Joe disappeared.

It made no difference to us seeing as we never saw much of him anyway. There was suddenly a lot of concern in the Clash camp as to his whereabouts. Why had he left? Was he unhappy? Would the band split? He supposedly hadn't told anyone where he'd gone. He hadn't told *me* anyway. The news was carefully leaked to the press who were also speculating and reporting various sightings. They'd seen him here, they'd seen him there! Spain got the most votes apparently. I no longer gave a fuck. I was sure his royal highness would resurface when required. Bernie told us that he'd broken up with Gabby and had taken time away to sort himself out. Gabby told me months later that he'd simply gone away to write more songs for the forthcoming album. She was surprised to hear there had been a rumour of a split between them.

One day Kosmo turned up to rehearsal and told us a tour had been lined up in Italy.

The idea came to me to get some funky clothes made up for the Italian tour. As I was still only getting £150 a week I had to confront Bernie for the money. Amazingly I got it! £500! Perhaps he thought these clothes would make me more 'happening'. He seemed happy I was showing initiative. A tailor in Berwick Street, Soho made up two Elvis style draped suits in a red and a green tartan. *I* was made up. Those clothes gave me some sense of definition. I had no idea what my purpose in the band was anymore. I was discouraged from writing songs. Supposedly I couldn't play. Every time I opened my mouth I always seemed to blurt out the 'wrong' thing. But hey! Who needs a fucking purpose in life so long as you *look* great?

We arrived in Milan at the beginning of September for the start of the Italian tour and Joe still hadn't materialised. I think it was around this time that things began to get a bit weird. It was a turning point for the new Clash. Alienated, frustrated and fed up I had long since resigned myself to trying my best to play out some kind of part that seemed to fit into this insane drama. I began wearing dog tags and brothel creepers. Things began to take on a dark twist. Something around the periphery of reality was manifesting itself and it truly began to unnerve me. I was lying face down on a deserted beach. In the near distance there is a flicker of movement. Out there are these malevolent creatures like shiny black eels slithering through the sand towards me. My thoughts have become crabs inching their way around looking for a rock to hide under.

I don't know about evil and I prefer to keep it that way but I felt there was *something going on*. I hoped that behind it all there was some method behind the madness.

Was it all something Joe and Bernie were deliberately orchestrating in order for us to be 'creative'? I seriously began to doubt it. I really couldn't see how anything good could come of it. Things were getting uglier and uglier by the day and I could feel myself getting swept away by the insanity around me. My sense of self was fading in and out of reality and being …………..replaced by what?

Joe turned up at our hotel in Italy a day after us and the tour commenced starting in Salerno, then Rome, Reggio Emilia and on to Genova. He was out in the stratosphere. Not a space cadet exactly but more like the Galactic General. Detached and aloof from the group onstage he began the mysterious task of isolating, picking on and grilling each one of the band and the band's entourage one by one offstage. Tour manager, art director and anyone else he felt the need to victimise. He'd managed to reduce our art director to tears. Paul had typically taken it all in his stride and it was great to watch him sometimes. None of this stuff ever seemed to faze him. I guess he was just used to it. It was water off a duck's back. I wished I could be like him. Everything seemed to penetrate. You need a strong psychic shield in this type of life and my shield was barely adequate. As to what happened to the others I didn't know. Nick and Pete had been picked on separately too and somehow they dealt with it. Nothing had happened to me and so with characteristic optimism I just assumed I'd been made exempt for some reason.

The gig, sorry, the *show* in Genova was a riot. I focused all my attention on the audience. There I felt I could connect. There was nothing on stage except ego, paranoia and enmity. Paul had taken to strutting and preening in front of me every time I was in the middle of playing a guitar solo and it was really beginning to get on my tits. I began banging into the cunt to get him out of my way. All the way through the show the crowd went mental.

In 'Tommy Gun', I would take a sudden run towards the edge of the stage, stop, lean over and fire an imaginary salvo. It was great fun. That is, until some bright spark in the audience grabbed the guitars' machine head and wouldn't let go. Other arms flayed out and grabbed on. Try as I might I just couldn't pull it back. I lifted the strap off my back and tugged as hard as I could but it was a losing battle. I was like holding a bone with a with a thousand dogs. It was either me or the instrument and so in I went. Hands groping all over tearing and mauling and screams as I hit the ground clinging for dear life to my beloved white Les Paul. It was scary. The boot went in once or twice. A couple of fists as well. I suppose it was a sign of affection. The bouncers were quick off the mark and got me out fast and in no time at all I was back up on the stage shaking and trying to compose myself. My lovely new suit was fucked. One jacket pocket had been ripped down around my knees. A lapel hung sadly over the other side. I lost a brothel creeper as well as a sock. I hobbled about the stage with one brothel creeper on and one bare foot trying to finish the rest of the song. I pulled off the other shoe. I wandered barefoot over to Joe like some deranged rag and bone clown.

' Fuck this! Let's get off now and come back for the last song. I wanna change. I look like a cunt.'

Joe glared menacingly at me. I don't think he saw me. Not at bit. It was eerie. Eyes glazed and like the messiah calling his followers to prayer he stooped low, pulled the microphone to his lips and slowly announced:

'I ....want......a ....riot............A
..........RIOT..................OF
...........................MY............OOOOOWWWWN.

The crowd erupted. I started smashing out tuneless chords in wild abandon. A few people jumped up on stage and started leaping around. I quickly forgot about how stupid I looked.

OUT OF CONTROL: The Last Days of The Clash

Suddenly all the madness made complete sense. The bouncers tried to throw people off but there were far more bodies climbing up than they could deal with. Soon the stage was so full of people I could hardly move or hear a thing. I couldn't see any of the band. No one could see me. I played the guitar solo where my fingers remembered it. But nothing mattered now. Sweaty bodies were climbing all over me. A beautiful Italian princess suddenly appeared and pushed her model lips against mine. She disappeared. Where did *she* go? The end.

Incredible roaring cheers and it was house lights, off stage towels, and back to sulking in the dressing room again.

That night Joe, me and Kosmo, Nick and some others headed out to a bar. I didn't have a clue where I was. I just needed to get drunk. Badly. I caught sight of a young, pretty looking blonde sitting with her friends.

I whispered in Joe's ear.

'Hey Joe, check *her* out.'

'What?'

'The blonde.'

No sooner had I opened my mouth than he began creeping over to their table like Quasimodo. He beckoned me slyly with his finger.

Leaning over her, he pointed at me.

'I give you the *boy*. Can *YOU* give *me* the MAAAN!'

There wasn't the slightest trace of irony in his voice.

'Oh fuck.' I thought. 'Will this shit *ever* fucking end?'

Joe walked off and left me to deal with it. I looked at the girl. I looked at her pretty big deer eyes suddenly caught in the glare of the Clash headlights. I hung in. I was hungry for some action. She didn't speak a word of English and I spoke no Italian. I got her number quickly and regrouped with the others. Another shot of brandy. Then another. A beer. Then another shot. Then another. More beer.

By the time we got thrown out onto the street I was fucked and Joe was just getting in his stride. Leaping up on top a parked car and standing proud he began railing the small crowd that were hanging around outside. I couldn't make out a word of it. It was incomprehensible gibberish. Part pigeon Italian and English. Waving his arms about madly he scolded them with the kind of power, authority and intensity not seen since the Roman days. The crowd roared their appreciation. I looked at their faces They looked like little children mesmerised at a Punch and Judy show. As the wave began to subside Joe jumped down. He decided it was time to move on.

'Let's get some prostitutes,' he snarled.

'What?'

'Prostitutes', he repeated, evilly.

I'd never been with a prostitute before but, hey! I'll try anything once. Just for the Clash! Joe assured me that it was great. A real experience. It had to be tried. So for a couple of hours Joe, me and Kosmo ran around town from bar to bar on a mission asking everyone we met. Kosmo made calls. Bar owners made calls. No luck. We'd left it too late. All the hookers were tucked up asleep.

Dawn was beginning to break. Everywhere was either shut or closing. The three of us wandered around pissing in the street until we found a small café that would serve us more booze. They weren't really open but we made them an offer they couldn't refuse. WE ARE THE CLASH!

It was a proper little homely Italian affair. Nice management. Respectable. Little wooden tables. There was no one else in there. Joe selected a table near the toilet and we ordered coffees and brandies. We got talking. Passionate spirit going this way and that. Everything falling into place. Laughing and joking and good times and vibes when suddenly it started.

'So………….. *Vince*, what I wanna know is, what makes you think *you're* so special to be in this band?' Joe suddenly asked.

'Hey! *You* asked me to join. *You* tell me?' I replied, still laughing, half drunk.

Kosmo took a long pull on his cigarette and the two of them began to eye me darkly. I tried to keep things light.

'What do you mean?' I asked, smiling, pretending. I didn't like the feel of where this was going.

'There are *thousands* of guitar players out there who can play better than you. What do you think makes *you* so special?'

What were they getting at? I loved rock'n'roll. MAN, I ROCKED!

'I don't know what you're on about. I'm me. I do what I do. What are you getting at?'

'What makes you think *you're* good enough to be in *this* band,' he insisted.

'I'm the bollocks! I'm fucking rock'n'roll! It's my fucking *life*, man,' I went on lamely. I could feel myself losing ground fast. I didn't see this coming. It must've been about 6 in the morning.

Joe and Kosmo both broke out in a loud chorus of sarcastic laughter.

'Look, I wanna make a *difference, OK?* You know, be a part of something *real*. I remember listening to these songs when I was younger. Bands like the Pistols and the Clash were like the light at the end of the tunnel for me. They still are. Like a home. They made sense where nothing else did. Nothing has ever made sense. Nothing. My father was an abusive cunt. I've never felt at home anywhere. School. The whole world is so full of crap. So much bullshit.'

Joe leaned back and sneered. Kosmo leaned back and sneered. He took another long drag of his cigarette.

I'd said the 'wrong' thing again. What was the *right thing?* From somewhere deep down I began to feel a surge of power. A sudden separation. People were shit. It was always the same thing. With everybody. These fucks too. Who the fuck do they think they are anyway? Who the fuck are *they* to keep looking down on *me*? Quickly, I caught myself and remembered. These were the people who could fire me just as easily and unceremoniously as they had Mick Jones and send me right back to the blue labels or the dole queue. I sat back in my chair and lit another cigarette.

Joe went off to the toilet. Kosmo suddenly changed tune and became a bit warmer. It was good cop, bad cop.

'Vince, I *understand* you. This band has a job to do, right? Joe's *concerned* that's all. He's under a lot of pressure to deliver.'

Behind his friendly attitude I sensed something mean. I knew I was being interrogated just like the others. Despite all the evidence I still refused to believe they had anything but best intentions at heart. I resolved to stay cool and stand my ground. Joe came back from the toilet and looked at Kosmo.

'Are we getting anywhere?' he grunted.

'I dunno. I think Vince is beginning to realise something but I'm not sure.'

Neither of them looked at me but their minds were on *something*.

Realize *what*, exactly? I thought. I kept quiet. What the fuck was going on?

'The point is that we're not sure you're cut out for this, Vince.' Joe began slowly in a deep, grave voice. 'We don't think you've got what it takes.'

I did my best to maintain some composure.

'Well? What *have* you got to offer?' he continued. 'That's what *I* wanna know.'

'Yeah, well what about *me?*' I suddenly blurted out, really beginning to lose it. 'I'm still only getting £150 a week dragging my sorry arse about backing you up. Taking endless amounts of shit from Bernie. What's in it for *me*? Eh? What do *I get?*'

Without missing a beat Joe began singing the Buzzcock's tune.

'*What do I get…..woah woah-oh …What do I get?*'

The pair of them sniggered smugly. It would have been funny but it wasn't. Joe continued.

'You see, Vince, I've been watching you for some time now and I'm not impressed. Take your girlfriend for instance.'

The hairs on my neck stood up. What did *she* have to do with all this?'

'What's *she* got to do with anything?'

'What do you have to offer *her*? I see her around in Camden and she doesn't look at all happy. I think it would be in *her* best interests and this *band's* best interest *and yours* if you *left* her. Without this girlfriend of yours, you might become a more *happening* person. Then you might realise something. You'd be doing *her* a favour.'

I was dumbfounded. Was this the same Joe Strummer? Was he serious? He looked it.

'Yeah,' he continued, 'I remember a time recently I was in the Lock Tavern and we were going to a party, right? You weren't there but I asked her if she wanted to come along. She said 'no', she couldn't, but it was so bloody obvious that she was *up for it!*'

What did he mean? She was *up for it*?! Was she up for *him*? Did he *shag* her? Fucking hell! Something was happening in my stomach. It wasn't nice.

'I'm sorry,' he said, ' but unfortunately and……. I hate to say it, Vince, but the bottom line….. is……….. that …..….I…… don't…… need you. You can GO!'

Joe dismissed me suddenly with a wave of his hand. He leaned forward towards Kosmo and they went on talking, ignoring me. I sat still for a couple of seconds just trying to take it all in. What was going on? Was I out of the band now? Should I just leave it, go back to the hotel and let things cool off? Did he fuck my girlfriend?

I get the sudden realization that it all means absolutely nothing at all. The Clash. Rock music. Strummer. Lots of stupid people dancing about. Bits of black plastic.b I don't give a shit anymore about this stupid boy band Clash Shitty fuckers crap I'm being force fed, we're so cool rock'n'roll '50's Chevrolet I like a vintage this and that and always 'wow! *that's* so cool!' with a brothel creeper and an army dog tag stuck up my arse. It really *could* all go to straight to fucking hell!

I rise slowly from my chair to leave. I don't hesitate. I take one pace forward and swing my fist as hard as I can. I hit him hard in his stupid fat nose. You stuck up fucking phoney! I watch him roll backwards off the chair and then jump on him, fists flying determined to do as much damage as possible. Tables and chairs fall about the room. Joe puts up no resistance at all. I'm surprised. I expect more. I'm whipping a dead horse! Kosmo steps in quickly and pulls me off. But before I know it, it's all make up time and we're standing outside in the street in the morning sunlight and Joe is laughing deliriously and hugging me.

'Brilliant Vince! You're the only one who came through! Aaah! Brilliant! Fucking brilliant!'

He begins kissing me on the cheeks. I'm fully creeped out. I'd rather get back to fighting. But I don't. I guess I'm just too curious.

OUT OF CONTROL: The Last Days of The Clash

Come through? What was that? Had it all just been another *test*? Had I *passed*? I really didn't know. I didn't *feel* as if I'd passed or achieved anything.

I felt sick. Lost. Isolated. Confused. Insane.

Dazed and drained we made our way back to the hotel. I got to my room. I ran straight to the mini bar. Drained a couple of whisky miniatures and waited for them to kick in. I gazed out through the thick brown curtains. It was a beautiful morning. The sun was burning over the roof tops. It looked like we were in for another glorious Italian summer day. I closed all the curtains and curled up tight in the big double bed and slept all day.

I arrived in the hotel lobby later that evening. The next show which was the last on this tour had been cancelled for some reason. Everyone was just hanging around there waiting to see what was happening. After a while, Joe showed up. A lot of heavy talking was going on and there's that big atmosphere of serious importance as if World War Three has just broken out. And there we were. Just a punk band after all. No mention is made about the night before. I'm still all shook up about it still but I just concentrate my eyes on a spot on the carpet hoping this will keep my brain neurons firing in some kind of order. But we still head out there, to that venue, the football stadium in Torino walking around it with no gig to play. I'm told some famous football team plays there. But I don't care for football. More stupidity. I get hold of the blonde on the phone, the one I'd met who couldn't speak a word of English and drag her out there. The band and entourage head out for a big meal in some fancy restaurant that's been arranged for everyone seeing as we weren't playing. I bring her along. A huge long table has been created by pulling tables together that dominates the restaurant. The big display. The big power thing. I hate it. I have a strange, sick feeling low and deep in my belly all the time now. Everything gives me that sick feeling. The low lighting and the thick table cloths oppress me. Endless courses arriving one by one oppress me. The waiters obsequiously moving around. Bits of this and expensive that on plates. People laughing loudly at nothing. It's no fun. I hardly touch a bit of that food.

The girl's name is Paola. She seems pretty impressed by it all and I'm happy for her. It's easy to get off on someone else's excitement. And here she was, all for me, a great diversion from having to speak to anyone. I want to escape from everything. We begin trying to converse in French. I can't speak French but it doesn't matter. There's only one thing on my mind and that was to get drunk and get a piece of her. I keep filling my glass with red wine. A whole glassful in one gulp. Then another. I ask the waiter for a brandy. My French begins to improve dramatically.

Piles of food sit in front of me, uneaten. I pick at a few bits to be polite. I just want to get back to the hotel room with Paola. We move out. She really has the best looking arse of any girl I'd ever seen. What a lucky fucker I was! And the arse is the most important aspect when it comes to sex of course. Not just small and tight, but that particular shape that can make a guy lose too much sleep. I was relieved to be back in that hotel room alone with her. I spent quite a bit of time at it. Working it slowly. She was 19. And it turned out to be the most magic of nights. Desert sands and holy stars writhing together in voluptuous singing and dancing across timeless tight night I'm getting the only part of Renaissance Art finely established within the parameters of bliss and teasing until another retreat proves the starting point for more invasions and violation which is after all only the ebb and flow of all creation and the tension point of everything that exists and comes into being and……………..……..*more!*

After it's over Paola begins to cry.

'Keska say le problem?' I ask.

'Rein!'

The tears keep flowing. I think perhaps they're tears of happiness?!!! But for want of an explanation I start getting the guilt again for some reason. I don't understand it. Guilt and jealousy are two emotions I never normally feel. Except with girls. Somehow women have a clever way of making you feel them.

I begin singing.

'Whatsamatter with you? You gotta no respect! Whaddayou think you do? Why you looka so sad? It's a nots-o-bad. Its-a-nice-a place OOOOOOHH *SHUDDUPA-Ya-FACE!*'

More crying. She doesn't get it. But with that bit of half English, half French I soon find out that she's a virgin. I've plucked her cherry. Oh! So *that* was the problem I had getting it in!

On and on she goes, crying and crying. I want to run away. What have I done? I look at her lying there all that innocent perfect body all proper virtue and vulnerable. I'm a real shit. I imagine her getting pregnant. Maybe she has some real heavy family. I imagine the mafia tracing me all the way to Finsbury Park. The Whale will kill me. The band will sack me. I'll have to find some child support. I might have to find a proper job. Some screaming kid will appear. Oh fuck, my life is over.

After a bit Paola calms down and stops. Then she gets all close and cuddly all of a sudden and things are going all romantic for her and I can tell there are ideas in her head. The only idea in my head it to run away. From her. From the band. From everything. But the guilt passes and soon, after half an hour or so that black dog devil is on my trail and he's caught up with me again. I'm lying immobile in the road and he begins howling. What the fuck? To shit him up I'm back in there again with a vengeance not giving a fuck about anything or anyone but simply chasing the……….. MOMENT.

Next day we're leaving. The bus is sitting outside the hotel baking in the hot sunshine. The sun is making sharp shadows with everything. Everyone's aboard, waiting for me. 'Come on Vince! It's time to go. Bernie's waiting,' shouts Raymond. Paola stands under the Italian arches crying. She looks like a ghost planted inside one of De Chirico's paintings. I kiss her goodbye, give her my PO box address and run quickly onto the bus. The bus moves off. I watch that incredible arse disappear behind me. It's all so sad. Perhaps Bernie is right, maybe I am weak. I look around the bus. Everyone's laughing and joking at me. Fuck them. I was the only one who got a bit of tail on this whole tour, after all. But still, I hope she doesn't get pregnant. It could be a 'problem'.

Back in London things seem to get worse. I meet up with Joe and the others in a bar in Camden. We're drinking Cognac at lunchtime. Then on to beer and by three in the afternoon Joe drunkenly informs me that Nick and I should begin working on our own record. As far as he's concerned he simply feels we aren't good enough to play on the forthcoming Clash record. For Nick and me it's all a bit confusing. I shrug my shoulders. I assume it's just another wind up. Nothing he or Bernie says seems to have any foundation in reality any more. Things just change from one day to the next. From one beer to the next. One minute up, down the next. A sense of carelessness descends over me. Just don't bother even trying. It's depressing though. I've been working on ideas for songs. Bernie isn't impressed.

'What *IS* your function in this band, Vince? What do you have to offer?' says Bernie at rehearsal.

'I've got some tunes. I want to write some stuff. I think it's good. You heard what I did with the......'

'I'm not interested in your fucking tunes. *Nobody* is fucking interested. You should focus on your guitar playing. And getting your shit together as a *person*.'

'I'm alright. I'm sick of you going on like this all the time. I've got..........'

'The trouble with you Vince is you're..............do you know what he is?' says Bernie staring around the room at the rest of the band, 'this guy is a fucking FASCIST!'

'Don't give me that I......'

'You're an arrogant CUNT! I really think you should stop 'trying' to write songs and shut the fuck up and actually learn to do your job. Learn to play your instrument. Stop wasting mine and everybody else's time.'

'As you like.'

For some reason I didn't get up and walk out.

Joe began going on about Reggae after that. A few months earlier reggae was a no go area and now it's suddenly become the order of the day. We need to get our reggae act together. I've come in with a reggae part I like, that I came up with but Pete's not convinced.

'Well, I dunno. Sounds like WHITE reggae to me. What do you think Nick?'

Nick laughs.

'Could be, I'm not sure.'

'Yeah, *real* reggae has a different emphasis on the first beat doesn't it?'

They go on talking, ignoring me.

It's hard to become enthused. I suspect that the following week Joe will decide something entirely different anyway. Hip hop maybe. Or Balkan folk arrangements. Gregorian chants?

The next test was a singing test. Bernie instructed each of us new guys to sing a song. Nick picked 'Just My Imagination'. Pete sang some old rock'n'roll tune and I shouted 'The Harder They Come'. The results were pitiful. Nick sounded like a girl, Pete did his bit and I sounded like a rusty iron gate. Our efforts were dismissed. But being or supposed to being a punk band I really didn't see that it mattered too much. After all, Joe wasn't really a *singer*. Mick Jones had been no 'singer' either. Bernie described his singing as the sound of a demented neurotic housewife. But I thought it was the attitude that counted. If you could simply capture that with a kind of style. That was all that mattered. But attitude was no longer something that spontaneously vomited up from the heart and soul that had value of a humanistic kind but rather something that had to compete in the marketplace. And the marketplace in 1984 was quite a bit different from 1977. Bernie made it clear you couldn't get away with it anymore. There was a lot at stake. I had nothing to lose but Joe and Bernie and the Clash reputation had plenty to lose. And so the reins were on tight. Reins made of chicken wire. And they would get tighter still. The goose that was the Clash would be strangled to death as Bernie stepped up his campaign to get at those golden eggs.

A couple of shows were coming up at Brixton Academy in early December. It was all in aid of the miners. It was billed as Arthur Scargill's Christmas party. The miners were on strike of course then and it was a big socialist deal and a big turning point for Britain as it turned out. Thatcher wasn't giving in to their demands and all that. And the Clash were to perform in their honour. A concert for the workers. I didn't care about miners or Thatcher or Scargill or the working class struggle or fucking anything else for that matter. I remembered all the power cuts in the seventies when I was a kid. Eating by candlelight. No heating and freezing and catching a cold every week. It was a drag. I had little sympathy with miners. If something wasn't working then you just move onto something else. But I couldn't move on either for that matter. But some things you just can't go backwards to fix. The end would come one way or another for all of us.

We began rehearsals for the Brixton party. I'd bought a new bicycle for £200 out of money I'd saved from my £150 week wages. I cycled to rehearsals. Joe and Paul always caught taxis to go anywhere. I didn't care, I liked the idea of being normal and didn't care about playing rockstar. I couldn't afford taxis anyway and was tired of jumping the tube everywhere I went. I already had one conviction for not paying the fare. I parked my bicycle near the studio entrance door everyday. It must have set some precedent for one day Joe, too, arrived on a brand new sparkling bicycle and parked it right inside under the studio window. It was really on show. So there we were preparing to rehearse for the miners' benefit show in front of Joe's bicycle. I imagine Bernie had got that one together for him. And later Kosmo announced that Joe was flexible. That Joe was at home anywhere. Either in a limousine or riding his bicycle to work. That it didn't matter to him either way.

Rehearsals were important events when Lord Joe was to be present. One had been arranged for Sunday and Joe was scheduled to be at this one so it was important that we turned up. I liked my Sunday's free of anything to do with the band. At least one stress free day in the week. I made the effort to drag myself down there but when I arrived the studio was locked and

Joe never showed up. I and the others went home demoralised. He didn't give a shit and neither did we in the end.

I turned up to the venue in Brixton for the soundcheck. Sitting near the front of the stage was Wendy and the Whale in animated conversation. My heart missed a beat when I saw the two of them sitting there together. I stepped back into the shadows before they saw me and collected myself. This is it. I'm done for. Oh, well, whatever! I walked over. I had to go past them to get to the backstage area.

'Hi, Vince!' exclaims the Whale, smiling.

'Hi, how are you?' asks Wendy.

'RADIANT! See you later girls!'

I think I've got away with it.

I began letting go of things. We were to start the first Brixton show with the song 'One More Time.' It was a reggae song and that was OK. I loved reggae. I opened the song with a riff, something original I invented and let it howl out with feedback. It was moody and heavy and different. I had my own style now and was going to let it show whatever. It worked for a song. But Bernie was on the mixing desk controlling things. Soon the volume of my guitar would drop. Everytime I began to let rip Joe would silence me.

'Take it down. Take it down. Take it DOWWWWWNNN!'

And more sensitive little mumbles from Joe.

'I wanna go …….I wanna go ………..the frickle backed santi falling mesa backid all together esra sample dad said HEEEEEY! VINCE! Gotta mak a biga shap VINCE! Yeah! Wverybody knows what the RUDE BOY KNOWS! ……………YEAHHHHHH!'

And you pick up the sense of nothing that really is only music power and crash rising to the end and LOUD CHEERS of thousands of happy excited people.

OUT OF CONTROL: The Last Days of The Clash

Leaving after the gig and I'm in one cab with the Whale and Sammy and there is Joe in the next cab as we sail past him. And what has he got in his hand? A huge joint! So what was all that NO DRUGS POLICY he was always banging on about to the thousands of fans at shows and radio interviews and rags? That dope made you dull? That he smoked so much grass he nearly turned into a bush? He was sparking off in all directions.

I stick up a hippy peace sign to him as we pass. He's the star and no one really cares about anything and being TRUE to any PRINCIPLE whatever and it's just entertainment after all and why even *think* that things could or should be any different?

The separation between Joe and the band is complete. Separation is everywhere now. There's no healing it.

I look at my hand. My fingers are all cut and fucked up again from hitting the guitar too hard trying to get some volume from it. It's frustrating. I resolve to give it up. I'm hurting myself for nothing.

Reviews for the shows are unforgiving. Lack of meaning, vainglorious slogans, fatuous rebel posing, irrelevance. Nostalgia. And they were right of course.

I get away for a few days down to my home town of Southampton. My father is a greengrocer. He's on his best behaviour now his son is in a famous band. I go with him to the fruit market near the Southampton docks to buy things for his shop. In the fruit market everyone wants to meet me. Everyone has heard of the Clash. They're all excited to meet a member of the Clash. I'm famous. But no one knows me really. No one really knows anything about anything it seems to me but their faces light up at the person they have in front of them. I'm the same person that used to go there a few years ago that was completely ignored. I sign an autograph for someone. I really have nothing to say. It's an effort to speak. I stand there in my usual way not having changed from my usual nervousness of being around people and things trying to answer in ways that they might possibly understand. Lying all around me are wooden palettes full of crates of oranges. Boxes of bananas. The place reeks of mould and fork lift trucks whir and dart around madly lifting up palettes full of sacks of potatoes in 56lb bags. All this stuff has come from the ground from somewhere in the world and loaded on a ship and now on a lorry and is going into a shop and then into someone's house and down into their gut.

But my father is happy. He has respect from his mates. His son is a somebody now. And I guess that makes him a bit of a somebody too.

It's nearly Christmas. We have another band meeting back in Chalk Farm. Something is very wrong and it's down, down, down. Every day has become a battle. Life is a constant battle. No longer just to survive and get potatoes and oranges. It's a battle for mental survival.

'I have a question to ask. What would you each do if you had a million quid?' asks Bernie.

Silence.

'Well? Nick? What would *you* do with a million quid?'

Nick doesn't know what to say. He spends a bit of time thinking it over. Getting his answer right. He balances a bit of selfish with nice socialist.

'I'd set up a recording studio, I think, to give new bands a chance to record and get their ideas across. It would be a non profit making affair.'

'Ok.'

It was Pete's turn.

'What would I do with a million quid? I dunno,' he laughs. 'I could only know that if I *had* a million quid. It's a pointless question.'

'See. That's *typical* of you. You always evade the issue. You can't commit yourself. Look, you're being given a million. What are you going to do with it?'

'Oh, I dunno, probably give it to charity, I suppose,' he laughed.

Bernie nodded.

Damn. It was my turn. All minds were on me. What would I do with a million?

'Vince?'

It didn't take much thinking about.

'I'd buy a huge fuck off yacht and fuck off around the world on it. Get to some pacific island and have threesomes with young black hula-hula girls with incredible bodies. Get massages, sit on the beach and drink myself stupid everyday.'

I knew it wasn't the right answer but it was the truthful one. Bernie wasn't amused.

'That's the kind of answer we would expect from you, I suppose.'

It was Joe's turn to answer.

He had it all ready. The radio interview answer.

'If I had a million I would spend half of it buying the town of Corby,' he began hotly. 'The other half I would give to the F.S.R.I.'

He sat back importantly and took a drag of his cigarette.

What was the F.S.R.I.? I didn't bother to ask. Probably some obscure rebel militia 'freedom' fighters somewhere in Africa. Joe was pleased with his answer. It was the 'correct' way to answer such a question. Bernie was pleased.

I'm with Nick and Pete after in the pub.

'God these questions! What is Bernie getting at? It does my head in!' I moan.

'Million quid!' exclaims Pete, *'million quid!* Don't you get it, Vince? Don't you fucking *GET IT?'*

I looked at him.

'Get what?'

' Don't you realise that Joe *already HAS a million quid!* Whatever he wanted to do with a million pounds he's already *done it?'*

Nick nodded in agreement. I was stupid. It never occurred to me. He was right of course. Five hit albums and one giant seller in the U.S. must have netted him a lot more than a million when you thought about it. That five story house off Portobello Road he owned must be worth quite a bit. He'd told me he bought it outright.

'Why didn't you bring it up, Pete?'

Pete quickly changed the subject.

My answer predictably brought me grief. I was bourgeois and selfish to want a yacht. I'd be better off in Duran Duran. Their videos had yachts in them. It rankled. I didn't like being labelled bourgeois.

'Bernie, you go on about it but why are YOU driving around in that bloody great new Mercedes of yours? It doesn't seem very socialist to me.' I countered.

'The reason I have a Mercedes is so that the people I meet take me *seriously,'* he explained. 'I don't care about having a car like that but the people I have to deal with do. I achieve a result. It's a necessity.'

'Brian Clough is a socialist,' chimed in Kosmo. 'He drives a Rolls Royce. He reckons in a socialist state *everyone* can be a millionaire.'

'Vince, what you gotta understand,' began Joe, 'is that there's always two sides to a story. When I was younger I was like you. Everything is in black and white. There is right and there is wrong but now I've grown up a bit I think differently now. There's ALWAYS another side to consider. Take Ronald Reagan for instance. Before I would have thought smash the American state and all that but now, when I think about it……….well, ……….I have to admit.the guy has a pretty cool haircut.'

Bernie went on. He had a new task or a test for us new guys.

'Right, I want each of you to be responsible for different areas in this band. I don't want you to be simply playing your instruments. There's more at stake here. I'm giving you each certain tasks to take on and be responsible for. We need someone to take care of technical things to do with recording. To have the technical side of things to do with recording organised. That responsibility is Nick's.'

Nick nodded and seemed pleased. It wasn't a bad assignment, really.

'Pete, I want you to take care of all aspects of equipment. You are to make sure that all the effects, amps, mikes, and anything to do with the hardware this band needs is looked after. If anyone has a problem with their equipment, they go to Pete. OK?'

'OK.'

Everyone seemed quite pleased with this. It seemed normal. What was mine?

'And Vince, your area of responsibility will be……………….. politics.'

POLITICS! Oh mama! Christmas was coming! Just what I always wanted.

'What do you mean? Politics? Fuck politics! What do you want me to do?'

'To take care of politics. I want you to oversee all areas regarding it.'

'Yeah, but what do you want me to *do* about it exactly?'

'I've *told* you. I'm asking you to take this seriously,' went on with barely suppressed fury. 'If you're not up for it then you might as well just say so. I don't want to waste my fucking time with you. I'm sick of your bullshit. You either get with this or you don't.'

I slumped further into my seat.

'Joe will help you. Give you some pointers. Won't you Joe?'

'Yeah. I'll help Vince.'

Joe took me to a bookstore after the meeting. It was getting dark already and miserable winter was here. We walked into one of those intellectual bookstores in Camden Lock where everyone mills around very serious and gently and wears a pullover. Joe began pulling books from the shelf. He picked out a book about the disaffected youth of Britain. He handed it to me. It was called 'No Future'. Another book about the revolution in Cuba. I picked up something about Angola. It was all very depressing. I wasn't interested in any of this stuff. I mean, I was in a way, but the pressure was on. I was back at school again, learning. Joe seemed like he wanted to help. I took all the books he recommended plus a couple of my own and paid for them. I went home. Back to the Whale. I threw the books down on the bed.

'What's all that for?' she asked.

'Politics. I have to read them for the band.'

She didn't say anything.

'This band is doing my head in, baby. What can I do? I better read 'em I suppose. Everyone is expecting me to get this together. The Clash are political after all and now it's MY JOB!'

She came over and put her arm around me. I didn't think I could sink any lower. But of course there's always a way to get that bit lower.

'It'll be alright. Just give them what they want.'

'Well, yeah, but I don't KNOW what they want. *They* don't seem to know what they want.'

'Come on, cheer up. Wanna beer?'

'Yeah.'

That beer got inside me and I began reading some of the stuff in the book Joe gave me about why people from deprived areas of Britain become punks.

My grandmother dies. I go back down to Southampton again for the funeral. It's a beautiful day down there in the country. The sky is cloudless and everything in the air is sharp and clear and cold and the sun is bright. The trees all around seem more exciting and real for some strange reason. I've never been to a funeral before but I'm interested to see how it all works. The coffin is lowered into the ground and some words are said. People, family and that stand around awkwardly all dressed up in suits and best clothes. No one is quite sure how to behave. A bit of crying from someone in a dress. For some reason I'm overwhelmed with joy. I know I shouldn't be. I liked my grandmother after all. She was a real character and my only friend growing up. She was very human. But there it is. The end. The inevitable. A life of 89 years and now it's over. It's not about her but just the senselessness of life that touches me. Anyone's life. The stupidity of it. Coming from nothing and going back to nothing. And in between all that TIME eating and sleeping and dressing and fucking and playing and working and money and loving and hating and crying and buying and laughing and reading and drinking and singing and whining. The finality of it makes my heart soar happily. Being face to face with death puts everything nicely into perspective. And it's comforting to know that if things get too painful there's always an exit strategy. Nice.

I go to the reception. All these people are hanging around, family, I'm supposed to know. But I only ever met them when I was a kid. I don't recognize anyone and I keep calling people by the wrong name. Some fuss is made over my new found 'status' but then after a lot of polite conversation, one by one we all leave and go back to our lives. I catch the train back to London with Sammy. An uncle and aunt are on the train with us. We pull into the dark noise of Waterloo. I exchange telephone numbers with my relatives, we shake hands and say goodbye. We head off down into the underground, going our separate ways. I never call them. They never call me and I never see them again.

Our last meeting in the studio before Christmas. I've been given a £250 Christmas bonus. But Bernie has a few words of cheer to give before we run off to go eat turkey.

We're arranged around the room as usual fingering our guitar picks and drum sticks, nervously. But we've been given a bonus.

'I've been looking at the forecast and it's looking like snow. Christmas. I'm sure you're all happy to be having some time in this unbelievable weather. The signs are far in front of what one would expect considering the current climate. Someone told me there's a front coming. Is there anything anyone wants to bring up………………..?

There was nothing anyone wanted to bring up.

'How are we doing? Are we making progress? What's happening?' Bernie looks at Nick.

'I've been working on synth sounds with Fayne. We're coming up with some very interesting stuff, experimental sounds that could be useful. The DX7 is great. We've been through the entire program, listing sounds that we can use. We're making progress.'

'Good.'

'And we've been advancing our understanding of hip hop beats and working out some New York rhythms with the RX11. It's very interesting.'

'Yep, that's …………there's a definite area …….that could be useful……Pete?'

'I've been busy working out a schedule with the Reckless hire company. I've made an inventory of all the equipment we own and need for Germany. There are some problems with finding someone who can do repairs, there are a couple of guys I'm in touch with but they're SHIT! I've spoken to them but I know they haven't got their act together. I know I can find someone better. I have some other numbers to try.'

'Good.'

Nick and Pete were really getting down to it.

My turn. Bernie just looks at me.

'Uhm. I've been doing some reading. Getting information……….'

'About WHAT?'

'Political stuff. Socialism. There's an interesting ………'

'VINCE……………..now how can I say this…………..without ………………I don't know what to say.'

Bernie looks angrily at the ground.

'Have you any idea about how the dynamics of ………..there is only one thing I have to say to you…………………..do you not realise ………….?'

'I don't understand, OK, you said politics, me and Joe got some books……books *he* suggested and……'

'*You*, Vince, just don't seem to get it, do you? You don't get *anything* it seems to me. What did they teach you in that fucking college of yours?'

Bernie half laughed. I looked at Joe hoping for some back up. He was looking away. Everyone was looking away.

'You asked me to research politics. Joe suggested some……..'

'I'm telling you this, and I'm telling you………. as a friend………. GET YOUR FUCKING ACT TOGETHER. I can't waste my time anymore with your provincial liberal bullshit. With people who can't deliver. I'm giving you one last chance. I wanna see some fucking results from you?'

'OK. What the fuck do you want me to do? I'm sick of this. I'm sick of listening to your shit, I…'

'VINCE, you don't seem to understand something very important………….you gotta be careful………YOUR ARSE IS ON THE LINE.'

I went silent and stared at the ground.

'There's a fine line here. Between knowing what is cow and what is milk. You're consistently just sucking the tit and spitting out the sour. If there's one thing I know and that is you can't milk a cow and expect it to keep on giving without a fight. Even cows have standards. There are limits.'

Bernie went on and the pressure seemed to be off for a while. Then back in.

'If I give you a direction then it's up to you to make the most of it. If you………..you can't seem to take a ………….*responsibility* ………. and take that and contribute

OUT OF CONTROL: The Last Days of The Clash

something to this project?............ We're trying here to solidify something………......a…………….determinate. To work as a team to ………..'

'I think what Bernie means is that you have to work outside of just your guitar playing Vince,' says Joe.

It's so nice to hear another voice.

'You just think of lead guitar. This band is far *more* than that,' says Pete. 'There's more to consider. And CHRIST! It's not that hard if you put your mind to it.'

'Well, I KNOW that but what I ……….'

'It's about letting yourself go,' says Nick joining in now.

'And giving something more,' says Pete. 'I mean, is this band just a rock'n'roll band or what? I always felt the Clash had far more to offer the world than ……just GUITAR PLAYING!' exclaims Pete.

Bernie seems pleased that everyone else is joining in and lets them get on with it. There's a subtext to all this. The animals smell blood now and are ripping at the open wound. The pack mentality. Tearing at the flesh, ripping at it. All the hate and misery and frustration channelled into a wild bloody meat frenzy. *My* meat.

I know I should just walk out and tell them all to fuck off but I can't seem to do it. I wishfully think that things will still work out. These were days when I was still naively optimistic and idealistic despite everything. That deep down in every human being is a core of goodness. Of rightness. That it's there in everybody except they can't see it. That truth and honesty will win out in the end. I actually feel sorry for Bernie. I feel sorry for everyone in the room and every sorry human being that has ever had the misfortune to be born into this stinking mess called life. Myself included. It's plain and simple. But this kind of thinking just digs a bigger hole for myself. I'm removed from what's going on around me. It doesn't fit. I don't fit with it. And in a sense one becomes superior because you won't or can't stoop to a certain level. But it arouses resentment. Sensing that, the animals step up the pressure.

'You see, Vince, the *you* ……..well Bernie is trying to get the best out of this band……and he simply wants you to step outside of your comfort zone and… ……take a different approach to things………maybe one you've never taken before and stretch yourself in other areas,' says Nick, considerately.

'But what? I fucking hate politics! I want anarchy! You all seem to want something …….I have no idea what.'

'And that's just *it*,' says Bernie. 'How are you going to ………..move yourself into ……..becoming a …………figure……….move out beyond your mediocrity when you persist in taking it easy?'

'It really isn't all that difficult, Vince.'

'You have to open up. You're closed off. We're here to *help* you, Vince. Frankly, you act as if everyone here were your enemy. We're not.'

With that we depart. No one goes for a Christmas drink. I cycle back to Finsbury Park through the dark up the Camden Road. In Holloway I stop at some traffic lights. People everywhere are full of good cheer. Shopping and being nice to each other. Families getting their things, food and bits, being simple and happy. I hear the strains of Slade's 'Merry Christmas Everybody' coming from a shop filled with lights and warmth. It depresses me even more. I want to cry.

Back to my bedsit. I walk through the door and the Whale jumps up to greet me. She stops suddenly.

'What's wrong?' she asks.

'What do you think?'

'What? What happened?'

'Oh, you know, another band meeting. They've really got to me this time. I don't know why. All the time it's the same thing now. I'm a fascist……..I'm selfish……I'm a cunt…..…I can't play…….I'm unprofessional……….I'm a not happening person………I………this and that. On and on. I've had enough. I don't know what to do. I can't walk out. Can I?'

'Vince! Can't you see what they're trying to do?'

I looked at her.

'What? What do you mean?'

'They're trying to beat you down. They're TRYING TO BEAT DOWN YOUR EGO!'

I looked at her. She was crying.

'Yeah? What am I supposed to do about it?'

'Those fuckers! They're fucking JEALOUS of you. Why else would they carry on like that?'

I thought about it. But I couldn't figure it out. I no longer felt I could trust anyone or anything. Even the Whale. It had been made pretty plain and clear to me over and over that girlfriends were the enemy. Bernie had been clear on that point. You either had a family life or a career life. Which was it to be? It was a decision that Bernie made clear that Joe had to make too. So you had to make a choice. You had to be wary of women. They could split bands up telling their boyfriends how great they were and that they were better and this and that. That a women's jealousy would hold a guy back. I'd been told this many times. And it was in Spinal Tap too!

'But I don't think ego is a good thing, Whaley.'

'They're knocking you down, Vince. You gotta realise you're better than that. You're good Vince. Don't let them get to you.'

'I'm trying. It's just………….I got this bad feeling.'

I went out for a walk. I thought it might help. I walked around Finsbury Park for a bit and when it got too cold I found a café and ordered a cup of tea. Sat there looking out the window at the shoppers with their big bags full of goodies happily hustling up and down through the dark, damp street. There's something so unholy about Christmas. It can magnify a person's misery a thousand times. Nothing can make me more miserable than the obligation to be happy. My mind begins to wander. I imagine a huge crack in the sky forming. Through that crack a shiny spinning flying saucer descends gracefully down into the Blackstock Road. Right in front of me it's there. Everything, the cars, people suddenly freeze in motion. The street is bathed in an unearthly glow. Some weird alien beings emerge from that spaceship and walk straight into the café.

'VINCE! Well done!' they say, benevolently.

'What? What's going on? Who the FUCK are *you?*' I demand.

'We're you're friends! We blanked your memory. You made it, Vince! No one has made it this far. You got the highest score EVER!'

And so it turns out that it's all just been a giant test, this life on earth. All along. None of it was ever real after all, just as I suspected. It's all been just a kind of game. Life on earth is just a playground for spirit beings. I've made it!

I leave with the aliens in the spaceship and return to my home planet where I'm crowned 'Master of the Universe' and live happily ever after, melting with the Nova women. Golden angels of light. Every moment is a moment of sheer orgiastic bliss.

I sit there in the cafe a while longer and smoke another cigarette. Finish my tea. But the sky never opens. No spaceship. Nothing. It's getting late. I pay for my tea and walk back to the Whale.

VERSE:

WORKING FOR THE CLAMPDOWN

Shitsmas came and went. Just another non event as usual, eating, presents and TV but that was OK. It was a welcome rest. But it was quickly over and I was back to the grindstone. New year arrived and I found myself inside 1985 and the band is getting ready to record the new Clash album. It was to be recorded in Munich, Germany. Lots of sessions in the studio in Chalk Farm were going on before going to Germany. Getting as much together as possible before the proper recording sessions started. I was summoned to a couple but it was mostly Bernie and Joe and sometimes Nick in there working with sound engineer Faynie playing around with machines. Bits of this and that. Long tiring hours were spent in there. It was good that Bernie was busy. It took the pressure off. My politics thing got forgotten. I wasn't required and so I kept out the way as much as possible and got drunk with my mates most days. Sometimes I would be allowed into the studio and hung out at the back. I wanted to be more involved but I was only involved to the extent that Bernie required me. Which was pretty much nothing. I heard some bits and pieces of songs with experimental synth stuff going on but it didn't excite me. The worst part of all of that was the depressing atmosphere around it all. It was all so serious. No fun at all. All I wanted to do was turn my guitar up loud and ROCK OUT!!! But that would've been too easy.

In January, Joe, Bernie and Nick and Fayne fly out there to begin recording sessions. Laying down the basic rhythm tracks. A few weeks later I was summoned, together with Pete to join them. Paul would fly over later to do something or other.

It was a long, uncomfortable road trip for me, Pete and our driver. We'd been sent over to Munich by Transit van with some of the band's gear in back. For some reason Pete and I hadn't been allowed to fly. Another of Bernie's ideas. Perhaps he'd decided that if we made the trip overland then Pete and I would 'bond' or something. Was he was trying to make a point? Keep us in our place? Make us suffer for our art? Save money? It was always guesswork.

By himself, away from the others, Pete was a bit friendlier than usual though he didn't have much to say. I didn't have much to say to him. Just cordial stuff and some complaining about our situation. A drum machine was being used so Pete wasn't going to be playing on the album apart from a few fills here and there. I didn't know if I was going to be used. I guess Pete was disappointed. He didn't show it. Paul wasn't playing on the album either. It came as a bit of a surprise to me to find out he'd never played on a Clash album before except the first one. Norman from the Blockheads was doing bass. I'd been told Norman had played on nearly all the Clash albums. He was responsible for the famous 'Magnificent 7' riff. God knows what was expected of me. We were still excited though. A new Clash album was being recorded after all and *we are the Clash!*

It got colder and colder as we rolled through the bleak German countryside. The temperature outside dropped to around minus 20 degrees. At some point the heater packed in.

'What's going on? There's no heat in here. I'm fucking freezing!' I moaned, shifting up and down, hugging my leather jacket.

'Well, it's so cold outside that the engine isn't using any water to cool itself,' our driver explained. 'So there's no hot water to make the heater work.'

'Fucking hell!'

Condensation inside the cabin began to freeze. My fingers began to freeze. Pete and I moaned relentlessly. Why was this happening? Small icicles formed on the roof and the windscreen kept freezing over. You couldn't see a thing. We had to keep stopping every few miles and get out in the subzero temperature to wipe it clear.

It was early evening after what seemed like days of driving by the time we arrived at the hotel. It was such a great feeling getting there. Just getting warm. Thawing out. Having a drink at the bar. Some hot food. The expectation. But it was short-lived and a mean vibe around the hotel lobby soon gave me the chills again.

There was that familiar, heavy seriousness in the air. Joe was dark, miserable, aloof and uncommunicative. And Kosmo. Nick. It was heavy. *No one* was speaking.

I got my key and found my room. Oh well, *whatever*. I had a small, clean and *warm* room. It was enough. *I* was happy. I looked at my bed. On that bed lay the biggest white feather

downy duvet thing I'd ever seen. Big feather pillows. I checked my reflection in the mirror. Punk rock star! I got in under that warm duvet and started dreaming.
  Next day, Nick was back in the studio laying down more rhythm guitar tracks. I wasn't required so I thought I'd have a look around Munich. I still hadn't been told whether I would actually be used on the album or not. I'd stopped worrying too much about it.
  I walked outside into a bright blue day full of promise. All around the snow was lying about four feet deep. The sharp air hit and I felt clean and invigorated. I jumped in a taxi and we drove for a few miles through these great white fields towards the city centre. By the time we arrived the sky had clouded up. It hung over my head suddenly like a giant slab of concrete. I paid the cab and began wandering around. I instantly disliked the whole fucking place. I've no idea why. After all, wasn't it just another European city? Lots of architecture you're supposed to find fascinating. Art galleries. Museums full of dead things. The same blank faces everywhere. Eyes that don't see. Little piss holes of hell. People moving this way and that. All cities are the same. Hundreds of years of fighting, cruelty and suffering and all that death, pain and struggle and for what? Buildings. Museums. Art galleries.
  Here people seemed a lot more together than at home though. Functional. And bloody rich! My mind began to wander. How come this lot were supposed to have lost a war? It seemed they hadn't lost anything. Everyone secure. Sure in themselves and determined. Immaculately dressed in expensive clothes. Jewelry. Expensive cars. I wondered what the world would be like if Hitler had won. Perhaps everything just evens out in the end, I thought to myself. I mean, in spite of all the atrocities and that. I suddenly saw the whole of humanity marching on some predestined course and all the wars and leaders just splashes in an inevitable stream of things. I stopped by the new

McDonald's. Inside, the German youth were happily getting their taste of freedom.

I trudged on. No, it's all inevitable, I thought. Why have one dictator when you can have groups of them. They're all out there. Everywhere. Throughout the Western hemisphere. Throughout the *world*. You just wouldn't know them or be able to recognise them, that's all. A whole bunch of anonymous, psychopathic, faceless fucks sitting behind corporate desks deciding everyone's fate. Committing unanswerable atrocities on the human spirit. Come to think of it, I thought, there was another one back at the studio desk orchestrating a new Clash blitzkrieg.

I shuddered with the cold. Time for a beer. If there's one thing Germany's got it's great beer. I caught sight of a small doorway with a neon sign, walked in and up to the bar. Around that bar were about ten fit muscular guys wearing mostly leather trousers and tight white t shirts. *I* was wearing leather trousers and a white t shirt. Four of them were wearing caps. *I* was wearing a cap and a studded leather biker jacket. A guy around forty years old smiled and tried to lock eyes with me.

'Oh, uhm, I …..er……forgot something………back later,' I mumbled to the bartender, embarrassed. I ran out of there.

Bloody hell!

I walked along a bit and checked my reflection in a shop window. All that leather shouted back at me. Was I a closet or something? Maybe subconsciously? Fuck it. How could you know? Who cares?

I found another bar and got a beer. Then another. After that I cheered up a bit. I'd had enough of Munich. I caught a cab and went back to the hotel.

It was late afternoon when I got back. Kosmo was excited and concerned.

'Where've you been? You're wanted in the studio.'

'So I *am* playing!'
'Yeah. We'll be going over in an hour or so.'

Kosmo seemed pleased for me. Kosmo was alright. We waited an hour or more in the hotel lobby and then drove over to the studio.
There was a hushed silence as I walked in. Importance and excitement. There were some hello's and polite inquiries about the trip over from Bernie. I felt I was meeting more long lost relatives at another funeral. Joe nodded at me.
What was all that polite stuff about from Bernie? Was he taking the piss?
I looked around. It was all very impressive.
. Bernie and Fanie sat behind this enormous mixing desk that seemed to fill the entire room. Joe sat in behind them quietly at the back. Nick sat to my left. Opposite was a big window that looked into a big live recording area. Flanked on either side of this window were these GIANT SPEAKERS filling the entire space from floor to ceiling. Four massive cabs in each, each one must have been at least four feet across. It was my first time in a 24 track studio.
I jumped up on a stool. Nick handed me my guitar and I tuned up.
Bernie suddenly announced:
'We want some lead guitar. Right, I'm going to play a few tracks and I just want you to play along. Don't think too much about it. Just play along. Have a listen first.'
The first track started. I can't remember which one. I think it was the 'Fingerpoppin'' or was it the 'The Three Card Trick'? All I can remember is it came at an ear shattering volume and nearly blew me off the stool. Raw guitar and pounding drum machine. I heard Joe's singing the song properly. There were no backing vocals. It was impressive. Mind you, with those

speakers he could've been singing the 'The Three Blind Mice' and I would have been impressed.
'What do you think?' asked Bernie.
'Pretty impressive,' I remarked, excited. Bernie looked pleased with my reaction.
I got a guitar sound together with Nick's help. Not too distorted. Not too clean. Sort of crunchy. Nice.
'Here it comes! Just play along.'
The tracks began rolling.
'Fingerpoppin'', 'We are the Clash', 'Are You Ready For War', 'Dirty Punk', 'Dictator'. I had nothing worked out. As far as the newer songs were concerned I just knew the chords and the arrangements Joe had given us. It was easy to just start playing and get lost in all the noise.
I picked a bit here and there looking for a few notes that would fit. Some wild rock'n'roll bits. Bendy notes. Feedback. Picky bits of riffs I'd got remembered in my head that seemed to fit. Whatever came to mind. It was all a bit ragged and I was sure I hadn't done very well.
'Good,' exclaimed Bernie. 'Now, I want you to do the same again. Don't worry about it. That was good.'
'Alright.'
'Here it comes!' he shouted.
I remembered some of the bits I'd done first time round and added some new ideas. A few embellishments. I played some single note picking siren thing and more bendy-bendy feedback with Chuck Berry coming in for an encore. I was having fun. No one interrupted me. When it was over Bernie looked extremely happy. He looked over at Joe.
'Interesting.'
'Yeah,' Joe replied, nodding.
The atmosphere in the room shifted. No one showed much emotion but I could sense a certain cloud had lifted. I did

another run through. Then another. After that, Bernie decided to call it a night.

We drove back to the hotel in silence. Kosmo quietly confided to me that everyone had been very impressed with my playing. Why? What had I done? I was just fucking around! Fucking hell! I'd done something *right* for a change. I was a *part* of things.

A great sense of possibilities and a feeling of my self worth quickly returned. That night I got under that big downy duvet thing with some peace of mind. I was wanted back in again the next day. I couldn't wait to get in there and tighten up that stuff and really give it the bollocks.

Next morning I got in there early, guitar on lap, all keyed up and ready to rock. Bernie and Fanie began messing around with stuff. Buttons were being pressed. Leads going in here and there. Out there. Bits of this and that. Tweaking this. Tweaking that. A few seconds of a song would suddenly blare out from the speakers and shock me. Stop. Start. Stop. Start. An hour passed. Another hour passed and I hadn't done a thing. By the third hour it all began getting on my nerves. I sat there, patiently smoking.

Finally they got it together and decided to concentrate on one track. 'North and South'. It was a song Joe had written all about the economic divide between the North and the South of England. The South had it all good and the North was getting the shitty end of the stick. As far as I was concerned the South was just as shit as the North. It was all shit. But it didn't matter, the track had a nice feel and it seemed like it meant something. The track began to roll. I had a melodic picking bit for it I'd played back in London that everyone seemed to like. I was pleased with it too. It had a sad feel that fitted well. Half way through the track stopped.

Bernie looked up at me, annoyed.

'That's NOT the way you played it before. It was different. Play it like you did.'

'I'm sure it's the same. What do you mean?'
'It was *different!* Here it comes.'
The track rolled. I played the picky bit. The track stopped.
'NO! NO! NOOOOOOO!' exclaimed Bernie getting hot under the collar. 'It's not *right*. Do it PROPERLY.'
The track came back at me and this time I varied the rhythm between the notes slightly.
The track stopped.
'Are you taking the fucking piss?'
I had no idea what he was on about. I really wanted to get it right. I wanted that same feeling I'd had the night before. I thought long and hard about that riff. I went over and over it in my mind. It was something I'd come up with in my bedroom to nothing in particular. I knew I simply couldn't have played it any other way.
'I don't know what you mean. It's the *SAME RIFF!*' I yelled, exasperated.
I played it again and again, each time changing it a bit. No go. Bernie sighed. Move on. We tried different tracks. But nothing was good enough anymore. Everything wrong. Don't do it like that. Do it like *this*. Like what? And in between, just endless fiddling with knobs and dials and crap. Stopping. Starting. I looked at over at Joe. What was he thinking? He sat quietly in his chair, detached, reading the newspaper not looking up or saying anything. It really was Bernie's show.
I suddenly remembered Joe telling me how they'd recorded the first Clash album. I was a big fan of the first album.
'We went in there not knowing shit!' he'd confided, reminiscing. 'I got this big roll of masking tape and we stretched it right out over the mixing desk covering all the dials on the desk, you know, the level meters? The engineer went fucking crazy. "What are you guys doing?" he'd screamed. "You can't do that!" We didn't give a fuck. Just went in there and started banging it out. You should have seen his face!'

'You are fucking joking?' I laughed, trying to picture it.
'No.'
It was perfect. I could just imagine some studio engineer in my mind, some arsey student type with long hair losing it as they'd begun creating history. I believed him. It was so funny it HAD to be true.

I took a break.

'Where's the masking tape Joe?' I shouted.

Joe nodded but I don't think he got it. Suddenly, recording wasn't fun anymore. The stress of it all was getting to me. I walked out and left Nick to do something. I got a coffee. Lit up again. It was my last one. Fuck, had I really smoked a whole packet already? I looked at my watch. Nine hours had gone by. I found a cigarette machine and bought another packet.

I was determined to pick myself up and turn things around.

I went back in and 'Dirty Punk' was playing. Nick, looking like a lost and miserable puppy was trying to get a solo together. He looked how I felt.

'Why don't we try a kind of question and answer thing?' I suggested.

Bernie agreed with the idea and so we tried it.

The track began and we went at it. Nick played a bit of a riff. I answered it. He played the next bit. I answered it. It sounded pretty good.

'Yeah. But you can do *better*,' said Bernie, looking at *me*. It seemed Nick's part was OK.

I played more of the same but getting as much feeling into it as I could.

The man who invented Punk rock and put the Clash together looked up disgustedly. He knew something I could never understand.

'No! No! NO! You're not really………..I………*get*…… SOMETHING……………' he yelled, exasperated.

The solo bit came again.

I began looking for that something. I didn't know what it could be. I felt what I *had* was good. I put everything into it.

The track stopped.

'Look,' said Bernie, measured and quietly threatening. 'you're either UP for this or you're NOT. Stop fucking around.'

'Look, *I'm* happy with it. It sounds good to me,' I said, leaning back defiantly. I'd had enough of this shit. I looked at Nick for some support. He looked away saying nothing. He was watching his own arse.

'You're too DERIVATIVE. You wanna be second-rate you can. But you have no place being here. You can just take that fucking guitar of yours and get the fuck back to London.'

I tuned up my guitar, thinking long and hard. What could I possibly do? It was only bloody rock'n'roll after all. I pulled out another cigarette and lit up. My hands were shaking. I could feel the edge getting closer. Was that the idea? Get one so fucked up that from the depths behind the routines of consciousness some incredible and unique piece of never heard of guitar thing would spontaneously erupt onto the fretboard? Chuck Berry reborn for the eighties?

I turned to put my fag into the ashtray. There was another one in there still burning. God!

I collected myself. The track started. I began loosening hold of just about everything I ever knew about guitar playing. Looking for that creative *something*. My fingers began hitting the fretboard in all manner of strange ways. A kind of weird, punk jazz began to emerge. Odd discordant notes and sounds. If they were out of tune then no matter. I just repeated them. It was crazy. Pure noise. Pure avant-garde chic!

The track stopped. Bernie leaped out angrily from behind the desk and stood up in front of me.

He began shouting something loudly. Then quietly. Loudly again. I couldn't hear a word he was saying. Joe yelled out something from the back. I didn't hear that either. Joe ran up and stood next to Bernie, his mouth moving. My mind began floating out of my body. As I looked back at Bernie I got the distinct impression of a giant Jack Russel dog standing up in front of me. The *feeling* of one. All hard muscle. The mouth moving. Eyes like points of sheer hatred. Angrily yapping. It was surreal. I was no longer rationally aware of any of the forms and shapes of things around me. Just the *feeling* of things. And those feelings weren't too good. A hard and sharp reality had arrived that disturbed and threatened madness. A giant hole appeared in my consciousness. A bottomless black hole. If I fell into it I knew I could never return.

'I need a piss,' I managed to blurt out. I dropped my guitar, ran to the toilet. I locked the door. I leaned over the washbasin. I splashed water on my face and looked at it in the mirror. Splashed on some more. I sat down on the toilet seat with my eyes closed, head in hands. Specks of light were flashing around there in the blackness.

What to do? Should I fuck it all and run away? Running away seemed like giving in. I know my spirit was getting severely whipped. I knew I should tell them to fuck off. But I lacked the moral courage to do it. The idea of being a famous guitarist in a famous band had me by the balls. Even my parents after 24 years of neglect and indifference had at last begun to show some warmth and respect. I'd recently returned to my university. All those guys I'd studied with were now finishing their Phd's. They were about to enter astronomical research and embark on one of the last frontiers of science. They were about to divine the secrets of the universe. I respected them. They were pretty bright. Back then I couldn't keep up with them but when I went back they now sat around gaping awe of me. I didn't get it. They were doing something of value for humanity while I leapt around like an idiot night after night making a loud noise.

No escape. My heart was pounding. Every fibre of my flesh and bone screaming. After a while I calmed down a bit. I went back in there and got on with it. Started going through the motions. Doing what Bernie asked. No more. No less. Play this here. Like this. I'd play that there. Play that there. Like that. I'd play that there. It was a familiar feeling. Stoic, helpless resignation.

The days went by. Things were no better for Nick. He did something. I did something. We carried on with our ego's fighting and faking optimism. I'd completely shut down. I think Nick had too. We didn't talk much. I felt compelled to carry on but now something was now out of bounds. No one could touch it. Detached. Nothing gets in. Nothing gets out. A crack that had been forming was now so wide that it couldn't be repaired. It was a split between what I thought, what I said, what I felt and what I did.

Some days later, Paul arrived on a plane from London and we all got together to do a few live tracks with Pete playing live drums. 'Sex Mad Roar'. What was that all about?

Joe came in to demonstrate the feeling he wanted to get.

He jumped up and down wildly throwing his arms about.

'Yeah, yeah and POW! POW! POW!' he drawled and shouted. 'Like this!' He suddenly stuck his fist in the air, 'and then give it that *Bang! Bang! Bang!*' He punched the air above his head.

Bernie smiled and nodded supportively.

It was like being on an old Hollywood movie set. The eccentric crazy star and his mad director.

We ran through all the live songs in a few takes. Paul kept making mistakes but eventually we got them all nervously down.

After about a week of recording we all went out together on the town to drink. Some huge beer keller place where they hold the big Oktoberfest. Nick, Paul, Pete, Kosmo and me. Joe was somewhere else with Bernie as usual. It was foul. Some band was in there playing traditional German folk tunes. All dressed up in that stupid gear they wear. Shorts and hats and funny stuff. And the waitresses too. They wandered around like extras from the Sound of Music. We ordered these great barrel glasses of beer. The conversation turned to the subject of love.

Pete seemed pretty concerned about it.

'Do you think true love is possible or just a dream?' he asked Nick.

'I think it's possible,' Nick said, thoughtfully. 'With the right person. I just think it's difficult to find.'

'I haven't found anything like that. I'm not sure anymore,' he went on ruefully.

'What do *you* think, Vince?' he asked, looking over his shoulder, suddenly seeming to remember I was there.

I'd never really thought about it. I thought about it.

'Well, I think that in the beginning you meet someone you fancy. You fuck six times a day for a couple of months. You're in heaven. Then it starts going downhill. Six months later you're beginning to look at other chicks. After two years you've had a couple of one night stands and you're fucking maybe once every three weeks because it's become boring. By that point you're attached. You can't let go. It's too painful. Then one day it's 'Peeeeeete, I think we need to work on our relationship!' Hah! When that happens you *know* you're screwed. Most relationships are. They call it 'love' to give the thing a semblance of dignity. People get into relationships or married because they can't stand the pain of being alone. Loneliness is a drag.'

'You're so fucking cynical!' said Pete, laughing.

'Yeah, but that's probably the best case scenario.'

'What.'

'Most people don't even get the first bit. Settling down for them is settling for what they can get.'

'I dunno, I still believe in true love.'

He looked at Nick.

'Vince doesn't believe in anything. Does he? You don't believe in *anything*, do you?' he said, looking at me.
'No, not really,' I replied, truthfully.
They turned back round and they went on talking, ignoring me.
I didn't really know whether I believed in true love or not. One course of action was just about as good as any other it seemed to me. It was all the same pile of dung whichever way you turned. It all evened out. Damned if you do. Damned if you don't. Married people were frustrated and angry. They never *looked* all that happy. Single people were often sad and lonely. But having the freedom to do what you wanted seemed to be the better option. You could always get a dog.

We were completely fucked driving back to the hotel. At some point Pete stuck his head out the car window. Screaming at the passers-by.
'You fucking NAZI CUNTS!' he yelled, manically. 'We beat all you fuckers! WE WON THE *WAR!*'
I laughed hysterically and joined in.
'WE WON THE WAR!!! WE WON THE WAR!!!' I yelled.
'NAZI FUCKS!!!!'
Nick smiled. It wasn't politically correct but it was just brilliant letting go and being stupid for a change. I realised I hadn't laughed and had any fun like that in a very long time.

If the mind and soul were beginning to disintegrate, so was the body. When I got back to London I began having problems with my stomach. When I ate anything I would get a violent burning sensation down there. Sometimes I got it even when I hadn't eaten. It was happening everyday. I thought I might have an ulcer and better get it checked out. Health problems. You can die from ulcers. I was going to fitness training twice a week and couldn't understand it. I was only 24. I was sure of my body. I found it hard to believe it could fail me. I was referred to St

Mary's hospital by my GP. They decided to investigate by sticking this giant tube down my throat. A thick rubber thing with a camera on the end that could take pictures of my insides. They had to give me some gas first so I could swallow this massive bloody thing down or one could freak out and suffocate. When I came to and it was over and they'd got their pictures I found myself in front of the nurse saying all kinds of things. I just came to, swearing and saying all sorts of dirty sexy stuff to her without realising where I was. I wasn't sure what I'd said but I could remember my dream which involved tearing off some woman's clothes and taking her. I could hardly walk I was so groggy from the gas. I smiled at her. She smiled knowingly back. I got out of there as fast as I could.

One by one the band returned to London. The Clash began having meetings in the Kensington Hilton lounge. Band meetings were beginning to give me the nervous shakes. I couldn't trust my arms and hands. If I held a cup of tea I was worried I would shake so much I'd spill it everywhere. Not cool. The answer to that was a big shot of whisky beforehand. Or maybe two or three. When I had that whisky after a few minutes the fear of shaking would stop and most of the tension would go.
I told Joe of the tests I was having.
'I don't know what it is, Joe. My stomach's fucked.'
He looked at me, coolly.
'I wouldn't be surprised if you're going to need an OPERATION, Vince.'
'No, I don't think it's that bad. I just get this burning in my stomach. Not all the time. Just sometimes.'
Joe sat back and shook his head from side to side.
'No. No. I can tell you're going to need an OPERATION. It's obvious. They're gonna have to cut you. I'm sure of it.'
'Nah.'

But that day at the meeting I seem to be in everybody's good books for some reason I can't fathom. My guitar playing is getting very good. Even Nick agrees. I'm making progress. Things are looking good. We're gonna kick ass with this new album.

Back for the results of the test. I'm in the doctor's room. Young guy. Just a little older than me.
'I'm happy to say we haven't found anything.'
'Nothing? Are you sure?'
'Yes, the tests are conclusive.'
'No ulcer?'
'No.'
'But what is it then? I'm in agony.'
'What do you do for a living?'
'I'm a musician.'
The doctor began making notes. He looked up.
'Do you eat well? Vegetables and ……..'
'YES! And I keep fit twice a week.'
'Do you smoke?'
'Yeah.'
'How many?'
'Oh, a couple of packets.'
'40 a day? That's quite a lot.'
'Yeah.'
'How much do you drink?'
'Uhm, well, it varies, you know?'
'On average.'
'Well it's hard to say exactly.'
'Roughly.'
'About 6 or 7 pints.'
'A day?'
'Yeah.'

That was on a quiet day. I didn't want him to know how much I *really* drank. I didn't want to know either.
'That's quite a lot.'
'Nah, not really.'
'I think you should think about stopping. That could be your problem.'
'What! Altogether! Come on. You must be joking!!!'
'Seriously.'
'For how long.'
'Well, forever.'
'What? Forever?'
'Yes. And I think you're stressed. Find way's to relieve your stress. Try some meditation. Yoga. It's good for stress.'
'OK, thanks.'
. I took the results of the test, the pictures of nothing and went home. Yoga! Meditation! I'd tried that stuff before. It was supposed to relax and calm you. More con. It only ever made me more nervous and strung out than before. Stop drinking! Yeah right. Stupid doctors. Boring fucker. I'll see him in hell first.

The pain continued. But when it came I discovered that a good shot of brandy and a can of lager seemed to cure it. For a while. I decided to give up smoking instead. And I did. The withdrawals were terrible. But I didn't need to smoke. I could make it. Drinking was another matter.

The Clash were kicked out of the Chalk Farm Rehearsals as the council wanted to repossess the building. They had plans to extend the Camden market. At that time the Camden market was small and located just around the Lock but it was expanding fast. In another year or two it would become unrecognisable. The whole 'youth' alternative punk purchasing thing had moved away from places like the King's Road and relocated. Now Camden was where it was at for rock'n'roll. And punk.

You knew it was all over. Punk was something unrecognisable from its beginnings. It was something for foreigners. For the Spanish or the Italians who came flocking over looking to find something they didn't have at home. Punk was a postcard with a fat Mohican on it. A tourist attraction. It was history. The new foreign punks had little style or any glamour about them. Or the English ones. It had no vitality. It wasn't growing. The Clash wasn't really them or anything new either. Where was it going to go?

I found a rehearsal place for the band in Finsbury Park. It was a dingy basement my landlord owned in Blackstock Road. We took the place over and carried on. I liked it. It was dark and smelly in there. You felt comfortable there. We got all the amps set up and they could stay there for when we wanted to turn up. And it was cheap. It was better than going to one of the popular rehearsals that all the pop stars went to. But it wasn't really. It was still just me, Nick and Pete turning up and trying to fill in TIME while the recording was going on. The girls, the secretaries at the Clash office were sacked by Bernie for some reason. I never found out why. Some new people were hired. The Whale and I were now living apart. I was bored. I told her I needed my own space. But we carried on as an item just arguing more and more. Meetings, band ones were always in the Kensington Hilton. And drink meetings were in the Soho Brasserie in Old Compton Street. I think the Soho Brasserie was the start of the wine bar thing. Posh refurbished pubs that were ultra slick and clean with metal and glass everywhere. Bottles of exotic this and that behind the bar. Sophisticated types in there thinking they're a cut above it. Yuppies. No one looking at anyone else. No one talking to anyone else. Sterile. It was the beginning of a new era. If 1984 was the end of the worldthen the fallout came in 1985. I hated it. Why were we there?

'What the fuck you bring us *here* for?' I ask Kosmo.
'It's alright.'

'It's horrible. It's snobby. It's……pretentious.'

'You're in the Clash, Vince. You have a profile. You need to be seen. It's about standards, Vince.'

'There are no standards here. It's phoney.'

'The world is changing Vince. If you wanna get noticed you have to get with it.'

'I don't wanna get with this shit.'

'You can't keep hiding away in that sorry pub of yours in Finsbury Park.'

'I like it.'

Nick and Pete laughed. They didn't seem all that bothered.

Just then a bottle of champagne arrived at our table by a waiter in black. In a silver bucket with the white towel around. Kosmo had ordered it for us all. The big show. Loud laughter. The cork went off and my glass was filled. I didn't like it but it was alcohol after all. I drank it down in one go.

Kosmo sat back with a smug grin.

I was happy to get out of there and get home. The only good thing about those places were the pretty young women that went in there. Hot bodies in tight skirts. They flocked into those places looking for someone wealthy. But you knew it was all on the outside with those types. You'd go talk to them but the inevitable question was always: *what do you do?*

Meaning: what can you do *for me?*

No fun at all. The eighties.

CHORUS:

THIS IS ENGLAND

Bernie arrives back from Germany and we have another meeting. He's back from the recording studio. I'm told that Pete will be going back over to Germany soon to do something. But of course he never did in the end and the drum machine was there to stay. But there in the plush Hilton bar Bernie sets us a new test. We're to go busking. What? Where? Around England with acoustic guitars. You are allowed to take £10 with you as starting money. No more. No bank cards. The rest is up to you. You have to survive on what you earn, playing in the streets. If you can't make it like that then you don't deserve to call yourselves a band.
We were all up for it. It sounded like fun. One of Bernie's better ideas.

So there we are standing on the hard shoulder of a slip road onto the M1 holding our guitars. Paul has sneaked some pepperoni sticks into his guitar case. He tells me it's his emergency food supply. The sky is darkening. I've got a £10 note and a bar of chocolate in my leather jacket. A small flask of whisky. The rush hour traffic has built up now, everyone in a big hurry to get out of the concrete jungle. Shouldn't be too hard getting a lift. Joe suggests we split up. No one is going to pick up all five of us in one go. Especially the way we look. He reckons we're too intmidating. Our rendezvous will be in Nottingham.

'Ok. When you get there find the train station. We'll meet up in the nearest pub to the train station. Agreed?'

We all agreed.

I walked up the slip road near the top. We space out along the slip road. I take a nice slug of my flask. Looked back. There we all were. The world famous Clash, stadium rockers, standing with guitars, our thumbs out, one by one, trying to flag rides holding out bits of cardboard. The traffic streaming past. I've only been standing there for a couple of minutes when a car suddenly pulls up in front of me. I run up. The window lowers.

'Where you going?'

'Nottingham. You going anywhere near?'

'Yeah. I'm going *to* Nottingham. Jump in.'

'Brilliant!'

I wave back to the others. They yell back something I can't hear. I'm the first off.

My driver is called Rick. He's a computer programmer. He's a regular sort in a suit. I tell him we're the Clash and we're going busking around England. He's heard of the Clash but it's no big deal for him. Busking? Oh, yeah, really? Nottingham is our starting point. Can he drop me near the station? No problem. He's a very relaxed type, Rick. All easy. We smoothly slip down the motorway eating up the miles. He brings out a joint. Lights it up. Passes it to me. I think about it. Oh, ok, fuck it. I take a toke. Pull out my whisky. Insurance against paranoia jeebies. I pass the whisky but he declines. He's driving. Ok. I try a bit of conversation but things don't connect too well so I just kick back and watch the road. But that's OK 'cause Rick's cool with silence or anything it seems. Before I know it we're there. Nottingham station. We say goodbye. I shake his hand. Cheers mate! Right opposite there's a pub. That's got to be the one. I go in and start spending some of my £10.

But sitting there trying to string out pints and the £10 I wonder if anyone else will actually turn up. Have I been set up? Am I'm being tested by Bernie? What if no one else makes it? An hour passes. It's after 9. I think about it. I've only about a fiver left now and the only solution I can come up with is to find a girl. A girl will give me a place to stay. It's Friday night. I look around. There are only two other people in that pub and neither of them are girls. I'll wait till closing time. Maybe then I can find a club and score.

But one by one the rest of the band do arrive. First through the door is Pete. I've never been so happy to see him. Then Nick and Paul. It's looking good but there's no sign of Joe. It's nearly closing time when he suddenly appears in the doorway with two young girls. One on each arm all laughing and stupid.

'Hey, hey, HEEEEY!'

'May I introduce you guys to………..this is July……….and this is……...Elsa. Let's get a drink.'

So we sit around and Joe goes to the bar. After this we're going to a club the girls know and after that July and Elsa have kindly let us stay the night in their house. It's a big relief. We can relax. Joe has really come through. The Gods have been kind.

'Where the hell did you find *them*?' I ask Joe.

'I just met them this minute right by the station.'

'That's lucky.'

'Right. And tonight we're going to get DRUNK!' Joe stands up and announces to everyone, 'and tomorrow we'll find the shopping precinct. And PLAY!'

The next morning we're up early and find ourselves in need of some rehearsal for this. Walking around we find a canal bridge and get under it and out of sight. Pull out our acoustics. Pete has some drum sticks and begins tapping them against the brick wall. The morning sun is bright and casting ripply water patterns under the bridge.

'What can we start with?' asks Joe.

I suggest 'Stepping Stone', the Monkey's tune which is really the Sex Pistols version and begin playing the chords. Soon we've got it together and it doesn't sound at all bad with the sound amplified and echoing there under the bridge. We got 'Police and Thieves' too. What else? Pete suggests 'Come on Everybody.' Of course we have a whole repertoire of Clash songs in our heads too.

Joe decides that's enough to start. So we take our guitars and head for the precinct.

We're a bit nervous. How is this gonna work? It's a so sunny Saturday morning and shoppers are out already with their bags, moving around. They don't look like Clash fans. They don't even look like they listen to music. We find a place in a shopping area and start. Paul puts his guitar case out front for the money with a couple of coins in it to get us going. We start with 'Stepping Stone'. Shoppers eye us nervously as they walk past our shouting. Ladies with pushchairs walk by. A couple hand in hand. Jeans and white pastel colours are everywhere. An old couple walk by with a curious, hostile stare. What are we doing there making such a noise spoiling their quiet morning? We carry on stubbornly. Next song. 'Come on Everybody'. Come on somebody! Give us some money! But they all just walk past, oblivious. Police and Thieves. Surely *that* will bring in a bit of cash. The song ends but the guitar case still only has the couple of coins we put in it. Back to 'Stepping Stone' again.

OUT OF CONTROL: The Last Days of The Clash

After about twenty minutes a sweet old lady with a little dog with nothing to do comes by and drops 10p onto the case. She looks up with a do-goody smile. I smile back at her. She walks off. Ok. It's a start. We carry on. A middle aged guy wearing jeans walks past and throws in a couple of coins. A bit later, a few more. After nearly an hour we stop and check the balance. £2.38.

Joe decides we've got to find a better pitch. So we walk around and set up in what looks like the main busy thoroughfare. Marks and Spencer is there. And a record shop. We begin to do a little better.

We keep on playing and a few more coins get tossed in. We stop. We need some fresh songs.

'Rivers of Babylon.'

'How does it go? What key?'

'I dunno.'

Joe just begins to sing the song by himself. I find a chord that seems to fit the pitch of his singing. The main one. Nick and I quickly work out the chords and agree on something. It's simple and in a few seconds we get into it. Singing:

'OH, THE WIIII--CKID CARRIED US AWAY INTO CAPTIVITEEEE!'

It's works. It's the release and good soulful all hands on deck reaching into trapped hearts and minds. And suddenly pound coins start dropping into the guitar case. It's a beautiful sight to see those coins. And the sound as they hit the case. Plop! Chink! Dop!

Another song!

'What about ………..Not Fade Away!'

The Bo Diddley rhythm starts and jumps and soon we have a little crowd. Someone from the record shop comes over. He's recognised the Clash. More arrive. The word starts going around. More people appear looking on, curiously. More coins. It's time to stop. People move away. Joe starts talking with the guys from the record shop. Paul starts counting the money. Nick and I help him, crouching down and stacking up the coins into little piles. There's almost £20 in there. We're rich! We adjourn to the pub and order beers. Later we play again and get a bit more money. Then someone takes us to a tiny pub set into a cliff. It's built inside a cave. It's the oldest pub in the world apparently. We sit outside, the sun going down. We try a few more songs but our voices are shot already. There's a hoarse cracking sound in there. Joe reckons we better rest up or we're never going to make it.

So we sit there drinking our beers as the sun goes down and already a sort of camaraderie has developed. With no ten ton trucks and television sets and scaffolding and stage barriers and light displays and separate hotel rooms and soundcheck and tour itinerary and no Bernie we're stipped naked. We're in this together. Equal. Nothing to lose or gain. No competition. Just fun. I suspect the whole busking thing has been set up by Bernie for a bit of publicity but so what? Someone puts us up for the night. We sleep on the floor. The couch. Pete's got the bed. Lucky him.

Next day we make it out to the road to hitch to Leeds. It's a real drag standing there just waiting, hoping for a lift. The cars speed by. Joe groups us back together.
'This is too much. Let's pool the money and catch the train to Leeds. We could be here all fucking day.'
We all agree. Relieved, we head to the station.
From then on it all becomes a blur. We get to Leeds and give up on the shopping precinct idea. Clubs are better. We wander about on foot from place to place. See a group of victims queuing up to go in. We whip out the guitars and start strumming.

OUT OF CONTROL: The Last Days of The Clash

'AAAAAAHHHHH SSEEEEEEE A BAAAD MOOOON RAAAHSINNN! AAAAH SEEEE TRUBLE OOOOOORRRRRNNNN THE WAAAAAAY!'

It's fucking hilarious. The stupidity of it. Pete is bashing away his sticks on anything he can find. We're just yelling. People look on not knowing what to think. As soon as there's a bit of money in the pool we're off again. On the move. Where to next? Another pub. Another idea. We stagger, drunk out of a club and start busking outside the railway station. It's 2am. Another group then another floor somewhere. A blanket. Leather jacket for a pillow. Our host brings me a cup of tea in the morning. The word is out that the Clash are in town.

Someone tells us the Alarm are in town too. The Alarm of course are a big second rate Clash imitation.

'Right, I've an idea,' gleams Joe, 'there's gonna be a lot of Clash fans down there. We'll get them before the band starts. Play to *our* fans as they go in.'

We arrive outside Leeds University and get up on the steps leading in. Get out the guitars and begin playing to the queue. Word quickly spreads from the queue and into the hall. People begin piling out of the concert as soon as they hear the Clash are outside. We're only on our third song and a giant crowd has congregated. More than 500 people are there in front of us as we run through a set which had begun to include some of the new songs. 'Cool Under Heat'. 'Movers and Shakers'. Together with an acoustic 'White Riot' and 'Clash City Rockers'.

No one can hear too much. I can't hear a thing. Each ragged song ends to incredible applause. But suddenly I hear shouts and yells. Some liquid falls down from the sky splattering everywhere. I look at my arms. They're covered in red patches. Some security from the venue come out and roughly tell us we better leave. We're quickly out of there.

Walking back down the road I look at my leather. Streaks of red paint are all over it and my guitar. We're all baptised with it. No one knows who threw the red paint or why. Perhaps it was the Alarm security? They had cause to be upset of course, upstaging the main band like that. Then again, someone else says it's animal rights activists. What was their fucking problem? Then it was something to do with Clash's CBS record label and it's involvement in apartheid in South Africa. What? We run down the road, laughing.

But a large group kept following us down the road. There was Joe at the front, leading his followers like the Pied Piper. The blind leading the blind.

We stop somewhere. A car park or something and play a full set of songs to our followers. Mostly Clash songs for almost an hour. Then off to a another pub.

A time had been set for us to play and the word has been spread. Things are getting out of control. What had begun as a bit of busking quickly begins evolving into small acoustic shows. With the revenue from the bar coming in, from all those fans, the manager is more than happy to pay us. It would become a regular sort of thing. The bucket would go round but as well as getting money from the groups of fans we would get a couple of hundred quid from a bar manager too. But that was OK. It was good beer and train fare money. Money was no longer a problem. Next stop York.

And so a routine developed. Arrive in a town, busk the city centre. Get recognised. Play a 'show' in the evening and get a load of money for the train fare. Joe began giving radio interviews. A couple of the 'shows' had to be cancelled. There were just too many people stuffed into some bar or club for it to happen. Fire regulations. We couldn't sing anymore. Our voices are shot. No one can hear anything. I realise that people are turning up for the band name, the event. The further north we go the more angry it gets. It's not long before the left wing militants get in on the act. We're sitting in a pub in Sunderland and the Socialist Workers Party propaganda is out. Communist party newsletters.

'I understand where you're coming from,' Joe explains, patiently to a small group of SWP officials, anxious to recruit him. 'There has to be some CHANGE in this country. I KNOW that. How we can REALISE that ………..and put PRESSURE on the democratic process to EFFECT ………..A RADICAL SHIFT in PERSPECTIVE. I KNOW IT CAN BE DONE. It's a question of WILL. To raise the level of…….'

'Joe, I have a form here,' says one intense character, solid and steely, spreading it out in front. 'If you'll give your support to us it will make a difference. The Socialist Workers Party CAN CHANGE THINGS!'

'I TOTALLY *RESPECT* where your coming from, man. But I can't do it. I can't be seen to take sides on …….to affiliate with any particular party. But I VALUE your commitment and I…….'

'But Joe!.....it would mean so much if you would lend your support. Your support will help raise our profile. Look here, look at the issues we're tackling'

This guy's got another pamphlet out and is spreading it over the pub table.

I take another sip of beer. We've been in this pub now for fucking ages with these cunts. I'm tired. The whole thing bores me stupid. Joe goes on.

'See, *I've* been elected to do a job. And that's why we're here. I'm not a politician. You see, just by being here, on the *streets,* I'm raising the consciousness…….of people. Even if I affect one…….just ONE PERSON ……help to raise the consciousness………..if our presence here can affect ONE PERSON to THINK……..then I'm making a DIFFERENCE.

And that one person can affect another and another and ………you SEE?'

But the guy wasn't impressed. He wanted Joe's signature on the dotted line. But thankfully, it was time to move on. We regrouped leaving the commies behind. The five of us moved off down the street to our next 'show'.

'Thank fuck for that Joe. Those guys do my fucking head in,' I say.

'Vince,' Joe says, smiling, 'there's NO WAY I would join the SWP.'

'Glad to hear it. You know, I reckon if this was 1930's Germany, those guys……well frankly, they're the type would've been the *first* to join the fucking Hitler youth. It's the same dodgy attitude.'

'Don't be too hard on them, Vince. They're trying.'

'It's all the same to me. It's not the system that's wrong, Joe. It's *people*. *People* are wrong. The system is just like a computer program. You put shit in…..you're gonna get shit out.'

'It's not like that Vince. The system is unfair. It has to change.'

In Sunderland we go to someone's house. The houses in the streets in that area are mostly boarded up with metal and wood. Rows and rows of derelict two up two downs. It's a depressing sight I'd see over and over again in the North. Shipbuilding, cotton mills, mining towns. The whole lot had gone to pot. To me, trying to fix it with demands was a losing battle. But above this house is a pair of ears. The year before Prince Charles had visited the area. He was concerned about it all and had gone round talking to people. Those giant ears were a tribute to him. After he'd left someone had made these giant things out of papier mache or something and raised them right up on that flag pole. It was a surreal sight. Those giant pink ears set against a perfect cloudless blue sky.

Inside, it's quiet and nice. Our host make us some tea and we flop around the place. Nick picks up a guitar and tinkles. It's poorly decorated but homely. I can sense working class pride. And the serious, meaningful talk begins. Political socialist action is what's required. The Labour government, Thatcher, blah, blah, blah. Things are bad and the government is to blame for it all. Whole communities have been callously destroyed by this present government. I steered well clear of the talk. It was all too sad. The great British industrial wave had changed the face of the planet. Trains, ships, coal, cotton, bridges, steel, mining. But that tide had receded leaving vast communities high and dry. And those communities were just carrying on, going nowhere. And the worse it gets the more that community spirit seems to strengthen. It looked like another trap to me. Another con. I tried to put myself in their situation. What would I do? It didn't take long to work out. All I'd need was a suitcase and a train ticket out. To London. Easy to say of course. I had no roots. No family ties. No real friends. No culture. No community. No affiliation to country, people, things or place of any kind. The talk went on. I kept respectfully quiet.

Another show in another bar in Sunderland. And enough money for the train to Edinburgh. Out there on the main drag in Scotland we're alone again. The guitar case is out but the street is unforgiving. Joe puts his all into his singing. So do the rest of us. But we've hit a wall. Nicely dressed people walk past ignoring us. The sky is dismal and grey. Traffic in the street moves past. It's the end of the world. A couple walk past and laugh but don't even think about putting their hands in their pocket. We're there for nearly an hour and not a penny. So it's true what they say about the Scottish being tight? I start to believe it. Then a youngish guy walks past in a biker jacket.

'Hey! Man! Where's the local spot? You know, a club…….where's it happening?' asks Joe.

'What do you want?'
'Like..........for music……...entertainment………where do young people hang out.'
'ROCK'N'ROLL!'
'Well, I guess you could try the Boursonne.'
'Yeah? Where is it?'
The guy in the biker jacket gives us directions. It's sort of hip. University students. That kind of thing.
'OK! Thanks man!'
And so we find the place. More beer. Wait till after dark. Then we do our thing, playing to a small crowd. Joe's been told of another club we can play and he announces another show there the next night. And word goes around that the Clash are in town and of course hundreds turn up the following night. On some level it bothers me a bit. We're here to busk and survive on our musical merits. But the Clash reputation is there, everywhere, providing a soft buffer against any real hardship. It goes before us like an insurance policy. And you know that nothing bad could really ever happen with that reputation in place. Money, places to stay, girls, respect, autographs, food, adulation, beer. It's all there, waiting. It's only a matter of time before things catch on and we're safe.

We're taken to meet Jimmy Boyle, the famous Glaswegian criminal. I'd already read his autobiography. I thought it was badly written but the facts! The facts of his life punched you in the gut. He's in a building he's got going for drug offenders and he's helping these people get rehabilitated. He's gone good and positive in his life and putting something back. Helping the drug fuck ups. It's all good. We wander around respectfully. Jimmy is very polite and courteous. He's a perfect gentleman. But standing there talking and getting the lowdown on it all I'm shocked by his eyes. They leap out at me. Points of blue. Wild animal eyes. I remember in the book the part about him killing someone. Those eyes tell a story and I'm happy to get out of there.

In Glasgow it's the same thing. Only the pubs are open all day. In England they shut at 2pm. Open again at 7. All day drinking! I'm in heaven only the stomach starts playing up again. A few minutes after each pint and I've got this burning sensation in my gut again. There's nothing to do but live with it. And pile more beer on top.
We're hanging around a lot with this small bunch who are putting us up. Pure losers. We start the morning with a bottle of vodka. We drink all day. Everyone's on the dole. No one gives a shit and I like them. It's comfortable in their squat and Nick and I strum on guitars and smoke cigarettes. There are no girls. Joe is talking politics almost non stop. Where does he find the energy for it? On to the venue which will open later. I'm bored fingering my guitar, waiting. Joe is standing up with his chest out explaining how to sing.

'It's all in the breathing,' he suddenly explains to his little group. He always has a little group of fans around him, now. 'You have to breathe from the diaphragm. The sound comes up from there. He points to his belly. And up and round and OUT! It's YOGA! That's what it is! YOGA!'

'Don't give 'em that shit! What BOLLOCKS!' I yell at him. 'YOGA! Joe, stop being such a fucking HIPPY!'

Joe ignores me. So do his little group. He continues.

'The sound mustn't come from the chest,' he says with his chest sticking out proud.

'From here. That's where the sound comes from,' he says pointing to his belt again.

Everyone is so interested in what he has to say. He could say anything and they would be satisfied. That great singing is the result of mutilating babies. A diet of caraway seeds. Sticking a carrot up your arse. Whatever. They're happy to just to be in his presence.

We do the show. We get the money and it's onwards. We arrive in Manchester but it's not happening anymore. The orange buses suddenly seem so oppressive. The city centre with it's thousands of people moving around pointlessly. Shops. Tarmac. Grey sky. It's time to call it a day. We agree to call it a day and catch the train back to London.

'So how was it?' asks Bernie, back at the Kensington Hilton. 'Has this experience taught you anything?'

'Yeah,' says Nick, 'for the first time we really got to know each other. Properly.'

'It was fun,' I added, 'though it wasn't all that difficult. I mean……we're the Clash aren't we? So people…….you know……..they were always there to help us out.'

'We felt like a BAND. That's the most important thing,' says Pete. 'And we've seen things ……….that are ……INSTRUCTIVE……….we can build from this.'

'The thing is to keep it going,' adds Nick. 'We shouldn't let that evaporate and lose it. That's what I'm worried about.'

'Did you encounter any problems?'

'Not really. We dealt with anything we had to as it happened.'

Bernie was pleased. It was a convivial meeting. It was all a success. He was a success. It was his idea of course. We were a success for pulling it off. We'd had fun. The media were having fun with the whole thing. The people we met had fun. It seemed like win-win all round.

I thought it had been a great idea. I couldn't think of any successful bands who would have undertaken such a thing. Just go out busking and roughing it on the road like that. It leant some credibility to a band who really didn't have much left. It wasn't long though before things were back to 'normal'.

OUT OF CONTROL: The Last Days of The Clash

2ND CHORUS:

COMPLETE CONTROL

Studio dates had been booked in London to get the album finished. I had some rough demos of the Munich sessions and was working out guitar parts to round it off. Often I'd find myself round at Joe's in Ladbroke Grove working with Nick and Paul using his new Fostex 4 track cassette tape recording machine. Nick would lay down a bit. Then I would. One night I was alone with Joe. We really got down to it. I had a lot of stuff I'd worked out at home. I was playing guitar about 6 hours a day. My fingers tips had turned into bits of rock. The stuff I had was good. It *was Rock*. The demos from Germany didn't 'swing'. It needed something although it was hard to inject anything. The drum machine rhythm tracks were there and you had to put your parts on top and somehow get it to all fit in. You had to somehow add it on. But anyway we got down to it. Joe started rolling joints. Or spliffs. Or whatever. On and on we went. We went through track after track. Mostly I had half rhythm, half lead style pieces that bounced and lifted in a kind of Keith Richards meets AC/DC style. I liked it. It was what was needed. Hard rock guitar. It seemed to work. Joe liked it. After each track I finished he leaned back. 'Yeah, that's more like it,' he said. We went until the early hours. The dawn was breaking. We decided to call it a day. Joe rolled another joint. I had some too. And a beer.

'Vince, I know what you think about spliff,' he said, taking a long pull, 'but you know, I was under so much stress, like Bernie and that and the pressure and………..well………….a friend was round and it was there and………I just *smoked* it, you know? I just felt so much *release*…… and it all………..the *pressure* ……Bernie, the band and everything…………..just……………..DISAPPEARED!!!!!!'

'I know what you mean,' I said taking a short toke. 'Don't worry about it man! It's only fucking rock'n'roll!'

'I'm under so much pressure.'

'Don't worry about it. It's gonna work. We got some good stuff done tonight.'

'Yeah.'

In a couple of days we were round at Joe's again. Bernie had heard the tape we'd done that night. I waited expectantly. 'NO! That's NOT what I'm looking for. It's……………… ………..too……….DERIVATIVE!' he exclaimed. 'It's old fashioned. I want something MODERN.'

'Bernie, we need something like this…………these songs are fucking BORING!' moaned Joe. 'They need a lift. I reckon we've got something ………….'

'NO. It's too derivative.' He looked at me. 'All your talk of doing something *inventive,* Vince. Something *new.* And what do you come up with? Bum kissing guitar rock. Disgusting.'

And that was it. Days of working at home. Hours and hours of digging up and pulling out the best you could find and a whole night of soulful drinking and smoking and meaning that kicked ass and rocked was swept away in an instant 'NO'.

Joe fought slightly. He made a half arsed attempt to stand some ground. But it wasn't nearly enough. The law was winning.

'Vince. Your time is running out. You better deliver or you could be getting the fucking sack very soon,' said Bernie.

I didn't believe a word of it. I didn't really care. But I did. I wanted to be on the recording.

So there I am in another bazillion track recording studio a few days later about to put my parts down. I've been up another three days and nights getting this stuff worked out. I'm toning down the rock element and well, I've got my part worked out anyway.

'Here it comes!' says Bernie.

The track rolls. Fingerpoppin'. I play my stuff note perfect. The song ends.

'What do you think you're doing? That's NOT what's required here. Look……….'

'What do you want me to do for fuck's sake? What's wrong with it?'

'It's not what is required. Take that guitar of yours and play a note.'

'What?'

'A note?'

'What note?'

'Play a fuckin'note.'

I select a fret at random and pick the string. I wiggle my left finger a bit to sustain the note.

'Yes, that's good but don't do that ………..whatsit called………. that tremelo thing.'

I pick the note again but let the tone fall, dully.

'That's better. Now try another a bit higher up.'

I fret the same string a couple of frets up.

'Yes, now find another one.'

I select another note a few frets down on a different string and play that one.

'Here's the track again. Play those three notes together.'

'OK. But where? Where do ....'

The track begins playing. I finger the three notes. But it doesn't seem like much so I add a couple more, playing them somewhere in the track they seem to fit.

'Look. Just those three notes, OK?'

'OK.'

The track rolls. I play the three notes.

'Hold the first note a bit longer. It's too short a time gap. *Then* play the second.'

I hold the first note a bit longer. Then play the second.

'That's too long. Not so long on the first note.'

And on it goes. After about 20 takes the three notes go down where our manager who is also our record producer too, wants them. Even then he doesn't seem too happy. The whole thing has taken about four hours. Tired and dispirited I take my guitar and go home. .

Back in the rehearsal space in Blackstock Road Kosmo informs us there's this kid in a coma. He's had an accident of some kind. He loves the Clash. It's very sad. And perhaps we can help? Can we record some songs on a tape for him? Bernie and Kosmo, they want a tape to play to the kid to see if the music will bring him out of the coma. So for two days we record some stuff in there. Joe turns up to the rehearsal, puts down some singing and it's done. Joe disappears. The tape goes off. I never hear anything more about it. I suppose it didn't work. If it had I'm sure we and everyone would have heard a lot more about it.

After we go to a club down in Brixton. The band and girlfriends and some famous Hollywood actor is in there with us. Laughing and joking going on and pretending. It's dark in there. The Hollywood actor seems OK but I can't seem to bring myself to talk to anyone. All I can think about is beer. I drink the first pint straight off. Get another. I slip back into the shadows and start sipping the next. A band comes on. It's the same thing. Guitar and noise. Noise and guitar. Same *old* thing. The band finishes. Loud cheers. I say a few things to be a bit social. Make a joke. Slip back into the shadows. A man appears suddenly in front of me. He's right in my face and very angry.

'You FUCKER' he shouts. 'Who the fuck do you think you fucking ARE? The big VINCE now, eh.'

I realise it's Tony. One of my old school friends I haven't seen for ages.

'What? Hi man! What's happening?' I ask.

'Don't give me *that* you…………..you CUNT. We've been standing here for half an hour and you………….you're so fucking BIG now aren't you?............eh?.......... standing around with your famous friends? Can't even be bothered to come over and even say hello to your old mates. You know what you are? You're just a piece of…………'

'Look. I didn't see you Tony. I ……'

'FUCK OFF YOU FUCKING WANKER!'

With that Tony angrily walks off and back to his group. I look over. I see a few of my old friends and an ex girlfriend there. Tony's with my ex girlfriend now. I go over.

'Hi! How're you doing?' I ask. 'I didn't see you there. What's happening?'

But no one will speak to me. They're immovable. Locked into something proud and rigid. I try vainly to make things OK but they're not having it. They're convinced there's something very bad about me. They're probably right. I give up and go back to the bar. Drink another beer. I leave the club and everyone and wander out onto the street. I need to be alone. I grab a taxi back home. I get inside the house and crawl under my duvet wishing the bomb would drop.

Something has me in its grip now. A continuous sense of dissatisfaction with everything. Everyday a sense of irritation gets me at every turn. The Whale is unhappy. I begin having a go at her for the slightest thing. We argue non stop. No sooner than we meet up and it starts. She ought to do this and do that and become more 'happening'. Music is no longer about spirit and fun and neither is our relationship. One should have a career and be professional. I've lost contact with my friends from the warehouse. They've moved on. Phone numbers have changed. Whatever. They're not happening anyway. So what?

Round at Joe's house. We hear some new album mixes. I hear the 'Dictator'. Weird synthesiser is sprayed all over it. Out of tune.

'Joe. It sounds awful. Look, it's …………..a *mess*. It's out of tune. It sounds bloody ridiculous.'

Joe dances up and down as it plays, shaking his arms.

'No, Vince. It's brilliant! It's …………..wild! Listen to it. Cuba! It's the sound of mental break ………….'

Joe realises something and contains himself. He's convinced about this music. He's locked into his own world. He brushes me off. We go on.

Everything is beyond me. I have one bullet to shoot. My opinion. But the Clash machine is in full swing now and it has no time to listen. Driving ahead full steam. I'm insignificant. A real loser. Just a cog in the machine. My opinion used to count for something but now it counts for shit. An avalanche of madness is sweeping everything away before it. It's outside me and within me and anyone who gets close gets infected. Whatever it is, it's like a virus or a cancer spreading within and without and ………… GROWING!

It's time to put down backing vocals. We're in Pete Townsend's studio down in Shepperton. There are hundreds of little recording rooms. Each one has a CCTV camera in it. Wherever you are in there you're on television. I reckon Pete must be a bit para. We group in one of these rooms, the five of us and prepare to sing choruses. Joe brings in a sheet of A4 with the lyrics scrawled in magic marker. It reads: 'This is England'. At the bottom he's drawn a football with a foot about to kick it. We shout the chorus and move on to the next song. And the next and the next.

Another studio. The bulk of the album is recorded now. A great final singalong has been set up. About a hundred people are there in the large recording area to sing along with it all. I've no idea who all these people are. Anyone remotely connected with the group are there. But none of my friends are there. The one's I have left, that is. No idea what's going on. The lyrics are up there on a big screen and everyone shouts them out. I shout along with everyone. In a break between songs I go to the toilet for a piss. A stream of red liquid hits the toilet bowl. Searing razorblade pain in my cock. What is all that red? I decide it must be blood. I zip up and rejoin the throng. The pain in my cock stays. But it doesn't take too long before all the singing is finished. I better see the doctor. Next day I'm there. In the VD clinic.

'Ok, drop your pants. Lets see your man.'
'What?'
'Your Charlie. Let's see it.'
'Oh, ok.'
I unbutton my jeans and let them drop. I pull down my y fronts.
The doctor begins pulling around down there. Pushing and roughly fingering.
'What is it?' I ask, anxiously.

He sticks some glass prong into the little hole in the top of my cock. To get a sample.
The doctor lets my thing drop.
'Ok, zip up.'
I zip up.
'Ok. We have to do some tests. We'll let you know the result in a couple of days.'

A couple of days later and I'm back in there.
'What is it?'
'You have a U.U.D.' he says, writing stuff down on a sheet of paper.
'A what?'
'An unspecified urinary disease.'
'Is it dangerous? How did I get it? Have I got Aids? Herpes? Will you have to amputate.'
'No, no,' he laughs. 'It's very common.'
'But the blood?'
'You'll be OK.'
'What caused it?'
'Mostly it's stress, this kind of thing. Take these. Drink lots of water. You'll be fine.'
He hands me a prescription for antibiotics.
'But the blood?'
'You'll be fine. And don't drink any alcohol.'
'None at all?'
'None.'
As I leave I say thank you.

We have a concert lined up in Denmark. The Roskilde festival. It's one of the biggest apparently. We begin rehearsals for it. Paul turns up but no Joe. Paul goes home leaving Nick, Pete and me walking around Finsbury Park. We wander around, sulking.
'This is bullshit!' exclaims Pete. 'A fucking joke.'

'Yeah, but what can we do about it?' says Nick. 'We're nothing but hired hands. Hired fucking help. We've no choice.'

'We've got to do *something*. We've got to put our point across. I'm bloody sick of it.'

'All we can really do is get a meeting together and stand up and say enough is enough,' I say. 'We're either in this band or we're not. I'm sick of it too. We have to stick together.'

We walk along in silence feeling a bit braver. It's funny how misery can begin to bring people together.

So we have another meeting with Bernie.

'None of us are happy,' begins Nick. 'We're never told anything. Like what's going on. We turn up and do our bit but we're not involved. I think if we're in this band we have a right to know.'

Bernie listens patiently. Then:

'I have decisions to make. Joe is disappointed with all three of you. Did you know that? You think that busking tour was so great? Well I can tell you that that's not what Joe thinks. In fact he's said to me that being out on the road with you was really boring. He thinks all three of you are boring. What can I do with that? You want to be included more. But I think that really it's down to *you* at the end of the day. I have to manage this band and ……………it's up to you to ………….*deliver*. I can only deal with the hand I'm dealt. To make the best of it. There are some issues here that you seem to be completely unaware of.'

The three of us sat in silence.

Another meeting. Down in a café in the West End, near Piccadilly Square. Nick, Pete, me and Bernie. We're waiting for Joe. Joe arrives late and takes his seat around the table. He looks depressed. He's been recording more singing on the album. Bernie has been sending him for singing lessons. Bernie's none too happy with Joe's vocal performance apparently.

We sit there in silence. The three stooges have things we want to get off our chests but suddenly it doesn't seem appropriate all of a sudden looking at Joe's face. He sits there huddled like he's trying to climb inside his leather biker jacket and disappear.

'Well, these three have some axe to grind or other, Joe,' begins Bernie. 'I don't know what to tell them, frankly. So I've brought you here to help resolve the issue.'

'What's the problem?' asks Joe quietly, seriously.

'They feel excluded. They think they should be more involved. But well………..I don't know what to tell them. I thought maybe *you* could shed a bit more………..*light* on the subject.'

'Light? I forgot to bring my torch. But the tunnel may appear at any moment. Hey presto! There's plenty of light down there.'

Joe looked me directly in the eyes, suddenly. Staring intensely.

'What's fucking going on?' I ask.

'Something has to change. You know what, Vince?'

'No, I fucking don't.'

'I'm depressed. That's what.'

Silence.

'Have a fucking beer, man. That will cheer you up. Lighten *up* for fuck's sake.'

'A beer? You think it's that easy? That simple? There's no way I can't do that. One beer leads to two. Then three and another and another. I'll end up drinking ten. Or twenty. Or fifty. It won't stop.'

I looked at him. Boy, he really did look depressed.

'Now what *I* think, Joe, and it's something you should know……..and that is that *you* are a *GENIUS*,' says Bernie. 'You have created music that has changed the world. *YOU!* ……..*YOU HAVE DONE IT. YOU!* You have *changed* peoples lives. Throughout the world. You've sold millions of records and affected the course of events in the world. Think about it.'

Joe began to straighten up. There in that café chair. His chin lifts bit higher. He expands his posture. Leans back a little.
'YEAH! YEAH! YEAH!' he shouts, suddenly immersed in something within himself. 'That's RIGHT! YOU KNOW, YOU'RE RIGHT!'
I wondered if Joe was joking. Suddenly changing like that. His face had lit up like he'd just had a line of cocaine. But he wasn't joking.
'And I know these guys are ......well,' continues Bernie. 'They *mean* well, but...........YOU'RE the creative source. YOU,' he says, leaning forward a bit. 'I think you should remember *that* first and foremost before engaging in any superfluous, distracting ....*destructive* elements...........that may sabotage this project.'
'Yeah, you're right.'
'You have a job to do. You don't need to be wasting your time and energy where it's not required.'
'Yeah, you're right.'
Joe had to leave for some reason. He got up suddenly and bounced out of the café leaving the four of us sitting there. Nick got up and left soon after. He mumbled some excuse. He had to be somewhere. I sat back, shocked. Silent. Dumfounded. It was so insane. I thought of my bad acid trip. A tight wall formed around me. What was the answer to all this?
Bernie went on now there was just me and Pete there.
'Underlying ....all of this is.............a............do you think that ....*LOOK*........things are created within a sphere of activity and what begins as a drama can resolve itself into meaningful exercise...........a..........productive experience that can become *REVOLUTION.* You think that can happen by sitting on your arse? There are *thousands* of individuals out there who would give their right arm to be in your position. To have the OPPORTUNITY.............*you* have........*you*

VINCE!……and ……..the thing I realise about you now…… is how fucking UNGRATEFUL YOU ARE!'
There was a rizla packet lying on the table. Bernie pointed to it.
'You see that rizla, Vince?'
'Yeah, I see it.'
'Well, if the surface area of this whole table is the album recording then I would have to say that that area………. covered by that…….. packet……. is approximately *YOUR* CONTRIBUTION to this album project.'
Bernie leaned back, pleased with himself. It was a clever put down. In that moment it did put me down. Months later I realised how possibly these were the kindest words he ever spoke to me.
But there's not much to say. I'm covered in a strange nausea and can't speak.
'This situation requires some……….
meaningful…….*understanding* of the current …….. social *awareness* of what's happening. Do you understand this? Do you really think you can skin a dog by its tail? Even when it's begging for it? There are ten million people on the dole. What are they going to say to you when you arrive empty handed with your basket of ashes and your empty rizla packet? When I managed the Sex Pistols there was a simple resolution to the situation. We got rid of the problem. What is the problem?'
Silence.
'I don't understand you Vince. You sit there like a clam. I think it's time you spoke up. You don't express yourself. You gotta realise your arse is on the line. You better *say something*.'
I sat and waited for something to happen. Bernie sat and waited for something to happen. Pete sat and waited for something to happen. Nothing was happening.
I looked at the door. I wanted desperately to run out of it. But I couldn't. I seemed to be frozen. All the tables were frozen. The waiter was frozen. I looked at my coffee. The black liquid was

frozen. I heard the hum of the outside traffic. It was the soundtrack to a frozen world.
'WELL?'
Something managed to stir.
'What can I say?............all I can say is I'm sick..............sick of it all..........from the very beginning of this ....at the outset the first thing I find out is Nick and Pete want me out of the band before I've even started. And from then on there's been nothing but paranoia. Suspicion. Backbiting. Hate. Bullshit. Bullying. Mind games. I can't ....*deal* with it. You're asking me to speak up. But everytime I do it's the same thing. I'm sick of it all. If you wanna fire me then please do it. Put me out of my fucking misery.'
'Ok. Well............ At least that's something I can understand.'
Bernie paid for the coffees and the three of us left. We begin strolling down the road. The traffic is getting busy. People everywhere are going places as fast as possible.
'What do you guys want out of life?' said Bernie.
'I want to make a difference in the world,' said Pete. 'This band is an opportunity to do that. To create some equality in things. SHIT! We *have* that opportunity. Let's do something with it,' he says, animatedly. 'This is our chance. We have to make the most of it.'
'I see.'
I knew it was my turn. What *did* I want out of life?
'I want to fuck as many girls as possible. I want to fuck a girl from every country in the world. I want to get a map of the world and to shade in every country on it with a felt tip pen before I die. When are we gonna tour Russia?'
'Seriously.'
'Oh. I dunno. Just to be fulfilled in some way. Be happy I guess.'
'Fulfulled? Uhm.'

We carried on walking.
'It's obvious to me you don't know who you are, Vince. Your problem is you don't *think*. You don't think about the consequences of what you say. Of your actions. It's time you took control of your life.'
'CONTROL! There's no such bloody thing. People just do what circumstances permit. What you're able to do. What you're conditioned to do. Control is an illusion.'
'What do you mean? Control is an illusion?' screams Pete. 'Don't you *get* it?'
'Get *what* exactly?'
'The whole fucking world! That's what people *do*. Everybody is attempting to …..control their circumstances, their environment. To affect and manipulate…….. their………. relationships………. and have power over their surroundings. That's the way it is.'
'Well I don't. I don't want power over anything or anyone. I want to be left alone. I prefer to let things just happen.'
'Oh, yeah, right! Don't give me that. You *do*. Everybody does. Whatever you choose…'
'I don't believe in choice.'
'What? I don't believe the shit you come out with sometimes, Vince. God! Fucking hell!'
'Having a choice implies a chooser. It's all illusion. A person decides on a course of action they believe will bring the most pleasure. And avoid the most pain. Some are just more clever than others at it. They think of the future. I want it now.'
'Oh! JESUS FUCK! JESUS CHRIST!'
Pete threw his arms in the air in exasperation. He was wasting his time talking to such a moron. Maybe he was. It was late afternoon. People were running around us in the grey concrete around Piccadilly. Going this way and that. Everyone in such a

hurry. What were they all doing? Fuck. In a hundred years of Time we would all be dead.

I was sinking. Sinking lower and lower. How far could I sink? We stopped. I stared at the ground.

'I have to tell you, you have a serious problem, Vince,' began Bernie.

What else was it now?

'Oh yeah? Really? What's that then?'

'Paul wants you out of the band.'

'Oh, really?'

'Yes. He's not prepared to work with you anymore. He doesn't like your attitude. I suggest you call him and try to resolve it or you're out. I'm not joking.'

'OK. I'll give him a call.'

'The way I see it you don't have a single friend in this band. What do you think Pete? Has Vince got a friend in this band?'

'No. I don't think he has a friend in this band.'

'Have you got a friend in this band Pete?'

'Yes. Nick is my friend. And Paul.'

'Who is your friend in this band Vince?'

'Well, Joe's OK. I get on alright with him. When he's on the planet.'

'Do you have a friend in this band?'

I thought about it. I looked at Pete. No, he wasn't my friend. Especially now. Nor Nick. Nor Paul. Joe was way too much the star to be a friend.

'No. I don't have a friend in this band.'

'You have a problem. I suggest you sort it out,' said Bernie.

With that we parted. I took the underground back to Finsbury Park. Through the rush hour madness. Who were all these people sitting there? Standing there. Did they have real friends? There were a couple sitting in front of me train talking. They were talking about the business in their office. A girl and a guy. The girl was attractive in her black office skirt secretary way.

OUT OF CONTROL: The Last Days of The Clash

The guy was obviously interested in her. They talked on and on. Politely. She liked him but you knew it wasn't in *that* kind of a way for her. They laughed a bit. Talked a bit more about people they knew in the office. Were they friends? I didn't know.

The next day I called Paul. We arranged to meet up and have a talk. We took a boat trip down the Thames. Went down to Tower Bridge. Walked around. Sailed back. Paul was very friendly. He didn't seem to want me out of the band at all. He had no idea what I was talking about. We talked about this and that.

'It looks to me like it's gonna end soon,' I say, 'the way things are going. Nick and Pete think it's over for the Clash. What do you think? It would be a shame.'

'Vince. Ever since this band began it's had been on the cards. There hasn't been a single day where it might not end at any moment.'

'Really? Even in the beginning?'

'Yeah. Even in the beginning. I don't worry about it. I just take each day as it comes.'

'But you're not on the album. Doesn't it bother you?'

'Bernie knows what he's doing. He's…….difficult …..but……it's for the best.'

I knew Bernie liked Paul. Paul liked Bernie. There was no conflict there. I gave up thinking about it all. We watched the city moving around us from there on the river. Things seemed to look much better when you were floating on top of water.

Driving by bus from Copenhagen to the festival. From the window outside I see people sitting around by the roadside. They're wearing plastic macs with hoods. I decide I really hate Europe. Everywhere the same bland blank stupid idiots. Hippies. But not even hippies really. At least hippies thought they had some reason to exist. Here it's just stupid youth with no style or thought. Armies of jeans and kagouls. Come for the party. Come to make sure. I realise I've aged so quickly. I'm only 25. Going on 45. I want to shoot them. Whatever the Clash is or was or supposed to be has no meaning any more. I just know it. It's just the thing to do. The famous band. Guitars. Loud noise. A bit of excitement. Meet a boyfriend or a girlfriend in the excitement of it all. And a relationship may come out of it. Eventually they get married and a few years down the line rock'n'roll is a distant memory. It's no longer a way of life. Something to die for. It's just candy for children. Empty.

As the bus pulls into the arena it gets swamped by thousands. Before I would have been a bit excited by all this. Now it just produces a feeling of disgust. Bernie moves up and down the bus aisle, barking out orders to the bus driver. Someone else. There's something wrong. We've come in through the wrong gate. The bus backs out to find the right entrance. It takes a long time. We're directed through to the backstage area and to some caravans. Here we get ready.

Showtime. At the ramp leading to the stage. I'm standing there holding my white Les Paul. I'm ready. There are more than a hundred thousand human beings out there waiting for amplified electrics. The show. The spectacle. Excited. Yelling. The sound is like nothing else when you know *you* are what it's there for.

'Look at it Vince!' whispers Joe in my ear, breathing deeply. Long and deep. In and out. 'What is it ALL ABOUT? All of THIS! WHAT'S GOING ON? IT'S INSANE.'

'I dunno,' I laugh, a bit nervous.

'It's there. And we're here. And in a moment..........'

'All I know, Joe, is I hate beetroot.'

Kosmo finishes his introduction and we're on. It's a while since we've played a live show. Apart from busking. It seems that 5 to 9 hours of guitar playing a day and endless rehearsals have paid off. I don't miss a shot. Swooping in and out and back to the mic for backing and solos note perfect and not a bum chord throughout. It's pretty much a greatest hits package. No new songs in the set Joe has drawn up. I guess he's just sick of the new songs now having his arse whipped in the studio trying to sing them. But the set goes down well. I'm pleased with my performance. There's a fine line on stage between getting into it being spontaneous and getting carried away but maintaining some control, some ability to play the music at the same time. I seem to have found that line. I've really got my shit together at last. We play 'Pressure Drop'. A was a busking favourite. It seems that we're beginning to come together as a group. Live at least. After the show someone backstage comes up to me and he's disappointed. He likes Mick Jones better because he didn't always play the solos note perfect like I did. Really? Why? He made mistakes and this guy liked that. It was more real for him.

Two weeks later and there's another concert in France. Another festival somewhere in Brittany. I think it was called Rockscene. I walk around during the soundcheck, out across the grass. Looking back I see a giant banner across the stage. The banner reads:

SEX STYLE SUBVERSION

in huge red. Oh my God! I think. Who the hell put *that* up there? I ask Pete and Nick. They just shrug their shoulders. They know it's wrong. I know it's wrong. It *is* wrong. They don't want to talk about it. We find a football and kick it around. Waiting.

We play another greatest hits set with no new songs. Before the show Joe pulls me to one side in the caravan.

'There are things going on Vince …..I'm …..realising something about Bernie and we may not be able to………..carry on this way………..'

'What way do you propose to go? What can…'

'Thing is ……..something has to change…….I don't know if I can ……..'

'What are you talking about? I don't understand.'

'You see, you gotta keep something for yourself, Vince. I give Bernie nearly everything he asks for. But only 99%. I keep 1% for myself. That's what I've realised. Always keep something for yourself.'

'Yeah. I'm doing that already.'

'I've been spending some time thinking about things. Moving into other areas and reconsidering what I'm about. What rock'n'roll is about. You know?'

'No. Not really.'

'I can't seem to get it right. There's so much……I'm always reconsidering the fight……and the meaning of the fight and it's ……getting too….. unrealistic.'

'Yeah, tell me about it.'

'Look at Nick,' he says, whispering in my ear, 'he's so fucking *boring*. 'He could be a fucking …… a conservative candidate. What do you think?'

Nick was laughing loudly and talking about something to Pete. I wanted to agree with him but didn't.

'Nick's OK,' I say. 'Why are you saying that? Why don't you say it to his face. Don't say it to me. I don't wanna hear that.'

'Oh, fucking hell!'

Joe walked away. We were nearly ready to go on. Standing there before the stage, waiting. Joe had a few more words to say.

'Vince. You have to drop your EGO.'

'What?'

'I can see what's going on with you,' he says. 'It's easy to fall into the ego trap. Get it under control. It's the biggest trap of all. You need to drop your ego.'

I thought this was all a bit strange coming from a man who had an ego the size of the known universe.

'Fuck off, Joe. You know, you're so full of shit. Stick it where the sun don't shine.'

But were being called on now and there's no time to finish this. It gets forgotten. It was a bad show. Something was wrong. We flew back to London straight after. In and out in a day.

Another show has been lined up in Athens. We begin rehearsals for it. But rehearsals have become really boring and especially without a singer. We have our stuff down. It's pointless going over and over it. We know the songs backwards. I arrive at Heathrow at 9am but there's some shit with the tickets or the plane or something so we can't leave.

It's hot out there on the runways. The sun is beating down. We sit in a little booth waiting for the flight. There's a TV screen in there up near the ceiling. Live Aid is on the TV. Up there on that TV we watch all the famous rock'n'roll bands doing their bit to save lives. It's a good cause. Not some anti this or that political rally but a real humanitarian event that will raise money for the starving. The destitute. People who probably don't even know what a ballot box *is* let alone seen one.

On the plane I'm sitting next to Joe. His head is buried in the inflight magazine.

'Joe. How come we're flying off to Greece? This Live Aid thing is looks pretty good. How come we're not involved? We'd steal the fucking show!'

'We weren't asked,' he replies, tartly.

'Weren't asked? You could have just insisted. You could just *tell* them we want to play! Make them an offer they couldn't refuse.'

Joe went on reading his magazine. He didn't want to talk about it. I asked Kosmo about it. I wasn't happy we weren't playing. After all, the Clash was supposed to support humanitarian causes. It didn't get bigger or better than this one.

'Well, it goes back a while,' says Kosmo. 'Joe and Geldof have had some differences in the past. The punk past. Some rivalry there. Geldof didn't like the idea the Joe had become the spokesman of a generation. They both saw themselves as that. They don't get on.'

'Surely they could put all that aside. I mean......it's all a bit childish, don't you think?'

'They hate each other. That's the way it is.'

'Oh, OK.'

Kosmo walked off. I sat down.

The Whale was taping the show for me. I'd watch it when I got back.

Big meal that night after we arrive. Long table. The band. Discussion.

'OK,' says Joe. 'Who on this table has ever had a homosexual experience? Hold your hand up if you have.'

Joe puts his hand up. Nick puts his hand up. Pete puts his hand up. Our art director puts his hand up. I don't put my hand up. I look around the table. A couple of other hands are up. Only Paul and I don't have our hands up.

What is this? One by one, stories are told of these experiences. In the bath. At school. Whatever. I search my mind but there's nothing. Not even in a dream. Bernie is not at the table, but I wonder if he's had a homosexual experience like everyone else. Back in my hotel room I think hard about it. I'm a bit shocked. Are they making it up to be cool. I don't know. I don't believe in bisexuality. Women are bisexual. But men aren't. In my mind a guy is either gay or straight.

After we go to a club. I'm sitting down nursing a beer. Joe and Pete stand over me leering.

'I'd love to fuck Vince. What do you think Pete? Would you fuck him?' says Joe.

'Oh yeah, definitely. I'd fuck him,' Pete agrees.

'Get out of my face you fucking poofs,' I yell and jump up quickly.

I get away and go find Paul. Joe and Pete are laughing away.

I spy Paul near the bar and go talk. Paul and I start having a 'Clash' conversation. This is cool. That's cool. Being careful to talk only about 'cool' things. Nothing substantial. There are lasers in the club. Quite a show. I'm bored with it. So is Paul. We wander out together into the car park.

'Let's get a car!' whispers Paul.

'Good idea, but how?'

'Hotwire!'

'I don't know how.'

'I do.'

We sneak around the car park. There are security around the club. We have to be careful. I begin trying doors. No luck. Paul is trying doors. I push the door button on one and it flies open.

'Here! I've got it!'

Paul moves in, head down. Gets in the car and begins fumbling around under the dashboard. I wonder if he really knows what he's doing. He's taking his time in there. I'm keeping lookout.

'What's happening? Get it started you cunt. Oh shit. Paul! Get out of there! There's someone coming!'

A couple of security men walk towards us. We run away laughing and get back in the club.

Thousands of people in a big concrete Olympic stadium. More than 40,000, I think. I'm not too up on the numbers. But it's a lot of people. Little do I realise that this will be the last concert the Clash will ever play. 'Complete Control' is the first song on a list Joe has scribbled down on a scrap of hotel paper. We gather around backstage and work out an intro. Joe suggests we go out one by one and build the song up. I reckon it's a good idea. It's different. I like the way Joe thinks on his feet. Spontaneous and always game to try something. We'd played a show in the States where we'd done three encores. The house lights were up and the DJ had begun playing records at the end. Most of the audience had filtered out of the hall by then.

'What do you think, Vince? Another song?' he asks me, backstage.

'Fucking right! Let's do it!'

So just for the hell of it we'd run back out on the stage and begin playing 'White Riot' in a brightly lit half empty hall. People began scrambling back in to try and catch it. Mad.

I'm to go out and start with the riff. Pete will be next with the bass drum. Nick with guitar. Then Paul. Then Joe will appear and start singing. It's a good plan. I've decided not to drink anything before this show. Drink and adrenalin don't mix. It's like mixing drugs and you get confused. I'm worried about walking out there alone. Boy George got bottled off the stage earlier. The people are here to see the Clash and they don't want to be disappointed.

I walk out in the dark and plug in my guitar. Turn up the volume. I hear a low hum. I'm electrified. My hands are shaking a bit. I look out over the audience. All I can see is a sea of little lights out there in the distance. Candles or matches or something in the blackness. There's just me and 40,000 people. Facing it off. Here it is you CUNTS!

BAH-BAH..........BUH...-BAH , BUH BAH-BAH.
BAH-BAH..........BUH...-BAH, BUH BAH—BAH!
I play the refrain over and over. The audience begin screaming. Pete arrives quickly with the bass drum.
DUH....DUH....DUH.....DUH.....DUH......

It seems ages before Nick arrives and starts playing the opening chord. Over and over it goes. Paul arrives and it all goes to plan. Where's Joe?
Joe arrives and …………..
'They said……that it's REMOTE CONTROL! We didn't' want it…………..'
And we're off. It's a blinding show. Being sober is good. Thinking is quicker. Notes are struck and movements are synchronised and effortless. I'm on the wave all the way through. There's room for experimenting too. At the final count I realise I've played my personal best. And as the newer live band we've reached out best. Even Nick and Pete are complementing my playing to Bernie. We've been given a tour itinerary for next year. Japan and the Far East. Things are looking up.

Back in England Bernie decides I should get a Mohawk haircut. I don't want a Mohawk haircut. Only a few weeks ago he wanted me to grow my hair long. Someone had to have long hair.
'You all look the same. You've all got short hair. One of at least has to grow your hair long. Decide amongst yourselves.'
I didn't want to grow my hair long. Or get a Mohican. I thought Mohawks looked a bit contrived. I didn't think it was the Clash to have a Mowhawk. Or punk in fact. I didn't like Joe's half flat one. I thought Mowhawks were dumb. But again the pressure was on. Everyone began making a big deal of it and a lot of effort went in to encouraging me to do it. I became the centre of attention and people were being friendly. I liked it when people were friendly. I couldn't resist that. In the end I thought 'what the hell'. I could always grow it again if I didn't like it, couldn't I?

So Kosmo got his hair cutters and I was done again. I looked in the mirror. Well, it wasn't so bad. I'd never had a Mohawk before. Now I had one. It was different if nothing else.

A photosession was arranged and the five of us were in the studio again for pictures for the forthcoming single. There I was again with a make up girl putting touches to my face. Some eyeliner. Face powder. She's so warm and so *female*. Big tits pushed up against me and somehow the whole thing reminds me of being fussed over when I was a kid by your auntie or something. The nostalgia of that and the female presence is so strong and nice. But I don't like any of this stuff. I'm a punk rocker. Rough and ready. I'm a fucking geezer. I like the dirt and the gritty side of things. The underbelly. Isn't that what the Clash are about? But the feeling of being around women and being pampered is intoxicating and I'm assured that it's better for the pictures. To get a better shot. We need it for the camera apparently. But I see the polaroids and I'm not convinced. We look plastic. I look plastic. Sweet pin ups or something. But fighting all of it takes too much energy. It's a losing battle so you just roll with it. Hey, what the hell?

I'm sitting in my flat when the buzzer rings. I lift up the window and look out. Down there on the pavement is Joe.
'Hey Vinnie! Can I come up?'
'Yeah, sure.'
'Sure you're not busy or anything?'
'No, come on up.'
I go down and let him in. He walks in.
'So for what do I owe the pleasure of this…….'
'Fucking hell Vince. This place is a mess. I thought you'd be a bit more tidy than this!'
I looked around but things didn't look too messy to me.
'Tea?'
'Yeah, thanks.'

We sat, drank the tea and talked for a bit. It was a bit weird. Joe had never come round to my place before. He seemed a bit agitated and nervous. He was only there about ten minutes when he suddenly jumped up and left. He had to go somewhere.
    When he'd gone I went and sat down. What was that all about?

    I'm back in the doctor's again. I've stopped pissing blood but my stomach is still so bad. I've stopped drinking for a while. Because I'm able to stop drinking I decide I can't possibly be an alcoholic. The pain in my stomach is a never ending source of discomfort. They take X-rays. In another session I'm given a scan thing. It's the latest technology apparently and the doctor rubs this device over my belly and I can see my insides on a TV screen. Again the results show nothing and I'm dismissed. The pain continues.
    There's nothing to do now and more boredom. The album is being mixed. The single will be released soon. I reckon it's time to get away for a bit and relax. On the spur of the moment I decide on Berlin. I tell the Whale we're going to Berlin. What? Berlin? I dunno. I haven't got……..
    3 hours later we're on the train. We can't fly of course. We don't have the money for a flight but it doesn't worry me. Everything is an experience. Roughing it is experience. That's the way *real* people do things. I'm a punk! Surface travel. It's the only way to feel life and really *see it!*
    The train pushes through the countryside. We cross into East Germany past a line of criss cross things and barbed wire. We're in the communist bloc! But it's almost 3 days to the city and when we arrive we're exhausted. We find a cheap hotel and sleep. We wander around West Berlin the next day and within minutes I'm miserable. I hate it. Soft. Affluent. Dull. I think of David Bowie and art for some reason and we go round the town looking for *something* a bit exciting. But there's nothing really. Just empty shiny metal bars. There's a film showing there. It's

starring Madonna. I forget the name of the film. I hate Madonna. I hate all that popstar trying to be an actress thing but we go in anyway. It's something to do. It's an awful film. We come out and sit in the main square. I have a beer. I realise it's all been a mistake coming here. Everything is a mistake. It's a mistake trying. You can go here and travel there but in Europe but it's always the same thing. Limited choices. People do it, travel I mean, and what do you end up with? The same thing you have at home. Museums. Art Galleries. Historical buildings. The cinema. Bars and cafes. Some dodgy European band trying to do rock. Embarrassing. Endlessly walking around looking at nothing. Absolutely fuck all. A dead end.

So we decide to venture into East Berlin. Past the wall. I want to know what goes on behind that mysterious wall and so we catch the train over. At the checkpoint we have to show our passports. Sitting behind this desk is this ugly guy in a grey uniform. He looks at my passport. In my passport is a U.S. stamp. It's there because I lost my other one on tour and it's a U.S. replacement. He looks at me. He throws the passport back at me and says something dismissive. He goes back to looking at something and writes some stuff. I don't understand. But it seems I can't continue into the East side. I refuse to leave. He says something angrily and points back the way we've come. I'm not having it. I begin arguing with him. Before I know it two armed guards are up against me and they have their rifles out at the ready. One of them pushes his gun into my sides and the Whale and I are pushed out the way we came.

There's always another way of skinning a cat so we book on a tourist tour. There's no problem getting a ticket. Get in a bus. Go through Checkpoint Charlie and we're there. On the other side. I look for something mad to shock me. But there's nothing there except blocks of buildings and the cars are all small and the same. It's dreadful. Even worse than the West. Some loonatic woman is saying stuff on the bus tour about how great the East is. More brainwashing. But the West is brainwashing too. What's the difference? We see a war memorial. It's there for the millions of Russian soldiers that died in WW2. I don't care. I have no sympathy with any of it. I can only sympathise with myself and the utter dreary nonsense of it all. I'm so happy to get back to the West side and get in a bar and drink beer. The Whale and I go to the stadium where Hitler rallied or where the Olympic Games were, some such shit like that, and we sit there in that great historical theatre and the mood isn't good between us. I'm miserable and pissed off. So is she. We fight and argue. Somehow we make it back to England.

I'm told the album won't be released. There won't be a tour either. Forthcoming dates have been cancelled and everything is on hold. It's all because Mick Jones is suing the band. And copies of the single are out in circulation. It seems everybody has a copy except Nick, Pete and me. But a couple of days later we each get one. Kosmo presents us each with a copy of 'This Is England.'

I run home with it and put it on my turntable. The sleeve shows a picture of Piccadilly Circus with the adverts changed and bright red colour and the new Clash logo. I think it looks pretty good. On the back are a lot of black and white photos of English life in the fifties or sixties. Old cars and some women in a bus queue. Our art director has done a good job, I think. Although I've no idea what it's all supposed to represent. Somehow those old black and white photos make me feel a bit depressed. It says written by Strummer and Co. I wonder who the Co. bit is supposed to be. Is it the rest of the band? If it is then will we get some money? Then it says produced by Jose Unidos. Who the hell is Jose Unidos? Has Bernie changed his name too?

I put the record on my turntable. It starts with the soundtrack of a girl selling potatoes. I listen to the whole thing trying to imagine I'm not involved and I'm a fan listening to it. It's not hard to listen to it like that. I decide it's not the fast and up beat kind of thing I would have liked to hear but there's a certain power and strength in the song. Despite the drum machine it seems to work. I decide it's not a bad record at all. It's loaded with nostalgia and melancholy. It works in a miserable kind of way and seems to say something although I've no idea what it is. I decide it's not an amazing record but a good one.

A week later I speak to Pete on the phone and he tells me that Joe doesn't want to work with Bernie anymore.
'What? Hold on? Has the band broken up?'
'I don't know.'
The three of us decide to meet up round at Pete's place.
There's more bad news.
'We've heard what the album is going to be called,' says Pete, mournfully.
'Lay it on me, what is it?'
'It's called 'Cut The Crap'.
'WHAT! YOU'RE FUCKING JOKING? *TELL* ME YOU'RE JOKING.'
'No, he's not joking,' says Nick.
Nick and Pete sit miserably. Something wells up inside me.
'We've got to *do* something. We can't allow that to happen. Cut the Crap! My God! We have to ……..'
'It's too late,' says Nick.
'Why?'
'It's already gone to press. They're pressing the album as we speak.'
A strange sound erupts from my gut.
'AAAAAAAHHHHHHFFFFUCKKKKKKKEEEEENNNNNS AAAAAAKD…….SHIT!'
Then I try to compose myself. Make sense of things.
'Why weren't we consulted…….I mean……'

I stopped bothering. I knew then that it was all over. So did Nick and Pete. We sat in silence. All three of us were at that point where all you could do was to watch things in motion. In fact we'd been there all along but now there was no deluding ourselves.

'CUT THE CRAP! I mean………….it's INSANE! What does he think he's doing?'

'Yeah.'

We couldn't take it anymore and each of us went home.

OUTRO:

TRAINS IN VAIN

A meeting has been arranged with Joe to find out what's going on with him and Bernie. I meet Nick in Nick's flat beforehand. Later Pete turns up and we head off to Ladbroke Grove. We get there and ring Joe's door bell. The door doesn't answer. We ring again. Still no answer. The phone doesn't answer either and so we go home. There's nothing to do now except see how things play out.

Kosmo calls and we're asked to do some filming. It's for a video for 'This Is England'. We catch a train down to Southend with Kosmo at the video controls. But Paul doesn't turn up. It's just Kosmo and the us three. We walk around the fun fair and amusements getting filmed, keeping up a brave face. Any minute Joe could change his mind and we'll have something ready, won't we? Kosmo is full of positive energy and he does a good job of keeping our spirits up. And the way things are it doesn't seem improbable that Joe will suddenly appear and the Clash ship will resume sailing.

Back in London I find myself round at Nick's flat and get given a copy of the new album, 'Cut The Crap'. I look at the sleeve. It doesn't look too bad. Only the title gives me the creeps. It has the word 'Crap' in it and that doesn't feel good. It's produced by Jose Unidos. Who's he, I thought? Bernie? Then it says songs written by Strummer and Rhodes. So Bernie is the songwriter too?!! The inner sleeve is a bit odd. It has a 'communique' in it. I read it.
It says: wise MEN and street kids together make a GREAT TEAM. but can the old system be BEAT?? . no……not without YOUR participation………. RADICAL social change begins on the STREET!! So if your looking for some ACTION…….CUT THE CRAP and Get OUT There.
I'm horrified. More soap powder rebellion. I want to die. Can this really be happening? I'm in the picture on the back of the album. That picture makes me officially a part of all this.

I go back to Finsbury Park and put the record on my stereo. I listen to all of it. Despite the fact that my powers of discrimination have been by now pretty much reduced to zero I'm still able to realise something. Drum machines aren't cool. Loud throaty football terrace choruses aren't cool. Synthesisers aren't cool. It's hard to hear Joe's vocals in the mix but from what I can hear he's struggling to make it anyway. There are some good bits here and there but the whole thing stinks of desperation and neediness. I hate it. It's fucked.
'This Is England' charts at number 34.
Kosmo is keeping up a big front as usual. He tells us that it's a good position for a record with no promotion. We take another train to Oxford to film more video. Again it's just Kosmo, Nick, Pete and me. Truth is, we all like 'This Is England' and reckon

the song has a chance. It sums up our busking experience and we reckon it needs a video. No record can make it these days without a video and some sort of promotion. So we wander around the historical buildings still wearing our dog tags under grey skies getting more footage. I'm told Oxford has the highest suicide rate in Britain. It's all to do with students at the university and the pressure they're under to perform well. Something happens inside their brains and they start leaping out of windows.

The following week 'This is England' charts at number 24. Not as high as 'London Calling' but higher than 'Rock The Casbah' anyway. Not bad for a record with no promotion.

When I get back to London the Whale and I split up. My indifference and callous attitude has got to her. Her flat is sprayed with aerosol slogans. The 'Blues' is scrawled everywhere all over the walls of her room in dayglo. It's a cry of desperation but I can't seem to hear it. I think it's pathetic. She's crying non stop. I have no feeling inside. I'm hard and dead to her and everything. All I can say is: 'OK, see you around, babe'.

I figure I really don't need some moany old cow doing my head in. I'm miserable enough as it is. I figure what I really need to know is whether I have any rights to any money. There's a single in the charts and an album coming out. I join the musicians union and then go to the office get some advice. I'm still getting £150 a week. What about royalties? It turns out that as I'm not signed to anything then all I'm entitled to is union rates. What's that? £8 an hour for the time spent recording. Fuck all, really.

The Kensington Hilton. Now there is only Bernie, me, Nick and Pete at the meeting.

'Joe is *mad*,' announces Bernie. 'I'm afraid he's completely lost the plot. I've tried to communicate with him but the fact is he's not capable anymore.'

'What do you mean, he's mad?' I ask.

'Mad. He's lost touch with reality,' Bernie says, almost friendly to me now. 'See, Joe believes in ....some kind of fate..........that's how he runs his life..........think about this....................I mean, we could be having a meeting..........but beforehand I've called up one of his friends, someone he hasn't seen in a while and tell this person to come round past our meeting. See, Joe would leave that meeting and walk out and see his old friend and think that seeing him was some sort of fateful encounter. Like it was meant. Significant. Joe has no base in reality.'

None of us have mouths. What can happen now?

'I've come to a new resolution of the situation. The Clash is more than any one ....it's more than any *individual* member..........the Clash is an *idea*......it has always been an...... *idea*..........now, how to take that idea to the next level? ......that's the opportunity presenting itself.'

'What are you proposing?' I ask.

'You..........each of you have a choice. I'm prepared to take this project to ....I can *make* this project successful. I will make it successful with you or without you. What I'm proposing, given the fact that Joe is incapable of delivering is to continue the Clash message to the people..........this is *crucial*..........I ....propose that *Paul* become the singer. We can get a new bass player. Or one of you can play the bass. Failing that we find another singer. *Nothing* will stop me from realising this project.'

It seemed incredible. Paul as the front man?

'What does Paul say about that?' asks Pete.

'Look, I'm giving each of you a choice. Either you stick with this or you can each take £10,000 and go. It's your choice.'

At the end, Pete announced that he would take the £10,000. Neither Nick or I agreed to take £10,000. I still felt that at any moment things could abruptly change and Joe would suddenly arrive full of enthusiasm and would begin promoting 'This Is England' at any moment. Maybe Nick did too. Taking the money seemed like admitting failure. I'd seen Joe do far stranger things. But Joe didn't turn up. Days went by. It was up to Bernie to straighten things out and there was nothing to do but wait.

I went home. I thought about calling Joe. I tried a couple of times but there was never any answer. I gave up calling. I'd had enough. I didn't really care. Something perversely malevolent and destructive was embedded deep inside. A big part of me wanted to see the whole shitty lying house burn down.

With the rock'n'roll ship floundering on the rocks I decided there was only one thing to do. I turned full heartedly to my other favourite loves, drink and women. I decided to cheer myself up and have as much fun as possible. Joe had suggested to me earlier that I go out to clubs by myself.

'Why?' I asked.

'You are in a great position, Vince. I can't do it. If I go out then I'll get recognised and it will be impossible............'

'What would be impossible?'

'I think you can learn a lot. Just go out alone, Vince and see what happens. See it as an experiment.'

I thought I'd try it. I went to one club. Paid my money and went in. Stood around and hung out by the bar, alone. Drinking. Trying to forget. I thought I understood what Joe meant. Like it was nice to by yourself and free to do what you want without accommodating people. But it got boring just standing there with no one to talk to. Then a girl with dark curly hair caught my eye across the bar. She was with her friend. She kept looking at me. I kept looking at her. Fuck it. I went over.

'What are *you* fucking looking at?' I ask.

'Where did you get those?' she laughs, looking at my dog tags.
'I'm in the army. They're standard army issue.'
'Oh, so you're a fighter, then?'
'No, I've deserted. The general just went absent without leave. I don't care about fighting anymore.'
'What *do* you care about?'
'Oh you know, the homeless, starving orphan children in Africa. Female equality and fluffy puppies. That kind of thing. What's your name?'
'Star. And this is Gina.'
'Buy me a drink, Star.'

Back at my place I find out a bit more about Star. She's from Reading. She has a boyfriend. They have a mortgage together on a house. She works in town. He works in Reading. She's real hot looking, slim in jeans and dark curly hair. She does the whole bit riding on top with little pouty smiles and she's dirty, dirty, dirty. In the morning she writes her phone number down and swings out the door and off to work. Tonight she'll be back in Reading but when can she see me again? I look at her writing and the number. Poor boyfriend. I imagine him cooking up a special meal for her that night for when she got home. Giving her massages and telling her he loves her. Stuff like that.

Something is snapping inside. But it's nothing that drink can't cure. I go back to my university bar and get pissed. I see a girl I used to like the look of but at that time I couldn't do anything because of the Whale. I'm back in her halls of residence within minutes of meeting. It starts to get stupid. I'm flying at the edge non stop, careless and desperate at the same time. Perhaps these girls mistake my desperation for some kind of bravery? I don't know. The only thing to do is to push it as far as it will go. The next night I meet Nick and Pete in a club off Piccadilly. The talk is depressing. The end of the band and all that. I can't deal with it. I see a blonde at the bar. Nice figure. In a second I'm next to her.

'Let's go,' I say, grabbing her arm, and pulling her towards the door.
'What? Where?' she asks. But she doesn't put up any resistance. She looks quite happy in fact. Just walks out the club with me. In seconds we're standing out on the cold street and looking for a cab.
'What are you doing? Are you mad?'
'Oh, probably,' I laugh. 'What's your name?'
'Silvia.'
'Nice to meet you, Silvia. What does your mother say?
'What?'
'Oh never mind. I'm Vince. Hey! Hey!'
I wave my arm and the cab pulls over.
We go back to her place.

The next day I go meet Pete in Kings Cross. We stand outside the train station.
'Nick is auditioning singers at the Electric Ballroom,' he tells me.
'What? So Paul wouldn't go for it, eh? Don't blame him. So Nick's really doing it? He's really auditioning for a new Clash singer? Fucking hell!'
'Yeah, we'll, I thought I better tell you.'
'It's insane. How about you? Are you going for it?'
'Nah. No way.'
'Me neither. What about Joe? Has anyone spoken to him?'
'I think Bernie has given up. I guess Joe's waiting to see how well the single does. Maybe if it goes in the top ten he'll be interested again.'
'It's all bollocks. Look, I gotta go. See you later.'
'See ya.'
Pete walked off. I tried to imagine it. A whole new Clash with a new singer. Without any of the original members. The Clash

was just an 'idea' was how Bernie put it. How far could he push it?

That week 'This Is England' dropped from the charts. But none of it interested me anymore. I put it all out of my mind. My new found sex life seemed far more interesting.

I met another girl at a party in Holloway. And another on the tube. By now had a small group of about six girls to see. I frantically ran from one to the other. I set up meetings with each, spacing the time so I could keep the whole thing together. Juggling things. No sooner had I finished with one then I was with the next. It was intoxicating and a great distraction. The more sex I had the more I seemed to want it. Even after a long night I'd come home and beat off another one looking at porno. I got names confused. Things I'd said with one I'd forget and sometimes tell the same story over and over to another. No one cared. I didn't care either.

The road of excess is supposed to lead to some wisdom. The road of excess seemed to lead nowhere except death. The death of my cock. After a few weeks of this it stopped working suddenly. Leaning over some tart who had no real existence outside of her daily work commute and the belief that her friends were the most important thing in her life, I ground to a halt. I tried to use my imagination to keep the ball rolling. I thought of whatever I could. Crazy stuff involving leather and bondage. It worked for a while. The girl wasn't there anymore. Just the insanity inside of my mind.

Then the Whale called me and said she wanted to give it another try. I told her to piss off.

Joe and Bernie hadn't been in the same room for weeks. We pushed for a meeting. We were entitled to know what was going on weren't we? Hear it from the horse's mouth. Nick got through to Joe and he agreed to meet and we met at Paul's house. We sat around the same table where only weeks before we'd done the photo for the back of the record. Joe arrived and sat down.

Joe didn't waste time getting down to it. It was all very formal.

'I have come to a decision. I've decided to call it a day. I've finished dealing with Bernie. I've decided to reform the original band. I've been talking to Mick and .... I want to put the old band back together.'

No one tried to change his mind. I only thought of one thing. Escape. This was it. Freedom. I was strangely happy.

Hardly a word was said. It was simply accepted. I think everyone else was relieved too.

'What about the record?' I asked.

'I'm trying to stop it being released.'

'What happens now?'

'Each of you will receive some money. I've arranged for each of you to be paid £1000.'

I didn't think £1000 seemed very much after two years work with a world famous rock band but money was the last thing on everyone's mind.

We left and went to the Gaz's rocking blues club in Soho.

'Well, that's it,' says Nick.

'Yep. I wish him all the best of luck,' says Pete.

'You know, I can't think that lightning can strike twice, now. In the same place,' says Nick.

'Hah! Things have a way of making themselves felt one way or another.'

'It's all fucking rubbish,' I say. 'I don't give a fuck. I'm just glad to be out of it.'

'Yeah, me too.'

The following day Nick, Pete and I were each handed an envelope with the £1000 in it and we went our separate ways. A

couple of days later my phone rang. It was Kosmo. He asked me to do a TV interview to promote 'Cut the Crap'. I declined. Kosmo started on at me, really pissed off. I hung up. Then Joe called. We met that night for drinks at a club in Soho.
  'Don't worry, Vince,' he said. 'I'll see you're alright. I'll have a word with Kosmo and make sure you're sorted and get some money. You all will.'
  'How much?'
  'Thirty grand. I think that's fair.'
  'Ok. I'm happy with that.'
  'So what's happened? What about Bernie?'
  'I can't work with him. See, Bernie thinks you can make a record………you can create something like you'd make a tin of beans. You manufacture it and put a label on it and it goes on the supermarket shelf…………like it's …….functional………….. creating, it's not like that.'
  'Yeah, obviously! But it never had to be like that. You've gone along with it this far, Joe. YOU allowed him to operate like that. To produce the record. It's your bloody fault.'
  'Yes. Yes. Yes. You're so *right*. It's ALL MY FAULT.'
  There was no arguing with Joe. He just agreed with everything you said. Even if what you said was wrong.
  Joe then went on giving me advice about how to put my own band together. And then:
  'Vince. The best thing you can do now is get married.'
  'WHAT???!!'
  'Yeah. Seriously. Get married.'
  'Why?'
  'It will do you the world of good. Trust me.'
  'Fuck off!'
  'It will. Get married, Vince. I assure you it will make a better man of you.'
  'No fucking way!'

I walked away from that meeting feeling really sick. Get married! Maybe Kosmo was right and Joe really was bananas. Despite myself, I began to really dislike the cunt. I realised what a reactionary he really was. What a bloody coward. He had no faith in himself, in life, in letting go or anything. What did he know about being a punk? How did he become one? Everything for him was always in the past. All that '50's crap he was banging on about all the time. He was a rock'n'roll FUNDAMENTALIST. Somewhere deep in his mind I reckon he felt mankind had fallen from grace. From some Elvis drape suited Garden of Eden that we all had to try and get back to. Back to basics. Back to the piano, a glass of scotch and some Joolz Holland boogie woogie bluesy pub rock safety. Now he was running back to Mick Jones to try and resurrect something else. Get married! What a fucking prick!

News of the band splitting came out in the Sun's bizarre column. 'Cut the Crap' was released and was slayed in the papers. It didn't do very well in the charts.

My telephone stopped ringing. The £30,000 never materialised despite several phone calls. My £150 wages stopped suddenly. There was nothing for it but the job centre. I went down there to sign on.

I went in and sat down. My interviewer looked at my form.

'What was your last job?' she asked.

'I was a musician.'

'Why did you leave your former employment?'

'I was made redundant.'

'Well, we have to verify that you were made redundant first or you won't be entitled to any benefits. Can you give me the details of your previous employment, a name and contact number?'

'Sure.'

OUT OF CONTROL: The Last Days of The Clash

I wrote 'The Clash' down on the form. Next to it I wrote: 'Joe Strummer' and next to that his phone number.

'Thank you, Mr. White. We'll contact you as soon as we've verified your status.'

'Thanks.'

I got up, walked out and went home.

Next day I got call. It was the dole.

'We've been trying to contact your previous employer.'

'Yeah?'

'We made enquiries regarding the circumstances of your leaving your former position.'

'And?'

'Well, they were very uncommunicative. They wouldn't talk to us.

'And?'

'Someone put the phone down on us. They were very rude.'

'So what happens? I have no money. I need money to *live on*. I didn't leave of my own accord. Effectively, I was dismissed.'

'I understand Mr. White. But we still need to verify your position. We'll try again and let you know.'

Days went by. I had no money. After a long day waiting and some pleading and shouting in the dole office I finally got a giro. My stomach was playing up more than ever. I had some X-rays taken. Still nothing was found in there.

I sat for hours, alone in my flat, looking out the window at the houses opposite. Stupid houses with stupid people living in them. The bleakness of the day stretched out before me each morning. Thousands of seconds, one by one flicking by. Things changing but nothing changing.

I tried to assess my situation. The thousand was long gone. I had no band. I had no money. My old friends had disowned me. No girlfriend. Girls I'd been seeing suddenly disappeared as soon as they found out the Clash had split. I'd stopped pissing blood but my guts were fucked. But the biggest problem was my brain. There was something in it. The Clash virus. Frustration and anger just dogged my every step. I was Clash programmed. I was brainwashed. I needed to deprogram my brain. How could I do it? I threw my dog tags down the toilet. I gave away my Clash shirts and trousers. I burnt a pair of brothel creepers in the garden. I had stacks of fifties rock'n'roll albums and shit I never used to listen to before. I decided to give them away. I did. I grew my hair a bit longer. But it was no use.

Then I got a call from Ashley, an old friend who was just back from Canada. We agreed to meet up round his house. I hadn't seen him in over two years.
'How're you doing?' he asked me.
'Shit.'
'What's wrong?'
'I dunno. Not enough love as a child? Genetic mutation? Bad potty training?'
'I heard the band split. What are you going to do?'
'I dunno. Get something else together I suppose. I've written some songs.'
'I heard the album. It's not that bad you know? Not considering it's effectively a new band. You shouldn't feel disappointed.'
'Well I do. It's shit. Well it's not *all* shit. When she's good she's fairly good. But when she's bad, she's worse than horrid. It's fuck all to do with me. I'm just a rizla packet.'
'Just move on. Get a new band together.'
'I can't sing.'
'Yes you CAN! I've heard you sing. You're a good singer.'
'I've no motivation. I'm sucked dry, Ashley. I can't see the point anymore. I can't see the point in anything.'
'There is. Just find it.'

'I used to think so, mate, but not anymore. I can't delude myself. All I see is emptiness behind everything. Don't you see? It's all illusions. All of it. Art, music, everything. It's all con of one form or another. These things only exist and have value because everyone agrees to make the same assumption. What they're told. It's just a form of mass hallucination and hysteria.'

'Oh come on! It's not just like that. There's been some fantastic music been made that stands by itself. Bowie, the Beatles, the Pistols……….'

'These things filled a social function. They're a product of their time. If the fab four had never been born I'm sure there would've been something else similar in its place. Same with the Pistols or the Clash. There's a demand in the market place and it gets filled with something. Don't you see? It's all over.'

'I don't believe it. There will always be a demand for social commentary through music.'

'Society?!! There's no such thing. It's abstract. The reality is there are several million individuals living on an island. And their minds are degenerating, Ashley. There's a new force taking over. Ideals and values are being eroded. The sensitive and intelligent will slowly commit suicide and deplete the gene pool. In two hundred years time there'll only be robots left.'

'No way!'

'Yes, way. And I blame women for it. They ultimately choose who they're gonna fuck don't they? What do they choose? The guy with money and social status. The top dog, that's who, the guy who's all power show without a fucking brain cell. We're doomed I tell you, *doomed*.'

'You've got it bad, my friend. What about the Whale?'

'We've split for good.'

'I can't believe that. You two are really good together.'

'Not anymore. We can't be in the same room together without tearing each other apart.'

'You know what I think you should do?'

'No, what?'
'Get away. Take a trip somewhere. Sort your head out.'
'You might be right. It's good to see you, Ashley. Thanks.'

I took Ashley's advice. It was a good idea. A trip away really might sort my head out. The very next morning I went to the train station and bought a ticket for the boat-train to Dublin. That girl I met in Italy, Paola was living there. She was working as an au pair. I had her address on a letter she sent. We'd been corresponding. I didn't tell her I was coming. I just arrived on her doorstep, out the blue one evening around 10. Out of the black. Drunk.

I rang the bell. I didn't know what to expect. I hoped she was in. It was cold standing out there and it was raining. Maybe she was. Maybe she wasn't. It didn't matter either way really. If she wasn't I'd find something else to do. It was better to be doing something than doing nothing. Just about.

The door answered and there she was.
'Hi. It's me. Vince. Remember?'
She didn't seem to recognise me. Then she did. She looked pleased.
'Vince! Hello! Come in!'

I went in. It was a big old house and extremely expensive. High ceilings and bits of antique furniture around and classic looking paintings on the walls. The owners of the house were out. They'd gone to the theatre and wouldn't be back till much later. The children were in bed upstairs.

Paola got me a beer from the fridge. She looked incredibly good standing there wearing her au pair gear. A black skirt and white shirt pouring the beers. That arse was there just the same. I grabbed her and started kissing. Soon we were down on the floor and ripping each other's clothes off. It didn't take long. After about ten minutes we were finished. I lay back on the carpet looking at the ceiling. I felt good. I wasn't thinking of the

Clash. This was much more fun than pretending. Then I heard a noise of a key going in the front door.
'What the fuck's that?'
'Shit. They're back already. Vince, quickly.'
I heard footsteps coming towards us. I leapt up and ran out into the adjoining kitchen and out into the garden. I hid behind the patio doors leading outside. It was freezing out there. I had no clothes on at all. I stood still for a minute or so, naked and shivering. I could hear voices back in the house. Then I heard footsteps coming towards me. A man suddenly appeared and walked through the patio doors very quickly and right past me. He went out into the garden shed, out back. I stood completely still, holding my cock. He walked back. I stared straight ahead. He walked straight past me and back into the house. More talking. I couldn't believe he hadn't seen me. I waited. The talking stopped. I thought of my clothes. If I could just get my trousers on I'd be OK. I peeked around the patio doors. There was no one in the kitchen. Perhaps they've gone up stairs, I thought. I tip-toed into the kitchen. My trousers were only lying a few feet away past the kitchen door.
A middle aged woman suddenly appeared through that door. She looked at me. I looked at her. Her hand went to her mouth and she started screaming. The man appeared at the door and looked at me. He started shouting something angrily at me. Paola appeared too. Then the man and the woman walked out and went up the stairs. I quickly got my trousers and put them on. My shirt and stuff. Pulled on my boots.
'I'm sorry Paola,' I said. 'I didn't mean to………'
'Don't worry,' she said. 'It's ok.'
I was dressed. Paola and I left the house and went out to a club. I wanted to laugh. I was worried she might lose her job over it. I stayed a few days more at one of Paola's friends house. Paola didn't lose her job. I spent long days walking along by the beach. Hanging around in cafes and bars till Paola was free from

work. I got drunk continuously. Soon the drink wasn't working either. After a week I was sick of it and got the boat and the train back to London.

Months went by. The Whale and I tentatively tried to get back together. But things weren't right and nothing seemed to put it right. Too much bad water had passed between us. We were damaged beyond repair. I heard nothing from anyone. I think Nick had returned to Bristol. Pete was somewhere. I wrote some songs to fill in all the Time. Bernie had promised to help me get something of my own started if I had something recorded and so I'd sent him a few rough demos. But nothing was happening. Then he called me up and offered to take me to dinner and discuss a few things. I hoped something was coming of the songs I'd written. Maybe some record company people were interested? But songs were the last things on Bernie's mind when we sat down to eat.

'So, why did you do it?' he asked, suddenly.
'Do what?' I asked, shovelling down my lamb madras. I hadn't been in a nice restaurant in ages. It was nice being in a restaurant again for a change.
'Why did you do what you did with Wendy?'
'Wendy? I didn't do anything with Wendy.'
'Yes, you did. Why?'
I stopped eating. There was no getting away from it. But I really didn't know.
'Oh, I dunno. It just happened. What can I say? I did it because………. I ……………..could.'
'Because you *could?*'
'Yeah. I didn't think you were all that bothered about her. I thought you……………………………………………….. were…….like…..too………*PROFESSIONAL*………. know what I mean?'

'Oh, ok, I can see where you're coming from now.'
Bernie showed no emotion. But Bernie never showed any emotion. Except anger. He didn't seem angry and so that was ok.
We carried on eating.
'What do you think of the album? I think it was pretty good. Most people I've spoken to really rate it.'
'Yeah, it's not bad,' I lied.
'The real problem I had with it was Joe's singing. He just couldn't sing anymore. That was the real difficulty I had.'
Bernie went on to tell me about Mick Jones.
'The man is EVIL.'
'Evil, really?'
'Yes. EVIL. He is the most EVIL person in the world.'
'Why?'
'He's devious. A trickster. A conniving and a cunning, dangerous piece of work.'
'I dunno, I never met him.'
'But tell me, Vince, who do you think is really responsible for the end of this band?'
'Well, I guess we all had our part to play,' I said, diplomatically. I reckoned Bernie had the connections to help me get my demos off the ground.
'PETE HOWARD! That's who!'
'Pete?!! Why?'
'He's undermined this whole operation right from the beginning. Right from the very beginning he's been a destructive element. I never saw it at the time but I see it now.'
I didn't say anything.
We finished our meal and Bernie paid. He gave me a lift back in his Mercedes. We cordially said goodbye and that was it. I watched those same old grey half brothel creepers disappear. I never saw them again. I never got in touch again after that. I thought I better leave it.

CODA:

Time passed slowly and relentlessly. I heard nothing from anyone anymore. Kosmo, I believe, went to America and began working on boats. Nick went to Australia. Pete had joined a band. In truth I didn't really want to hear anything from anyone. The Clash virus was still in my brain and I wanted to be rid of it and get back to some kind of normality and be happy. I tried meditation and got fit and tried to stay off the booze and keep my head clear. Stuff like that. I had a certain amount of success with it but it was hard. Every time I went to out to a party or whatever, I would get introduced as the guy who played guitar with 'the Clash'. Someone showed up with bootlegs of some of the live shows. On those bootlegs were the new songs I'd had a hand in like 'In the Pouring Rain', 'Ammunition', 'Glue Zombie', and 'The Three Card Trick' played hard and live and they sounded really good. It made me feel worse to think of what might have been and the reality of what IS. Which is *my* picture instead of a rizla packet on the back of 'Cut the Crap'. But what can you do with speculation except drag it by the tail and stuff it down the toilet?

People kept behaving differently towards me. Some were jealous and be offish. Some just wanted to talk about the Clash. I didn't want anything to do with any of it. But I couldn't get rid of it. Every time I went in the newsagents there was some magazine or other with the band name and old pictures of the band on it. Sitting in a pub, 'London Calling' would suddenly blare from the juke box. The people I was with would suddenly go a bit quiet.

I knew I had to do something drastic and so I thought I'd get a job. I sold what few things I had and got enough money together to buy a car. A red Cortina Mk5 and what a beautiful car that is. I got a walky talky radio put in and began mini-cabbing around Camden. I heard that Topper was doing the same so I didn't feel too bad about it.

I took to it right away. It was low status compared to rock star but in my mind it was glamorous. I worked long hours like Travis Bickle stealing through the streets of London late at night. You got to meet all kinds of interesting people. People would tell you anything and everything about their lives. When I got home late at night and emptied my pockets; fivers, tenners and twenties popped out and went into a big pile on the floor. Tons of paper money. Tons of it. I left that pile there and everyday I watched it getting bigger and bigger. Bigger and bigger! I played the music I wanted in my car. No one told me what to do or what to think. No one told me how to dress. No one bothered about my hairstyle. I worked when I wanted to. My Time was mine. Most people I met were nice to the guy who was driving them home and seemed happy and grateful and it was nice to be around friendly people for a change. Within just a few short months I earned and saved more money than I had in my entire two years as Clash guitarist.

I took travelling trips around the world for months at a time. I could always just pick up work from where I'd left off when I

CODA

got back. I went to the Middle East, Africa, South America, India and the Far East, just bumming around. Out there, I realised, there's a fantastic big, big world with far bigger and better kicks and less traps. Out there, no one had heard of Elvis Presley or the Beatles, let alone the Clash. The only universally recognised world music hero seemed to be Bob Marley. I kept finding myself on some beach somewhere lying under a hot sun, curling my toes in the sand with nowhere to be. No one to be. No timetable. The only order of the day I had was to meet some fellow travellers and have as much fun as possible. No one criticising. No one-upmanship. I was the white man just looking for fun.

It took two years to save the money for a trip back to the U.S.A. I went back to Los Angeles and bought a black, 1965 convertible Ford Mustang. Got a fuck off stereo system put in. I drove it solo from coast to coast.

Of course, life still gets to you one way or another.

Like this woman I met in a bar in Tucson. She turned out to be a right psycho nut case. Within just a couple of days of meeting her she was already giving me hell. Why don't I do this? Why don't I that? Nasty stuff.

One morning, early, I collected my things and quietly sneaked out of the motel before she woke up. I stuck the stuff in the trunk of the car, pulled the top down and jumped in. Turned the key in the ignition. The V8 burst into life. I drove slowly and easy out the car park, found the Interstate 10 and headed east. I realised suddenly IN THAT MOMENT how easy it is to simply move off and leave things behind. You could leave anything behind and fuck it off if you really wanted to. Anything. Just drop it and keep moving. Shit doesn't cling to you when you're moving.

I switched on the stereo. AC/DC's, 'Shot Down In Flames' erupted from the new speakers. The morning Arizona sun beat down, lighting up the car's chrome and black metal. I pushed my foot down hard on the accelerator. The engine roared and the car jerked forwards.

I'd found what I was looking for.